MACROECONOMIC APPLICATIONS: UNDERSTANDING THE AMERICAN ECONOMY

Robert Paul Thomas
University of Washington

Wadsworth Publishing Company
Belmont, California
A Division of Wadsworth, Inc.

Economics Editor: Marshall Aronson
Production: Cobb/Dunlop Publisher Services, Inc.

Printed in the United States of America

1 2 3 4 5 6 7 8 9 10—85 84 83 82 81

Library of Congress Cataloging in Publication Data

Thomas, Robert Paul.
  Macroeconomic applications.

  Includes index.
  1. Macroeconomics. 2. United States—Economic conditions. I. Title.
HB172.5.T47   339'.0973   80–29051
ISBN 0–534–00963–8

Contents

CONTENTS

Preface

This book has only one goal: to aid the beginning student in bridging the gap between economic theory and application. Economic theory is abstract. That is the way it should be. The concepts that make up the heart of the principles of economics course must be mastered if a student is to think systematically about economic problems. Such an understanding is as important to the economic way of thinking as mastery of the rules of mathematics is to working algebra and calculus problems. But economics does not stop with a knowledge of economic theory. The ultimate goal is to employ theory to understand the contemporary world. This means application. The theoretical concepts that are presented in the principles textbook must be applied to a real-world situation if the true value of the economic way of thinking is to be appreciated by the student. Application helps the student recognize both the relevance of the principles of economics to his or her life and the way that theory can be used to explain how the world works.

There is, however, potential danger in attempting to apply theory for the beginning student. The example must be selected with great care to ensure that only the concepts the student has mastered are necessary to successfully analyze the problem. Should a student's knowledge be insufficient to understand the application, the result may be confusion rather than enlightenment.

PREFACE

Many current public issues require the simultaneous application of several economic concepts. This is all right, of course, if such issues are used at the end of the course. But in my experience the willingness of many students to learn abstract concepts is directly proportional to their belief in the usefulness of the tools, and much of the usefulness of learning economics through application is lost by delay. For this reason application should begin early in the process of teaching economics. In practice, this means at least one application for each chapter in the textbook and two or more for the core and summary chapters.

For each key concept commonly presented in teaching the principles of economics textbooks, this book contains an application at the student's level of mastery that demonstrates how the concept can be used to analyze a real-world situation. The applications are presented in approximately the same order as the concepts appear in most textbooks. For textbooks that differ in the order of topic presentation, a correlation table appears at the end of the preface.

Each chapter begins with a preview that introduces the problem to be examined and the major economic concepts to be employed. Following the preview is a list of statements that summarize the important points in the analysis. A list of readings following each application indicates where the student can find additional information about the topic.

The applications in this book were initially developed from classroom presentations. The material was class-tested by the author, and student responses were incorporated into this published edition. The author thus owes his thanks to the countless students whose classroom comments, criticisms, and test scores led to improvements in the level of presentation and in the analysis itself. The author also wishes to thank the reviewers of this book, whose efforts are reflected in the final product: Roy Grohs, University of Minnesota; Richard Rosenberg, Pennsylvania State University; G. Dennis Shine, Fresno City College; Robert Strom, University of Missouri.

KEY TO USING MACROECONOMIC APPLICATIONS WITH MAJOR INTRODUCTORY TEXTS

CHAPTERS IN MACROECONOMIC APPLICATIONS

	PART I INTRODUCTION TO ECONOMICS								PART II NAT'L INCOME, INFLA-TION, UNEMPLOY.				
	1	2	3	4	5	6	7	8	9	10	11	12	13
McConnell *Economics*	1	2	5	3	4	5	7	8	9	9	10	37	10
Samuelson *Economics*	1	2	3	3	4	4	6	9	10	10	10	5	13
Spencer, *Contemporary Macroeconomics*	In	5 7	2	1	2	2	3	4	5	5	6	3	6
Wonnacott/Wonnacott *Economics*	1	2 19	3 30	3	4	4	6	5	7	7	7	32	14
Mansfield, *Principles of Macroeconomics*	1 2	1	21	3 20	4	4	7	6	8	8	8	3	9
Dolan, *Basic Macroeconomics*	1	1	2 20	5	3	3	2	4	6	6	6	2	7
Lipsey/Steiner *Economics*	1	1	4	4	5	7	4	2	26	26	26	20	28 40
Gwartney/Stroup *Macroeconomics*	1	2	3	3	3	3	4	5	6	6	6	4	7
Miller *Economics Today*	1	1	2	8	3	3	4	6	9	9	9	31	7
Waud *Economics*	1	2	3	3	4	4	3	9	5	5	5	1	6
Baumol/Blinder *Economics*	1	3	4	7	4	4	24	32	17	17	6	29	6
Amacher/Sweeny *Principles of Macroeconomics*	1	2	3	3	3	3	3	3	4	4	4	4	8

KEY TO USING MACROECONOMIC APPLICATIONS WITH MAJOR INTRODUCTORY TEXTS

CHAPTERS IN MACROECONOMIC APPLICATIONS

PART III INCOME, EXPENDITURES FISCAL POLICY						PART IV MONEY AND MONETARY POLICY							PART V CURRENT MACROECONOMIC PROBLEMS					PART VI ECON. GROWTH INTER. TRADE			
14	15	16	17	18	19	20	21	22	23	24	25	26	27	28	29	30	31	32	33	34	35
11	11	12	12	13	13	14	15	16	17	16	16	17	18	18	18	18	18	19 20	41	42	43 44
14	11	12	12	19	19	15	16	17	17	17	17	15	41	41	41	41	41	37	34	35	33
9	7	8	9	9	9 16	10	11	12	14	12	10	13	15	15	15	15	15	17	20	20	21
8	8	8	9	9	13	10	10	11	12	11	11	12	13	15	13	13	15	15	25	25	16
13	10	11	12	5	12	14	15	16	17	16	15	14	18	18	18	18	9	20	22	22	23
7	8	10	9	18	14	12	11	12	14	12	11	15 17	15	18	18	18	7 16	7	22	22	23
27	27	28	30	31	31	32	33	35	35	33	33	34	42	41	42	42	40	43	37	38	36
7	8	9	10	15	15	11	11	12	12	11	11	13	14	15	15	15	15	18	16	16	17
7	10	11	12	5	12	13	14	15	16	15	15	16	17	17	17	17	17	19	37	37	38
6	7	8	9	9	13	10	11	13	13	11	11	12	14	14	15	15	15	16	29	29	30
5	7	9	7	10	14	11	12	14	14	12	12	13	15	14	16	16	33	43	37	38	36
9	9	9	10	10	9	5	6	12	12	6	6	7	13	14	14	14	14	14	15	15	15

I

INTRODUCTION
TO ECONOMICS

1

Introduction: Application of Economic Principles

Economics is a systematic way of thinking about a wide range of personal and social problems. Once a person has mastered the principles of economics, opportunities to employ them appear everywhere. These principles allow the thinker to sort out sense from nonsense in the daily reports of the news media, in the statements of politicians and special interest groups, and in the conversation of friends and neighbors. The application of these principles allows people to exert more control over their lives by increasing their ability to understand what goes on around them.

It doesn't require a Ph.D. in economics to master the economic way of thinking. In fact, this way of thinking rests upon a set of very simple principles:

1. Economic thinking recognizes that providing scarce goods involves a cost or sacrifice of other goods; scarce goods are not free.
2. Economic decision makers economize; they implicitly recognize that economic goods are scarce and always attempt to obtain a goal at the lowest possible cost.
3. Economic thinking recognizes that incentives matter in decision making. As the personal benefits from choosing an alternative increase, a person is more likely to choose that option or, if the costs increase, reject it.
4. Every economic action has several effects. In addition to the direct result of an action, there are secondary effects that also must be identified and considered.

5. Finally, the test of economic thinking is its ability to explain human behavior. This often reduces to the ability to predict future behavior.

Because all economic thinking is little more than the application of these principles to particular problems, the proper way to master this method of thinking is by application. The purpose of this book is to provide a connection that will allow you to proceed from a knowledge of economic principles gained from a textbook to the application of the principles to real problems and issues. The examples in this book thus bridge the gap between theory and application, demonstrating the ability of the economic way of thinking to clarify issues and point the way to purposeful action.

Each application in this book begins with a preview that introduces the problem to be analyzed and identifies the economic concepts that will be employed. Following the preview is a list of key economic points that alert you to what you should learn as you study the application. Then follows the application itself: a description of the problem, phenomenon, or issue to be explored and an analysis that applies the relevant economic concept. The task of explaining the economic concept itself is left to the basic textbook.

The best way to use this book is to first read the assignment in the basic textbook and master the theoretical concepts presented there. Then you should read the application assigned in this book. As you read, keep in mind the key economic points of the analysis. When you have finished, ask yourself if you understand each key economic point discussed.

It is hoped that the more than thirty applications in this book will convince you that (1) economics is widely applicable to contemporary social problems and (2) the discipline has much to contribute toward an understanding of how our modern society operates.

The list of past accomplishments of economics is impressive. The advances in knowledge about economics have guided the intervention of the federal government to moderate business fluctuations. As a consequence of this intervention, the post–World War II economy has been relatively free of economic recessions and another major depression has been avoided. The fact that recessions still occur and inflation has become a major social problem only testifies that work remains for economists to do.

Advances in economic knowledge have also guided government intervention to improve the performance of the economy. Economics has provided the guidelines for the regulation of pollution and the improvement of economic efficiency. Economics has also been in the forefront of the movement to improve the regulation process itself. It was the work of economists that directly led to the deregulation of the airlines, for example.

Private business has also benefited from economic research. Many, if not most, of modern business practices have their foundation in economic analysis. Recent advances in the process of business decision making, such as capital budgeting, inventory control, accounting practices, and business forecasting, were all developed from the initial efforts of economists.

Few public issues are debated today without the application of the principles of economics at some stage of the argument. At the very least economic analysis narrows and defines the issues; at best it allows an efficient and effective public policy to be developed.

During such debates it will be observed that professional economists sometimes disagree. It has become fashionable for the nation's press to focus on these areas of disagreement, but don't be misled. Conflict is interesting, hence newsworthy, while agreement is dull, therefore ignored by the media. Professional economists agree on most things! But they do sometimes disagree, so it is important to understand why.

Economists can disagree because of genuine differences in scientific diagnoses. These differences generally arise when the problem lies on the frontiers of economic knowledge. Economists disagree on the causes of inflation, for example, because the profession does not as yet fully understand the phenomenon of inflation. Just as biological scientists do not as yet understand the causes of cancer and are pursuing different approaches to finding the answer, economists are exploring the inflation problem from different directions. Until a breakthrough is made and a consensus develops among economists, disagreements as to how best to deal with inflation—and other unresolved areas—must be expected.

The opinions of economists may also differ because the basic facts are unclear. A difference of opinion as to the accuracy of economic facts could obviously lead to a difference of opinion among economists, as it would in any profession. Economists disagree on the correct policies to follow to deal with poverty, partially because the facts about the extent of poverty are not known. They disagree on what to do to ensure an adequate supply of energy in the future, in part because some of the basic facts are little more than guesses. Thus, where economic facts are elusive and cause and effect relationships unclear, it should not be surprising that economists disagree.

But even if there were basic agreements to how the economy operates and agreement on the basic facts, economists would still sometimes disagree on some matters of public policy. The basis for this disagreement is not the discipline of economics itself, but rather the differences in social philosophies held by individual economists. Such differences are reflected in the diversity of recommendations as to the appropriate policy the government should adopt. For example, economists could differ on what the government should do about inflation. One group might argue that inflation is such a social evil that the government should take immediate steps to halt it, even at the expense of temporarily increasing the amount of unemployment in the country. Another group of economists could argue that inflation is a social problem but unemployment is even worse. They would argue that the inflation problem must be attacked in a way that will not increase the amount of unemployment. The two groups of economists disagree, but not over the economics of the matter. They disagree on what they value most and on whether the benefits of immediately halting inflation exceed the costs to society. This is partly a matter of fact but also a matter of social conscience.

These possible sources of disagreement may also apply to the applications in this book. The views expressed may not be shared by every other economist. The possibility that disagreement can exist provides you, the student, with another reason to acquire the ability to think like an economist: so that you can analyze problems for yourself.

Preview

The nationwide 55 mph speed limit for highway driving was designed to save gasoline and human lives, but it does so only at the cost of increased driving time. This chapter employs the economic concepts of opportunity cost and efficiency to investigate whether the speed limit is the best way to accomplish these goals. There are always several ways to attain any goal. The best way is the one that does the job at the lowest cost.

Key Economic Points

Obtaining more of certain scarce goods, such as gasoline and human life, requires the sacrifice of other scarce goods, in this case, time.

Is the 55 mph speed limit the most efficient way to achieve the goals of saving gasoline and human life?

How does the employment of positive incentives compare with the negative speed limit as the means of achieving the goals of saving gasoline and human life?

2

The Opportunity Cost of Saving Lives and Gasoline: The 55 mph Speed Limit

By now everyone is familiar with the 55 mph speed limit. The law limiting highway speed to a maximum of 55 mph was passed at the federal level in response to the energy crisis of 1974, with the expectation that reduced highway speed would cut down on our consumption of petroleum. The National Highway Traffic Safety Administration estimates that since that time, besides saving 1 to 2 percent annually on total gasoline consumption, reduced highway speeds have saved 4,500 lives each year. Supporters of the reduced speed limit are now emphasizing the life-saving aspect of the law, relegating the conservation of gasoline to the status of an added benefit. This development has led to bumper stickers that read, "55 mph Speed Limit Is a Law We Can *Live* With."

Not everyone agrees. Bills have been introduced in several state legislatures and in the U.S. Senate to repeal the 55 mph speed limit. While none of these bills has been passed, it is clear that many drivers find the reduced speed limit intolerable. State highway patrols across the nation report writing citations in record numbers (8 million in 1978) in their attempt to enforce the reduced speed limit. Several state patrols have been able to pay for new airplanes and increased numbers of patrolmen out of the receipts from speeding fines. Despite increased efforts, general compliance has not been obtained, as a freeway drive anywhere in the country will attest.

The main reason that people do not voluntarily obey the 55 mph law (fewer than half do) is that it is personally expensive to do so. The principle is simple: time is money. The cost of increased travel time for many individuals is greater than the saving in gasoline and the personal benefits of reduced chances of having an accident. The time saved by exceeding the speed limit is for many also worth the risk of being cited for speeding by the state patrol.

An individual's time is a precious commodity because it is scarce, but life is precious too, and so is gasoline, as supplies become increasingly limited and expensive. It is clear that in the case of the 55 mph speed limit we cannot have more of all three. In this case, to save lives and conserve gasoline we must sacrifice time. But is the time well spent? Economics is particularly well suited to answer this question.

Studies have shown that commuters are willing to pay up to 42 percent of their hourly wage to save an hour of travel time. It is estimated that the 55 mph speed limit forces drivers to spend 2,710 million extra travel hours annually, which, valued at 42 percent of the average hourly wage rate, equals $6 billion worth of travel time per year.

What does this added expense purchase? We have already mentioned the savings in life and in gasoline. Saving a life by reducing highway speeds costs $1.3 million worth of time per life saved. Is this a bargain? How can anyone place a value on human life? As difficult as it seems, it can be done. Indeed, the legislators who passed the lowered speed limit implicitly did just that. For instance, they could have reduced legal highway speeds to 5 mph or to zero. If they had done the latter, the almost 50,000 lives currently lost annually on our nation's highways would be saved. The fact that our government chose 55 mph rather than zero suggests that the overall benefits to the nation of driving at 55 mph is felt to be worth the 47,600 human lives lost in highway accidents in 1977.

We can also look at the cost of saving a life by reducing the speed limit in terms of years of life gained or lost. If we compare the extra travel time to the reduction in traffic fatalities, we find that it costs 102 years spent in extra driving time to save the life of one person who, on average, could be expected to live 35.2 more years. This may suggest that the lower speed limit is an inefficient way to save lives. But society often seems willing to impose such a cost when it is spread, as in this case, in small amounts among millions of persons to avoid the violent early death of a few.

Almost all economists would agree that the value or worth of anything is determined by what a person is willing to pay or sacrifice to obtain the good. The personal valuation of a good, however, may not be the same as its social value or cost. There may be benefits or costs to society that are not included in the individual's valuation. This is certainly the case in highway driving. A driver's personal valuation of the benefits of driving at certain speeds imposes costs on others. A fast driver who has an accident may also harm or kill others. Thus a private determination of the benefits of driving faster than 55 mph may impose significant costs upon society. It would be useful to know whether the public values a human life at more or less than the $1.3 million it costs to save a life by reducing highway speeds to 55 mph.

There have been two serious attempts to estimate the amount the public is willing to pay to reduce the risk of death, which is the figure that a government decision maker would be interested in when evaluating whether the 55 mph speed limit is worthwhile or not. These two investigations both studied the job market. Individuals, since they spend a large part of their lives on the job, have an incentive to find out about job-related risks. Dangerous jobs will be less attractive to workers, so employers will have to pay higher wages to induce employees to accept the risks. One study used injury rates among hourly workers in manufacturing. After correcting for education, experience, and other factors affecting relative wages, the study found that workers in dangerous jobs received 1.5 percent higher wages than workers in jobs where the death rate was half as high. This estimate suggests that collectively workers were willing to accept $1.5 million less if employers took safety steps that might save even one life. The second study found that 1,000 workers in an occupation where the risk of death above the level normal in industry was 1 in 1,000 would each be willing to sacrifice $200 a year if the extra risk were eliminated. This implies that collectively a life was valued at $200,000.

The range between the two estimates is too wide for our purposes. According to the first estimate, the 55 mph speed limit is an efficient way to save lives; according to the second, a life saved by reducing driving speeds costs six and one-half times too much. There is yet another way of determining the willingness to pay, one that can be derived from peoples' driving habits. Buckling a seat belt reduces the risk of death by one in 5 million for the average trip. Even though over 20,000 deaths a year stem directly from not using seat belts, many people appear willing to take the risk rather than experience the minor hassle of "buckling up," and the small probability of death by automobile accident suggests that drivers value their lives at less than $500,000. If the $500,000 figure is accurate, the 55 mph speed limit collectively forces people to spend too much to save a life.

Another way to look at the economics of saving lives by reducing the speed limit is to consider the cost of alternative ways of accomplishing the same goal. What does it cost to save a life by other means? About 2 million Americans die each year, most (over 99 percent) from non-traffic-related causes. For instance, as many people die each year from fires as from motor vehicle accidents. It has been estimated that placing a smoke detector in every home would save almost as many lives as the 55 mph limit at a cost of only $40,000 to $80,000 per life saved. Heart disease presently accounts for 40 percent of all deaths. An additional mobile cardiac care unit costs only $2,000 per life saved. There are numerous opportunities to save lives for $20,000 to $100,000 each by reducing roadside hazards for drivers. In comparison, the cost of $1.3 million in extra travel time per life saved by a reduced speed limit appears to be too expensive a way to save lives.

The true cost of anything is the sacrifice that is involved in obtaining it. Economists call this concept the opportunity or alternative cost. In this case the opportunity cost of resources spent saving lives by reducing the speed limit is too high because there are other means of saving lives that cost much less. Efficiency in this case suggests that the government abandon the 55 mph speed limit and adopt alternative life-saving forms.

The efficiency of a reduced speed limit in saving gasoline can be analyzed in the same way. What is the cost compared with alternatives that would accomplish the same task? The government estimates that the 55 mph speed limit reduces our gasoline consumption by 9 million gallons a day, or 1 to 2 percent. This same amount of gasoline could be saved by switching every car to radial tires when existing tires require replacement, or by changing spark plugs at regular intervals, or by simply keeping tires inflated at the proper pressure. Each of these alternatives would save as much gasoline at a cost that is trivial when compared with the present cost of the 55 mph speed limit. Another alternative would be to convince just 4 percent of the drivers to switch to more fuel-efficient cars. The average car in the United States now runs about 14 miles to the gallon, but automobile manufacturers offer dozens of models that get much better gas mileage, often twice as much.

How can society induce people to drive more fuel-efficient cars? There are two traditional ways to influence human behavior: (1) pass a new law that makes the desired behavior compulsory or (2) increase the personal incentives for the desired behavior. In other words, the government can use either the carrot or the stick to alter public behavior. The carrot is in many cases a more efficient means of changing behavior because it is self-enforcing. If it is in a person's interest to do something, society does not have to check to see if it was done: self-interest takes care of the enforcement. But pass a law prohibiting a certain behavior on pain of punishment, and society not only has to constantly monitor people's behavior but must punish violators as well. The expanded state highway patrols needed to enforce the 55 mph speed limit bear witness to this fact. The cost of enforcing a law prohibiting behavior suggests that alternatives employing the carrot be seriously considered before the government resorts to the stick.

The government, however, has already taken steps that employ the stick. Automobile manufacturers now must produce a fleet of cars that average a certain gasoline mileage. That is, for every car sold that obtains poor gas mileage, a manufacturer must sell enough fuel-efficient cars to maintain a fleet average that complies with the government standard.

Numerous other options could be designed to provide incentives for individuals to voluntarily behave in the desired manner. One way would be to tax fuel-inefficient cars, either when they are first purchased or annually when the owners relicense their vehicles. Fuel-inefficient cars would become more expensive to drive, hence fewer people would be willing to drive them, choosing instead the now relatively cheaper-to-operate smaller cars. A second option, really a variation of the first, is to impose a gasoline tax sufficiently high to encourage individuals to put good gasoline mileage high on their shopping lists when considering the purchase of a new car.

A novel proposal made by Charles Lave (*Newsweek*, October 23, 1978) is to allow drivers of fuel-efficient cars to drive faster than the 55 mph limit, which would still be imposed for "gas guzzlers." That is, allow fuel-efficient cars to travel 65 or 70 mph, and issue two kinds of license plates, so that the state police would have no trouble telling the two classes apart. Would this approach work? The results of economic research on transportation, according to Lave, suggest that the fastest mode of transportation attracts all the commuters. The chance to drive faster would provide the incentive to choose fuel-efficient cars. The point is simple. According to Lave, if we insist on manipulating the speed limit to affect energy consumption, then we should do it in an efficient way. The most effective way to reduce gasoline consumption is to provide an incentive for individuals to drive more fuel-efficient cars. Any of the above incentives would both save more gasoline and cost less than the 55 mph speed limit.

The 55 mph speed limit originally imposed to conserve on gasoline had the additional advantage of saving lives, but only at the cost of additional travel time. The economic question is whether the saving in life and gasoline, both of which are scarce goods, is worth the sacrifice of time lost, which is also a good. The value of anything is determined by the willingness to pay or sacrifice to obtain it. The cost of the resources imposed by the 55 mph speed limit lies between various estimates of what workers are willing to pay to avoid the risk of death, and is substantially above the amount suggested by the behavior of drivers concerning seat belts. The opportunity costs of saving lives by a reduced speed limit is the number of lives that could be saved if the resources were used to save lives in the best alternate way. The 55 mph limit comes out poorly when this comparison is made. Mobile intensive care units, smoke detectors, and the removal of roadside hazards save more lives for the same resource cost. The same approach suggests that switching to radial tires, changing spark plugs regularly, or merely keeping tires inflated would save as much gasoline at much less cost.

The relatively high cost of enforcing the reduced speed limit suggests that alternative means of saving gasoline be explored. In addition to passing laws prohibiting certain behavior, society has the option of creating incentives that will redirect individual behavior in the desired way. The advantage of employing incentives over prohibiting behavior is that the former requires effort for the government to enforce. Taxes, for example, could be used to provide the incentive for drivers to switch to more fuel-efficient cars. A novel approach would be to allow only fuel-efficient cars to exceed the 55 mph speed limit. In any case, changing incentives would probably be a more efficient way to reduce the consumption of gasoline than the continued use of a 55 mph speed limit.

Additional Readings

Lave, Charles A. "The Costs of Going 55." *Newsweek,* October 23, 1978.

Rhoads, Steven E. "How Much Should We Spend to Save a Life." *The Public Interest,* Spring 1978.

Singer, Max. "How to Reduce Risks Rationally." *The Public Interest,* Spring 1978.

Tomerlin, John. "The 55 MPH Myth: Six Years of Speed Prohibition." *Road and Track,* May 1980.

There exists a widely publicized fear that the world may soon exhaust many of its resources. This fear is allegedly supported by computer studies that predict that within a century "a sudden and uncontrollable decline in both population and industrial capacity" will result from the exhaustion of our nonrenewable resources. There are, however, good reasons to reject these doomsday prophecies. The main defect of these studies is that they ignore the existence of a functioning price system. This chapter demonstrates how the price system can register and respond to the increasing scarcity of nonrenewable resources. When the effects of a functioning price system are taken into account, the future looks quite different from that predicted by the doomsayers.

Key Economic Points

The price system registers and reacts to scarcity.

An increase in price will affect the quantity of a resource demanded and supplied.

A functioning price system is incompatible with the total exhaustion of nonrenewable resources.

The appropriate question to ask about the continued availability of natural resources is not how long will they last but how much will they cost.

3

Function of the Price System: The Doomsday Syndrome

In the past it was not uncommon for persons of fervent religious belief to walk the city streets with sandwich boards proclaiming, "The End of the World Is at Hand." These individuals have recently been replaced by scientists and philosophers who for different reasons believe essentially the same thing. What distinguishes the current "doomsday syndrome" from its predecessors is the claim that predictions are based upon scientific estimates. Modern doomsayers don't merely state that the end of the world is at hand; they can produce a computer printout that demonstrates it!

The most famous of the modern doomsayers is a 1972 publication entitled *The Limits to Growth* sponsored by the Club of Rome. It has sold more than 3 million copies and continues to have a tremendous impact upon public opinion. This study found:

If the present growth trends in world population, industrialization, pollution, food production, and resource depletion continue unchanged, the limits to growth on this planet will be reached sometime within the next one hundred years. The most probable result will be a rather sudden and uncontrollable decline in both population and industrial capacity. (p. 23).

This study thus concludes that continued economic growth into the not too distant future will be impossible. Furthermore, the world as we know it will end with a bang, not a whimper.

The authors tell us why. The end of the world will come like one, two, three because one, the earth's natural resources will soon be exhausted; two, increased output will smother the world in pollution; and, three, growing world population will outstrip the capacity of the planet to produce food. Unless drastic changes are made, the world economy will overshoot the level of output and population that can be sustained by a planet of fixed dimensions and will in the near future suddenly collapse.

In this chapter we examine the conclusion that the world is going to run out of natural resources relatively soon. This dismal conclusion results directly from the assumptions incorporated in the doomsday model. The basic assumptions are (1) that the stock of the world's natural resources is fixed, (2) that the world's economies will tend to consume this fixed stock at an ever increasing rate, and (3) that there are no built-in mechanisms that will reduce the rate of consumption prior to the complete exhaustion of the resource base.

The first two assumptions are questionable and must certainly be qualified, as we shall see below, but the third assumption is simply incorrect, making the conclusion of the doomsayers almost certainly wrong. The theory used in the Club of Rome study ignores the existence of a functioning price system, which is the main social institution for registering and reacting to the existence of scarcity.

There are several ways that the workings of a price system will direct society's behavior to avoid the predicted catastrophe. Economic theory divides market forces into those affecting the supply of a good (or resource) and those affecting the demand. The role of price is to equilibrate the quantity supplied with the quantity demanded. As a resource becomes increasingly scarce, its price will rise relative to other goods. This will cause buyers of the resource to voluntarily reduce the quantity of the good they demand, thereby reducing consumption. On the supply side, a higher price will induce suppliers to offer more of the resource either by mining the reserves more intensively or by finding new sources to exploit. Thus increasing scarcity is translated by the price system into a set of incentives to conserve on the use of the resource, on the one hand, and on the other hand, find and provide more of it.

First let us consider the known stock of existing resources as a limit on the supply side. Almost everyone would argue that the world is fixed in size and contains a fixed amount of resources. Hence it must follow that once we have consumed all of a particular resource, it will be all gone. Luckily for us, when viewed in terms of the demands of human beings the total amounts of the earth's resources are virtually limitless. A cubic kilometer of the earth's crust, on average, contains about 210 million tons of aluminum, 150 million tons of iron, 150,000 tons of chromium, 7,000 tons of uranium, and 80,000 tons of copper whereas a cubic kilometer of seawater contains about 37.5 million tons of solids, mostly sodium and chlorine but also large amounts of magnesium, gold, cobalt, lead, and mercury. These are the amounts of minerals found on the earth's crust—only 4 percent of the total mass of the earth. Beneath the crust the amount of resources available staggers comprehension. While fixed in size, the earth can still provide people with virtually unlimited quantities of resources.

But not without cost. The important question is not the total amount of resources in existence, but how easily (expensively) can resources be obtained for humanity's use? This is the same as asking what it will cost to mine and supply the resource in the markets of the world. The Club of Rome study did not ask this question. Instead, the authors accepted existing estimates of mineral resources and calculated how long they would last at various rates of exploitation. Existing estimates of known resources are those reserves that we know about and that can be exploited profitably at current market prices. They found that known resources of natural gas, for example, were 1.14×10^{15} cubic feet, which they calculated would last 22 years. There were only 13 years resources of silver figured the same way, and 15 years of tin, 20 years of petroleum, 111 years of coal, and 93 years of iron.

But do we know the total amounts of all the existing resources in the world? The world's resources, in truth, remain relatively little explored. Consider the case of crude oil, which is the example that will be used throughout the remainder of this chapter. The known reserves of petroleum in 1970 amounted to 455×10^9 barrels of 55 gallons each. The Club of Rome study estimated that this resource will last 20 years. Does this mean that in 1990 the world's economies will suddenly consume the last drop of oil? Furthermore, is the known estimate today equal to the total world stock of crude oil? The answer to both questions is no for at least two good reasons.

In the first place, most of the drilling for oil has taken place in a very few countries. Fully 75 percent of all oil wells have been drilled in the United States. No geologist believes that 75 percent of the world's oil is or ever was in the United States. There are twice as many oil wells, for example, in Kansas as in all of Africa. Much of the world has simply not yet been systematically explored for oil. When the Club of Rome published its study, proven oil reserves in Mexico were considered to amount to no more than 2.8 billion barrels. Today proven reserves total 50 billion barrels, and private estimates of 160 billion barrels, equal in amount to Saudi Arabia's, have been made. Recent discoveries in China may well amount to 50 billion barrels also. A study recently done for the World Bank estimated total world reserves to be ten times more than the Club of Rome assumed. Actually, nobody really knows how much oil there is.

The world still remains basically unexplored for oil. The reason for the lack of exploration is that until quite recently oil was relatively easy to discover, and was worth more the closer it was located to the regions in which it would be consumed. Naturally, petroleum engineers looked in those places first. When oil was discovered in abundance in the Middle East, that discouraged further efforts to look elsewhere. All that was required in Saudi Arabia was to drill a hole in the sand to find oil that could be produced for less than a penny a gallon. Why look further?

Another factor that explains why much of the world remains to be explored for oil is that it doesn't pay to know about all the oil that exists. The larger the stock of known resources, the less valuable it will be to find more. Is it really worthwhile, for example, to spend resources now searching for oil that won't be sold for 20 years? The larger the known reserves, the less valuable it is to discover more. There is simply an optimal amount of known reserves. Once this amount has been found, it doesn't pay to look further.

There is a second reason that one shouldn't take the existing known resource estimates as seriously as do the authors of *The Limits to Growth*. Known resources are estimated as the stock of resources that can be profitably exploited at the current price for the resource. Under a price system, as a resource becomes increasingly scarcer its price will rise. When that happens, some deposits of the resource that are already known, but were considered too expensive to exploit, become commercially feasible. Known reserves thus expand automatically with increases in the resource price. Furthermore, as the price of oil increases, it will be profitable to find more, and exploration will increase.

There are other sources of oil not currently being exploited. Currently, it pays to abandon an oil field when only 30 to 40 percent of the oil has been extracted. More than half of the oil is left in the ground. As the price of oil increases, it pays to spend more to extract a larger percentage of the resource. As the price of crude oil increases, it will become profitable to extract oil embedded in other material. The tar sands of Canada could be exploited to produce oil, as could oil shale in the United States. There are 40,000 years of oil at present levels of consumption contained in these deposits alone. Coal also can be converted to oil and gas, further increasing the potential supply of oil. Talk about an absolute shortage of oil is therefore unjustifiable as long as the price system is functioning. As oil or any resource becomes scarcer, its price will rise, which provides an incentive to discover and supply more of it. The important question is not the absolute amount of oil or any other resource, but what it will cost to supply. The world will never run out of oil, but oil might become too expensive to use.

The second assumption of the Club of Rome study is that the consumption of resources will continue at an exponential growth rate. For an example of exponential growth, consider what happens to a number that doubles every time period. The exponential sequence 1, 2, 4, 16, 96, 9216, 8534016 will quickly exhaust the spaces available on a desk calculator. Exponential growth generates immense numbers very quickly. Economic growth rates do not often double each time period, but a growth rate of 1 percent doubles consumption in 72 years, a 5 percent rate will double in 14 years, a 10 percent rate in 10 years. A rate of increase in petroleum consumption of 5 percent means that we shall use twice as much oil in 14 years as we are using today.

Consider now the future demand for oil. The use of historical growth rates to predict future consumption ignores the incentives provided by the price system to reduce the rate of consumption. As a resource becomes more scarce, its price will increase, which will discourage its use. As a resource, such as oil, becomes more valuable, people will have a strong incentive to economize on its use. Individuals will insulate their homes. They will purchase smaller automobiles that obtain better gasoline mileage, or they will switch to motorcycles, bicycles, or electric cars, or ride public transit, or even walk more. Goods that use a lot of oil will become relatively more expensive than goods that use relatively little, and consumers will respond to changes in relative prices by buying less of the former and more of the latter.

As the price of oil increases, industrial firms also will conserve on its use. Electricity, coal, and wood will be substituted for oil as sources of energy. Waste heat will be recycled. The reason that so much oil is currently used is that historically oil has been very inexpensive relative to alternative sources of energy. As oil becomes more expensive, it will certainly be used more sparingly. Current estimates state that the demand for oil falls 1 percent for every 4 percent price increase while supply increases 1 percent for every 5 percent price increase. Thus the world is threatened not by the imminent exhaustion of crude oil, but with the prospect of higher prices for petroleum products. The world may well abandon oil, if its price rises too high, in favor of lower cost substitutes. But we will never run out of oil.

In summary, one should not have the slightest confidence in the predictions of a theory that ignores the operation of the price system. Relative prices provide the information for individuals and business firms to make economic decisions. As a good or resource becomes more scarce, its price will rise. The higher price will increase the quantity supplied of the resource. Higher prices will encourage the more intensive exploitation of existing resources and the discovery of new reserves. Conversely, higher prices will discourage the use of the resource, providing an incentive for users to conserve the resource, to employ substitutes, and to purchase less of the goods that use relatively more of the resource. Increasing scarcity will be translated into higher prices well before the resource is totally exhausted.

Additional Readings

Hall, R. E. and R. S. Pindyck. "The Conflicting Goals of National Energy Policy." *The Public Interest,* Spring 1977.

Maddox, John. *The Doomsday Syndrome*. McGraw-Hill, 1972.

Meadows, D. L., et al. *The Limits to Growth*. Universe, 1972.

Solow, Robert M. "Is the End of the World at Hand?" *Challenge*, March–April 1973.

Preview

Labor has always viewed technological change as a potential threat to jobs—with some justification. There is a long list of occupations that have disappeared as the result of technological improvements. So in one sense this fear is justified. But during the past century, which has been characterized by rapid technological change, the overall rate of unemployment has not risen. This paradox can be resolved by the application of the circular flow of economic activity model. This model suggests that developments in one sector have consequences for the other sectors of the economy. In order to accurately assess the impact of technological change in one industry, it is necessary to consider the effects it has in other areas. Within this context it can be seen that if technological change reduces the opportunities for labor in one industry, the increased productivity that results creates offsetting opportunities in other areas.

Key Economic Points

Households and business firms are linked by product and factor markets.
Technological change increases the productivity of the economy.
Economic efficiency requires the periodic transfer of workers from less productive activities to more productive ones.
The effects of technological change upon employment opportunities cannot be evaluated by considering only the industry in which it occurs.
The costs of unemployment to workers affected by technological change are compared with the benefits of increased productivity for the economy as a whole.

4

Circular Flow of Economic Activity: Does Technological Change Cause Unemployment?

Adam Smith, the first great economist, lived through the Industrial Revolution and apparently missed it, so gradual were the changes occurring. Today you don't have to be a great economist to know that we are currently living through the computer revolution, so dramatic are the changes going on all around us. Your college registration and grades, your purchases at the grocery store, your paycheck, and your utility and credit card bills are all processed by computer. The computer now predicts election results when only 2 percent of the votes are counted. The same computer that predicts the outcome of next week's professional sports contests is used to design automobiles and hi-fi equipment. The computer is now moving into the home in personal sizes; one is even called a Pet.

The computer is widely acknowledged to be a laborsaving device. The number of labor-hours saved by the computer in performing the tasks just described staggers one's imagination. It also raises the question: does the widespread substitution of the computer for workers cause unemployment? If it does, will the unemployment be permanent?

In order to understand the effect of technological change on the unemployment rate, it is necessary to understand how the various elements in the economy are related. Often the developments in one sector affect other sectors as well. Technological change is one of these developments. Economists have developed a theoretical construction called a circular flow model of the economy, which shows the relationship between households and business firms. This is a useful tool for analyzing the effects of technological change upon unemployment.

In this model business firms and households are related to one another by their transactions in product and resource markets. Households sell resources to firms in order to obtain income, and the firms use these resources to produce goods and services which are in turn sold back to households. The specter of scarcity haunts these transactions because households have limited amounts of resources to supply to business firms; thus their money incomes will be limited. This will allow the purchase of only some of the things households, as consumers, would like to buy. Also, because the amount of resources that business firms can acquire is limited, the amount of goods and services that can be produced, given the state of technology, is limited.

Technological change allows business firms to produce more goods with the existing amount of resources. Because goods now require fewer resources to produce, they cost less, which provides consumers with the incentive to buy them. Because consumers are never able to satisfy all their wants, there is always a demand for lower priced goods, hence always a demand for labor to produce goods. Therefore, technological change cannot result in a permanent reduction of the demand for labor in general.

But historically the working person has viewed technological change with alarm, if not fear. Technological change may be the introduction of a more productive way of producing goods and services, but it often takes the form of new machines that do the work previously done by several workers and machines. Workers see the machines as taking their jobs. The medieval guilds, which were associations of skilled laborers, had strict rules against employing other than traditional methods. In the 1790s a group of English cloth spinners, called the Luddites, actually destroyed the first multispindle textile-spinning machines which allowed one person to do the work of several.

Such fears on the part of the working person have often been justified. Glassblowers, typesetters, elevator operators, cordwiners, icemen, and puddlers are but a few of the workers whose occupations have all but disappeared; the tasks these people used to do are now performed solely by machines.

The disappearance of these occupations is part of the process of economic growth. The substitution of capital for labor accounts for much of the increased standard of living we enjoy relative to our ancestors and to much of the modern world. The productive capacity of each laborer increases as he or she is provided with more capital equipment with which to work. The increases in labor productivity, upon which increases in the standard of living are based, are in large part tied to the introduction of new technology embodied in new capital equipment.

There is little doubt that technological change has reduced the demand for some kinds of labor. The list of extinct occupations demonstrates this. But does technological change cause an increase in the overall unemployment rate in the economy? After all, what is true of the part is not necessarily true of the whole. It may be a fallacy of composition to argue that because the introduction of a computerized cold type process in printing eliminates the jobs of linotype operators, the widespread use of "smart machines" will increase the national level of unemployment.

Consider the example of American agriculture. In 1870 about 45 percent of our population lived on farms; one farm worker produced enough food to feed roughly five other persons. By 1970 the proportion of the population living on farms had declined to less than 5 percent; the vast majority of Americans lived in urban areas and were employed in nonagricultural pursuits. Despite the fact that the American population had increased from 40 million to 205 million over the century, there were less than half as many farmers in 1970 as there had been 1870, one-third as many as existed at the start of World War II. What caused the relative and absolute decline in employment in agriculture? It was the increased productivity of labor resulting from the development and introduction of new technology—improved seeds, fertilizer, irrigation, and the mechanization of farming. In 1970 one farmer produced enough to supply the food requirements for forty-seven persons.

The increase in productivity in agriculture during the last century significantly increased the amount of food and fiber potentially available. How was this increased availability enjoyed by the American consumer? The increase in productivity increased the supply of foodstuffs, which reduced the price of food relative to other goods. The American consumer could now buy more food with the same budget or could buy the same amount as before and have money left over for other things. Americans were already relatively well fed in 1870, so they tended to use much of their now surplus food budget to buy other things. More labor was required to produce the increased amounts of nonagricultural goods households now demanded. The temporarily technologically unemployed farmer moved to the city to become the employed industrial worker, a process that continued for a century. Despite the migration of millions of farmers out of agriculture, the long-term rate of unemployment did not change appreciably. If technological change causes unemployment, it would be expected that the unemployment rate would have risen significantly over the last century. But it didn't. The rate of unemployment fluctuated, to be sure, but this was the result of the fluctuation in national income as the economy experienced various business cycles, not of the shift away from agriculture by millions of Americans.

Technological change does not always result in the reduction of the demand for labor within the industry in which it occurs. Consider one of the most important industrial developments during the first half of this century: the development of the automobile industry. The rapid growth of the automobile industry was made possible by the introduction of mass production initially by the Ford Motor Company. Between 1909 and 1923 Ford pioneered and developed the techniques of mass production that embodied principles of worker specialization and the substitution of capital for labor in producing the famous Model T. Each person employed on the Ford assembly line repeatedly performed a limited specialized task and was provided with specialized capital goods that allowed the task to be performed more efficiently.

As a consequence, the labor hours required to assemble a Model T declined from 12.5 in 1911 to 1.5 in 1914, a saving of 88 percent in the amount of labor required. But the total number of workers hired by Ford actually increased despite the new labor saving techniques. The reduced cost of producing automobiles allowed Ford to reduce the price of the Model T from $1,000 to less than $400 over the same period. The response of consumers to the lower price was to increase their purchases of Fords by 650 percent. The increase in the quantity of Model T automobiles sold actually required the employment of more labor, not less.

As long as scarcity exists, there will not be a shortage of things for labor to do. The price system functioning through resource and product markets provides the incentives, when technological change occurs, for labor to move from socially less desirable occupations to socially more desirable ones. The argument that since technological change may reduce the demand for labor in a particular industry, the introduction of new technology will result in widespread technologically-induced unemployment is indeed a fallacy of composition.

This does not mean that unemployment is not a serious national problem because from time to time it certainly has been. It does mean that cyclically high rates of unemployment are caused not by technological change, but by forces that lead to business fluctuations in the aggregate economy.

Nor does this mean that the benefits of technological change are without cost to all members of society. The glassblower who after years spent acquiring his skill is replaced by a machine and decides to take a job at a lower wage as a warehouseman is certainly worse off. During the course of the century, labor has tended to become more specialized. Each of us can do fewer things better than ever. If technological change eliminates the demand for a specialty, the next best opportunity may be terrible in comparison. While the benefits of the improved productivity that results will be widespread, the costs may be narrowly imposed upon the few workers unemployed as a result of technological progress.

It is no wonder that skilled labor, when faced with such a threat, resists the change. Stokers are still employed by railroads even though diesel electric trains do not require people to stoke the furnaces. The longshoremen are currently resisting the use of cargo containers which would reduce the demand for their services. This resistance is for good and personally valid reasons, but if it succeeds as it has so far in these two cases, the full benefits of increased productivity will not be available to society. A case could be made for the compensation or retraining of technologically displaced workers provided the costs of such programs are less than the gains from the more rapid introduction of new technology and from the reemployment of retrained workers.

In summary, while individual workers and professions may have reason to fear the employment consequences of technological change, there is little reason to expect that the unemployment rate for the economy as a whole will increase. This becomes apparent when the economy is viewed within the framework of a circular flow model. The process of technological change increases productivity, allowing the prices of some goods in the product markets to fall. The fall in prices has potentially two effects. First, the quantity of the goods demanded will increase, which in the case of the Model T actually increased the demand for labor by the Ford Motor Company in the resource market. Even if the increase in demand for the products with lower prices is not sufficient to offset the reduced demand for the labor, as was the case in American agriculture, it will still increase employment opportunities elsewhere. The lower prices made possible by technological change allow people to satisfy their desires for those goods at lower cost and thus have money left over to satisfy other wants. The increased demand for these other goods creates employment opportunities in other industries for the labor initially displaced by technological change.

The U.S. economy has benefited from substantial technological progress during its history, but there is no evidence that the trend in the unemployment rate has increased. This fact should not be surprising because, since scarcity exists, there will always be a demand for the goods labor produces, and a functioning price system, described by the circular flow model, provides the incentive for labor to move from less productive jobs to more productive ones. Should labor that has been displaced by technology fail in a short time to take up alternative employment, the fault lies not with the introduction of new techniques but with impediments to the allocation of resources within the economic system. It is the removal of these restrictions rather than the attempts to impede the introduction of new technology that society should consider.

Additional Readings

Leontief, Wassily. "Is Technological Unemployment Inevitable?" *Challenge*, September–October 1979.

Mansfield, Edwin. *Technological Change*. Norton, 1971, Chap. 5.

Pauling, W. G. "Some Neglected Areas of Research on the Effects of Automation and Other Technological Change on Workers." *Journal of Business,* July 1964.

Silberman, Charles E. *The Myths of Automation.* Harper and Row, 1966.

Preview

During the 1970s adult Americans took to their bicycles. By the middle of the decade more bicycles than automobiles were sold in the United States. The phenomenon of millions of Americans riding bicycles has been called the "bicycle boom." The purpose of this chapter is to explain the "bicycle boom" by employing the economic tools of supply and demand.

Key Economic Points

Is it a shift in the supply of or the demand for bicycles that accounts for the boom? Which of the forces that could have caused this shift was in fact responsible for it? An expansion of industry output could be caused either by an increase in demand or in supply.

5

Supply and Demand: The Bicycle Boom

Today it is ordinary to see numerous adult bicyclists peddling along city streets and across college campuses. A decade ago it would have been unusual to see an adult on a bicycle. Bicycles were then conveyances for children. The most popular model sold was called the High Riser, a bizarre, garishly decorated vehicle with small wheels, a banana-shaped saddle, and handlebars shaped like the arms of an ape. It was an unglamorous product produced mainly by small, family-owned manufacturers.

Suddenly, as a new decade was dawning, adult Americans went slightly mad over cycling! The number of bicycles sold doubled in 2 years, increasing from 6.9 million in 1970 to 8.7 million in 1971, to 13.9 million in 1972, and to 15.3 million in 1973. The retail price of a basic ten-speed bicycle increased as sales grew during the boom. The average price of a bike in 1970 was $55; in 1971, $62; in 1972, $66, and in 1973, $74. If we employ the consumer price index to factor out the effects of inflation and express the price of bicycles in real terms (in 1967 dollars), we still find that the average price of a bicycle increased over the boom. In 1967 prices, the average price of a bicycle in 1970 was $48; in 1971, $52; in 1972, $55; and in 1973, $60. In 1973, despite higher prices, Americans were buying more bicycles than automobiles.

The bicycle people wanted was not the oddly shaped High Riser but the elegant English style, a lightweight bike with narrow tires and five, ten,

33

or more gears that allowed the rider to mount a hill without great difficulty. American manufacturers had for years produced a few models of the English type. The High Riser, however, had been the best seller because kids had been the ultimate customers for nine out of every ten bikes produced. This situation changed during the 1970s, when "cycling mania" swept through the adult population. Adults, defined as anyone old enough to drive a car, now purchased for their own use half of the bicycles sold. American manufacturers rushed to produce an adult bike in quantity. Meanwhile imports filled the demand. There were more than 100 manufacturers of bicycles in 42 countries selling bicycles in the United States.

Within the United States in 1973, eight major manufacturers produced 76 percent of all bicycles sold domestically. Murray Ohio, Huffman, AMF, and Schwinn were the biggest of these, selling over 1.5 million each. U.S. manufacturers in total produced 10.3 million bikes, and imports accounted for the rest, bringing the total sold during 1973 to 15.3 million. Britain's Raleigh and France's Peugeot were the best sellers among the imports.

The total number of bicycles in America increased over the 4-year bicycle boom from around 20 million to over 65 million, and the presence of vastly increased numbers made itself felt on the urban cityscape. More than 25,000 miles of bike paths from which motor vehicles are excluded have been built or set aside for the use of cyclists. The U.S. Congress in 1973 provided $120 million for more bikeway construction. Bicycle racks, always present at grade schools, became a common sight on college campuses, in shopping centers, and even on Fifth Avenue in New York. One Miami bank installed "pedal-in" teller windows at its suburban branches.

The great bicycle boom took everyone by surprise, including the manufacturers. In retrospect, it is possible, if the principles of supply and demand are applied, to understand what happened. It may seem at first glance that because sales increased by 220 percent in 4 years and prices rose by a quarter, the law of demand (which postulates that higher prices discourage consumption) had been violated, since sales increased in spite of the price increases. But first impressions can be deceiving and in this case would be. Such a conclusion involves confusing a movement along a schedule with a shift of a schedule, a common but often disastrous mistake. A combination of increased output and rising prices is consistent only with a demand schedule that is increasing (shifting) relative to supply. The bicycle boom, then, was generated by a sudden (apparently unforeseen) increase in demand which generated a movement of the demand curve outward along the supply schedule, the increase in output reflecting the increase in consumer demand and the higher prices reflecting the higher unit cost of producing an expanded output. The larger output coupled with higher prices was generated by a demand schedule moving along a fixed supply schedule, verifying the principle of supply which states that more will be offered only at a higher price.

The increase in demand could have resulted from a number of factors. The price of related goods—complements or substitutes—could have changed, causing the demand for bicycles to be affected. The price of substitutes, such as shoes or automobiles, could have increased, or the price of complements, such as locks and chains, reflectors, and backpacks, could have fallen. The income of consumers could have increased or consumers could have suddenly altered their expectations for future prices, fearing that prices in future would significantly increase. Or the tastes of consumers could have changed in favor of the bicycle. Any or a combination of these changes could account for an increase in demand.

There are several reasons to believe that it was the last of the four possible factors—a change in tastes—that accounts for most of the increase in demand. The first reason is that the demand increased so dramatically that it would require a drastic change in the prices of complements or substitutes, a large increase in consumer incomes, or well-publicized information that future prices would be much higher to account for the increases in demand. Significant changes in these parameters did not occur. There are good substitutes for a bicycle as a means of transportation: walking, motorcycles, public transport, and automobiles are examples. Neither the price of shoes nor alternative means of transportation changed very much, certainly not enough to account for a doubling in the demand for bicycles. While the period from 1970 to 1973 was a recovery period of relatively rapid economic growth in the United States, the median incomes of households increased only from $14,465 to $15,437, an increase of less than 7 percent. Such a small increase hardly seems sufficient to account for a large expansion in the demand for bicycles. Nor does it appear that there was any unusual development in the bicycle industry that would lead consumers to change their expectations about future prices. This process of elimination leaves only a dramatic change in the tastes of consumers to explain the bicycle boom.

Economists do not like to resort to taste change to explain an economic phenomenon because taste changes cannot be observed in the same way that changes in income or in the price of substitutes or complements can. It is possible to use changing tastes to explain anything. If demand increases, then tastes change to favor the good; if demand decreases, then tastes alter in the opposite way. Because taste changes cannot be measured, no explanation based upon taste changes can be falsified. Taste change can explain everything, so in fact it explains nothing.

Therefore, economists then will resort to changing tastes to explain a shift in demand only as a last resort. After all the other phenomena that in theory could explain the change in demand have been examined and eliminated, then a change in taste can be considered. We have seen that the prices of related goods (substitutes and complements), income, and expectations probably did not cause the bicycle boom, therefore changes in taste can be considered.

While changing tastes cannot be observed directly, supporting evidence can generally be found. Usually industries experiencing rapid growth have introduced a new product that catches the consumer's fancy, e.g., Frisbees, Hula Hoops, minicalculators, electronic watches, video games, and video recorders. This was not the case in the bicycle boom. The English ten-speed had been available to Americans since the 1930s. A possible inference is that consumers rather suddenly changed their tastes to prefer this product over other goods.

This inference is supported by the radical shift in the age composition of the final user of bicycles from children to adults. During the 1970s adults purchasing bikes for their own use accounted for almost the entire increase in demand for bicycles. An investigation into the uses to which adults put their new bicycles is also revealing. While the bicycle was the primary means of transportation for children, it was not for adults. The automobile remained paramount as a source of adult transportation. Adults used their bicycles for recreation. By 1975 almost half of the adult population exercised regularly, a significant increase from 5 years before. Walking was the most frequently employed exercise, but calisthenics, swimming, and bicycle riding competed for second place. More than twice as many people rode bicycles regularly for exercise than ran or jogged. The American people discovered physical fitness during the 1970s, and the bicycle fit in perfectly with many individuals' exercise programs.

Other evidence for selecting changes in taste as the major explanation of the bicycle boom can be found in the ending of the boom. Sales peaked in 1973 at 15.3 million and fell immediately thereafter to 13.8 million in 1974. The energy crisis, with gasoline in short supply and long waiting times at the pumps, did not spur bicycle sales as might be expected. In fact, bicycle sales fell by 1.5 million, or 10 percent. The rapid rise in energy prices in 1974 caused the worst recession since the 1930s, and the negative effect upon consumers' incomes simply swamped whatever positive stimulus to demand that substituting a bicycle for a car might have encouraged. The demand for bicycles, like the demand for most other goods, declined during the recession. The demand curve shifted in along the supply schedule. The result was as economic theory would predict. The quantity of bicycles sold fell, as did the average price of bikes—from $60 to $56.60 in 1967 dollars.

The recession of 1974–1975 did not in itself end the bicycle boom, which would have slowed down of its own accord. Americans' new proclivity to exercise was a once-and-for-all change, and so was the increase in demand for bicycles that it stimulated. The rapid increase in sales satisfied a virgin demand for bicycles from individuals who did not have one. Between 1970 and 1974, almost 60 million Americans purchased a bike. The size of the potential market of bikeless individuals was in the process reduced significantly. A used bicycle market developed to compete with manufacturers for sales. In the future manufacturers would depend increasingly upon replacement sales for their business. No one knows how long a bicycle will last an adult user. A child's bike lasts betweeen 5 and 8 years, but these vehicles are not very well maintained. An adult willing to periodically spend a few hours and dollars on maintenance can make a bike last a lifetime.

The bicycle boom would probably have ended of its own accord during the middle 1970s as the market for bicycles as exercise machines became saturated. When this occurred both the relative price and quantity of bicycles sold would probably have declined as the economics of supply and demand predicts.

The bicycle boom provides an illustration of how the economics of supply and demand can be used to explain past events. The pattern of rising prices and outputs is only consistent with an increase in demand (a shift of the demand curve) stimulating an increase in the quantity supplied (a movement along the supply curve). It is thus possible to investigate the potential sources of increased demand to identify the forces that caused the bicycle boom. The economic tools of supply and demand can, of course, also be used for prediction by reversing the process and inquiring as to what would be the effect upon the price and output if one of the sources that can cause a change in either supply or demand is itself changed. The basic tools of supply and demand are therefore widely applicable in explaining economic phenomena.

Additional Readings

"Bicycle Boom Still in High Gear." *U.S. News and World Report,* November 5, 1973.

"Boom Goes Flat." *Wall Street Journal,* October 24, 1974.

Louis, Arthur M. "How the Customers Thrust Unexpected Prosperity on the Bicycle Industry." *Fortune,* March 1974.

"Output Increased, But Still Can't Keep Pace with Demand." *Wall Street Journal,* September 2, 1971.

"Wheeling and Dealing." *Barron's,* June 11, 1973.

Preview

It is a common practice for the top rock 'n roll groups to price their concert tickets below the market clearing price. This practice results in a shortage and requires some nonprice means for allocating the available tickets. During the Rolling Stones' 1972 tour, concert tickets were priced below the market clearing price and the concert managers used means other than price to allocate the scarce tickets. The most frequent means was to sell tickets on a first-come, first-served basis. Other methods were also used: friendship passes, a lottery, even violence. Everywhere the Rolling Stones played, a black market appeared. This chapter investigates the efficiency consequences of employing nonprice mechanisms to allocate concert tickets and explores the question of who gains and who loses when a particular nonprice means is employed.

Key Economic Points

When a price is set below the market clearing price a shortage is created.

Some of the ways scarce goods can be allocated when a shortage exists are identified.

What are the efficiency consequences of using the various nonprice means of allocating resources?

Who benefits and who loses from each nonprice allocation method?

6

Nonprice Allocation of Scarce Resources: Touring with the Rolling Stones

Aside from the music itself, nothing provokes as much emotion in rock music fans as the way tickets for a major concert are distributed. After every ticket sale, concert promoters and local newspapers receive a rash of complaints and anguished protests from people who couldn't get tickets or who could only obtain "lousy seats." The problem is that there are often more people who want to hear a "major" act than there are tickets available at the price promoters set. Promoters of concerts by superstars, it would appear, do not price the tickets they sell so that the quantity supplied (seats available in the auditoriums) equals the quantity demanded.

This has always been the case on Rolling Stones concert tours. During the 1970s the Stones toured the United States roughly every 3 years. These tours were fantastic successes. The 1978 tour, for example, played to 760,000 people and grossed over $9 million. Everywhere the Stones went they played to packed houses, and still many people were turned away. Individual tickets were scalped (resold) for as much as $400 in an active black market. It was much the same on earlier tours.

Nothing, for example, in the summer of 1972 was more scarce than tickets to a Rolling Stones concert. Millions of fans between the ages of 15 and 35 wanted to see them perform. The Stones' business manager, Peter Rudge, was in charge of the tour. He saw that his problem was not to sell tickets, but to ensure that they were distributed "fairly," that they would not fall into scalpers' hands in large numbers, and that there was no counterfeiting and no riots. Tickets were to sell at $6.50 top, and less in smaller cities such as Seattle, where they sold for $6.

The demand for tickets at that price far exceeded the capacity of local auditoriums. Everywhere they played, they could have sold twice or three times the number of tickets actually available. *Life* magazine estimated that the Stones could have played in San Francisco for 3 months and in New York for 6 months to packed houses. In San Francisco there were only 18,000 seats available; in New York, 80,000; in Seattle, 28,000; in Vancouver, B.C., 17,000; and in Washington, D.C., 50,000. The available seats had to be allocated somehow among the considerably higher number of people wanting them. Some ticket seekers got tickets; many more did not.

The nonprice ways scarce resources can be rationed are numerous, and the Stones and their followers apparently tried most of them at one time or another during the tour. If a price less than the market clearing price is set, then scarce resources must be allocated by means other than a simple exchange of money. There are many possible ways this can be done. One way is on a first-come, first-served basis, which requires waiting in line or queuing. Another is friendship. Other means include bribery, violence, the use of some rationing system, or a lottery. Each of these methods, when compared with a price system, discriminates in favor of some groups over others, redistributes wealth, involves some inefficiency, and suggests an interesting investigation into who gained and who lost.

In Vancouver and Seattle, as in most of the thirty-two cities toured, the tickets were available on a first-come, first-served basis. Tickets were sold about 1 month prior to the performance. Each person could purchase a maximum of four tickets. Customers began to appear at both Empire Stadium in Vancouver and Memorial Stadium in Seattle 48 hours prior to the tickets going on sale. Hundreds actually spent the night in front of ticket windows. Hours prior to the windows opening, a crush began to form. In both places, the concerts were all sold out within 5½ hours. Many who had waited in line for hours were disappointed.

In Vancouver some who were disappointed vented their anger on Empire Stadium, attempting to raze the structure and doing several thousands of dollars worth of damage before they were stopped. The night of the performance 2,000 persons attempted to crash the sold-out concert. A riot ensued in which thirty police were injured, and the promoters were presented with a bill for $12,000 to cover the damages. The gate crashers did not succeed in their attempt to get into the theater.

Forewarned by the events in Vancouver, Seattle police took preventive measures and no violence occurred. In Seattle, 28,000 tickets were sold to 7,500 people who waited between 6 and 8 hours in the crush to obtain them. Thus the Stones got the $168,000 paid by buyers, and the ticket purchasers paid an additional $90,000 to $120,000 in time spent waiting. Many persons who stood in the lines expressed anger at the way the tickets were sold. One young man said that tickets should have been sold at normal outlets or at a location with more ticket windows. Another suggestion was that tickets could have gone on sale simultaneously at numerous locations. Some persons grew weary, and some nauseous, from waiting in lines for hours, and many left without tickets.

By the time the tour got to San Francisco the Stones had taken the man's advice. Tickets, 18,000 in number, went on sale via the computer-controlled Ticketron system, which allows tickets to be purchased at over fifty commercial outlets. One person scouted the available outlets and selected a Montgomery Ward store in Oakland. When he arrived at 7:00 a.m., he found the sidewalk jammed with the devoted who had spent the night in sleeping bags. When the store opened at 9:30, there was a rush to the ticket window and a crush formed. Precisely at 10:00 the computer went on-line and at 10:01 stopped working. All fifty outlets were trying to buy at once and had to wait their turns. This amounted to a delay of 12 to 15 minutes between two transactions at one place. Once again, not everyone who waited in line got a ticket.

However, not everyone who got tickets had to stand in line. At each performance, 500 seats were reserved for VIPs. If a person was someone who mattered or knew someone who did, he or she got tickets for free. Queues and friendship passes were used everywhere on the tour except in New York City. Everywhere the age of the majority of persons in the queues was between 15 and 17 years.

In Washington, D.C., one giant performance was given in Kennedy Stadium. Forty-five thousand persons, each paying $5.50, attended, and the crowd was handled like a sellout at a professional sports event, with crowd control precautions taken. Nevertheless, a crowd of 30,000 had formed by 4:00 p.m. when the turnstiles opened, 4 hours before the concert. By 5:00 there wasn't a good seat left in the stadium. The age of this crowd was considerably older, mainly in the 18 to 25 age brackets, but there were almost as many in the 25 to 30 group.

The same was true in New York, where a lottery was employed to distribute "fairly" the 80,000 tickets available for the four performances at Madison Square Garden. Winners were allowed to buy four tickets at $6.50 each. Persons who wanted the right to purchase four tickets sent in a postcard with their names and addresses. A CPA firm employed a computer to first check for duplicates and then select 20,000 names. It is reported that 560,000 persons wrote in, requesting the right to purchase tickets. Their chance of getting what they wanted was 35 to 1—a real long shot. The lucky audience was primarily made up of persons in their 20s.

Let's look closely at the Stones' pricing policy. It is clear that at every concert they could have charged higher ticket prices and made more money. They chose not to, and redistributed the additional income they could have had as a gift to some of their fans, those who could get tickets. They reportedly were interested in fair distribution of tickets and in preventing scalping, counterfeiting, and riots. The latter was accomplished with the exception of the disturbance in Vancouver. Counterfeiting was not a serious problem, but it was an everpresent fear.

Scalping, the process of buying a ticket for one price and selling it for a higher price, was present everywhere. The limit of four tickets per customer was an attempt to take the business away from the professional scalper and give it to the kids. In Seattle tickets were offered for $10 to $15; in San Francisco the price was one lid or $15, but one set of four tickets was sold for $120, or $30 each. In Chicago sales were made at $70 a ticket and in Los Angeles at $75. *Time* magazine predicted that tickets for the Madison Square Garden show would fetch $100.

The Rolling Stones thus provided employment for persons of relatively low opportunity costs to wait in line, purchase, and resell the tickets. If, for example, a person valued his or her time at $2 an hour and had to wait for 8 hours to purchase four tickets at $6, then his or her cost is $10 per ticket. If the ticket is sold for more than that, the scalper makes a profit. A person using one ticket and selling three for more than $13.83 would have his or her way to the concert paid.

The above situation also explains why in the cities that allocated tickets by long waiting lines the people in the lines were relatively young. This group has the lowest opportunity cost of waiting. Thus a ticket allocation method that employs waiting lines or queues will have younger people standing in those lines. Many persons who actually attend the concerts, however, would be older because of tickets being resold.

In Washington, D.C., where the lines were short and started near the end of the working day, there was a group in line whose average age was several years older than in other cities. In Washington, where the crowd on average waited for 4 hours, the cost of a ticket was the price in dollars, $5.50, plus the value of 4 hours time lost.

In New York City 560,000 persons tried to obtain tickets by sending in postcards. New York is bigger than Washington, D.C., but not thirteen times bigger. The reason more people tried to obtain tickets in New York was that it was less expensive to do so. Instead of spending hours waiting in line, one simply mailed a postcard. If one was lucky, one gained the right to buy tickets worth several times their cost. It was a giant lottery. This method of allocating tickets does not obviously favor any one age group, so a mixed age group got tickets.

Let's look at the economics of the various ways the Stones used to provide a gift to their fans, since that is precisely what they did when they offered tickets at less than their market value. The waiting in queues resulted in persons paying with time part or all of the potential gain available from tickets priced at less than the market clearing price. We also know that some people waited in vain and actually lost the value of their time. It is quite possible that the total cost of the tickets, the dollars paid plus the time cost of both the lucky and the unlucky, was larger than it would have been had the Stones instead charged the market clearing price. Clearly, society was worse off. Had the Stones charged the market clearing price, the people who wanted the tickets badly enough to pay the price would have had to create goods and services at least equal to the value of the tickets they wished to purchase. Society would have had both the Stones concert and the wealth created to pay for it.

The use of influence or friendship in ticket allocation, although reprehensible to many, is not nearly as socially wasteful as selling tickets below the market clearing price. It is merely a transfer from the Rolling Stones to the favored few. If these privileged persons could sell the tickets, and they could, then the Stones would have given them a present valued at the difference between what they could scalp the tickets for and what they had to pay to become a "favorite." If the tickets to friends were free, then the price a scalper could get is the value of the gift.

The lottery was to each individual less costly than the queues. It is not clear as to whether the social cost of 580,000 postcards, a CPA firm, and a computer's time is more or less than that of several thousand persons standing in line. In both cases resources are spent trying to qualify for the gift.

The scalping or black market was merely a way for people—either those in the queues with lower opportunity costs, or those in the lottery who were more fortunate, or the favored ones who got their tickets for free—to cash in on the gifts. Whenever a person is given the opportunity to purchase a good at less than the market price, an opportunity is also created for that person to gain by exchanging the ticket with persons who value it higher.

The only method the Stones employed of giving the gift that did not impose social costs was the friendship or VIP method. The queues wasted valuable time in waiting and the lottery ate up postcards.

Why do the Rolling Stones and other top groups price concert tickets below the market clearing price? Perhaps they want to share their wealth. It is also possible that they gain more than they lose by pricing their concert tickets below the market clearing price. The crowds and crushes generated caught the attention of the national press. Every major newspaper carried an article on the Stones tour at least once a week, as did many national magazines such as *Time, Life, Newsweek,* and the *Saturday Review.* National television followed their tour. The behavior of Stones fans attempting to get tickets was news, and it provided the Rolling Stones with millions of dollars of free publicity.

It is more than likely that the publicity of a successful tour would, in record sales, more than make up for the loss in ticket sales. A tour by a major rock group such as the Rolling Stones has as its primary purpose stimulation of the group's record sales. Publicity, and the opportunity to hear the group in person, increase record sales. The Stones employed a nonprice means of allocating tickets because the behavior of fans attempting to locate tickets generated publicity.

Most of the money the Rolling Stones, or any rock group, earns is through record sales. One "gorilla" record that sells several million copies easily earns more money with less effort for the group than an entire tour. The majority of records are sold to high school age buyers. This is a group with relatively low opportunity costs for their time, just the group that is favored by the waiting-in-line ticket allocation method. The Stones picked this method to allocate tickets in most of the cities toured. The Stones in effect chose the allocation method that increased the chances of record buyers to see them in concert. This is probably what Peter Rudge meant when he said he wanted to see the tickets distributed fairly. A person is simply more apt to collect the records of a group that he or she has heard live. Everyone in the record business knows this.

A nonprice method of allocating scarce resources is not without its costs—in this case to the Stones, to their fans, and to society. It cost the Stones the difference between the price charged and the market clearing price; fans who were successful in obtaining tickets paid the price of the ticket, plus the cost of the resources used to qualify for the tickets; those who were unsuccessful in obtaining tickets expended resources for nothing; and society lost the value of goods and services that could have been produced with the resources spent to qualify for tickets, plus the resources spent reallocating tickets in the scalper's market.

The problems and costs associated with employing a nonprice means of allocating scarce resources on a Rolling Stones tour are but a microcosm of the problems to be expected whenever some allocation scheme other than a market clearing price is employed, such as the wage and price controls sometimes employed by the government, or the current price controls in the oil and gas industry, or the plans advocated to control rising hospital costs. Whenever a nonprice means is used to allocate scarce resources, some costs, not borne when the market is employed, are imposed, and some groups are favored over others. Furthermore, there is no guarantee that the people who want the goods most (that is, who are willing to sacrifice the most) will obtain them.

Additional Readings

Flippo, Chet. "Life Ain't What It Used to Be on the Road with the Rolling Stones." *Rolling Stone*, September 7, 1978.

Greenfield, Robert. *S.T.P.: A Journey Through America With the Rolling Stones.* Saturday Review Press, 1974.

Lupoff, Dick. "Rolling Stones: Goodbye to All That." *Ramparts*, July 1972.

Preview

The dominant form of business organization in our economy is the corporation. Although there are relatively few corporations, in comparison with individual proprietorships and partnerships, the corporations do a majority of the business in the industrial sector and control most of the assets. Furthermore, their hold on business activity is increasing. Recently, large corporations have chosen to grow larger by merging with other large corporations. This situation raises the question of whether, in the absence of monopoly, giant size is itself undesirable. A number of social critics think it is. Some legislators and the Department of Justice agree and have asked Congress to pass a law prohibiting large corporations from engaging in mergers. This chapter explores the question of whether giant size is in itself bad for our society, considers whether the giant corporation has escaped from the rigors of the competitive marketplace as some critics suggest, and analyzes the efficiency of employing an antimerger law to restrict the further growth of giant corporations.

Key Economic Points

Arguments are evaluated for the claim that the large size of a corporation is itself bad for society.

To what extent does competition in the product markets limit the power of giant corporations?

Personal interests of the management of large corporations may be different from the interests of stockholders.

To what extent does competition in the factor markets, especially in the stock market, limit the power of corporate mergers?

The advantages of an antimerger law are weighed against the disadvantages of the reduced competitive pressures on corporate management.

7

Business Organization: Does Competition Control the Giant Corporation?

The corporation is the dominant form of business organization in our economy. About 55 percent of the nation's output is produced by business firms organized as corporations. The corporate sector is also highly concentrated. In 1974 the 500 largest industrial firms, all corporations, accounted for 66 percent of the total sales of the industrial sector and 72 percent of the profits. The largest corporations are very big indeed. The sales of any of the ten largest corporations are greater than the national income of most of the countries of the world.

The concentration of the nation's assets in the hands of a corporate few has been increasing. Three decades ago the largest 200 industrial companies held 46 percent of the nation's industrial assets. In 1978 the largest 200 held 64 percent. Mergers are one way the largest firms have grown at the expense of the smaller firms. In 1977 there were forty-one mergers that cost the acquiring firm over $100 million. In 1978 there were eighty, and the trend looks as if it will continue into the indefinite future unless stopped in some way.

The growth of corporate giants has alarmed not only social reformers such as Ralph Nader and John Kenneth Galbraith, but also members of the federal government. Senator Edward Kennedy has introduced a bill to limit mergers by giant corporations, and the Justice Department has requested a similar bill. Either bill if enacted into law would effectively prohibit additional mergers by giant corporations.

The rise of the giant corporation and the suggested legal remedy raise at least two questions. Is bigness bad per se, and if so, is a new antimerger law the way to counteract further growth? First, it must be demonstrated that there is a problem. Second, it must be shown that prohibiting mergers by giant corporations is the way to solve the problem.

Social critics feel that it is absurd for economists to analyze the giant corporation as if it were a Ma and Pa grocery store, only bigger. The giant corporation, they contend, is not merely an inflated version of a small firm but a different species entirely. The sheer size of the organization, they contend, allows it to dominate economic and social behavior. Giant corporations, it is alleged, can through advertising convince people to buy things they do not really want while at the same time excluding rivals from markets by predatory tactics or by combination with smaller firms. Stopped by the antitrust laws from forming cartels, the giant corporation has turned to mergers. The road to monopoly, in the words of one critic, has been paved by mergers.

Even when the monopoly of a market is not obtained, the sheer size of the giant corporation alarms many people. This fear is very old. Supreme Court Justice John M. Harlan in 1911 attacked "the aggregation of capital in the hands of a few controlling the production and sale of the necessities of life." Giant size, the concentration of a large part of the nation's assets in the hands of a few, is feared to be inconsistent with democracy. Big business has a political advantage because of the assets that can be brought to bear in any political debate. According to Ralph Nader, "The costs of corporate oligopoly and giantism to the consumer, to the small business man, to the worker, to the economy, are substantial."

This potential for doing ill, according to Nader, would not be so bad if the owners of our industrial corporations exercised their rights to govern these giant firms. There are millions of individual shareholders who come from all walks of American life. They own, but they don't control. Shareholders exert little authority over the corporations they own, leaving the running of the companies to professional managements who do not own what they control. The interests of the managers, who control, and the stockholders, who do not, often diverge. Shareholders would prefer the firm to be efficient and maximize profits, while managers may be more interested in security, power, prestige, personal income, and advancement. The best way for management to achieve its goals may be for the corporation to grow in size even if this implies a sacrifice in efficiency and profitability.

The larger the corporation, the more secure it is against bankruptcy, the higher the salaries that management can command, the more opportunities there are for advancement, and the more prestige, influence, and social recognition the managers will receive. The management of giant corporations are able to pursue these goals because the board of directors, which in theory represents the stockholders' interest, in practice represents the interests of management. Almost half of the directors of a giant corporation typically are employees (management) of the corporation, and another quarter are executives of other corporations who share the goals and values of management.

The critics of the giant corporation feel that bigness is in itself bad. It is possible, however, that large size is necessary to achieve economies of scale in production and management. Large size allows the corporation to produce at lower costs, to ensure the sources of supply, and to borrow money for expansion at lower rates of interest than smaller firms. In short, there may be economies of large size that allow resources to be used more efficiently. Economists have always been more concerned with the size of a firm relative to the market(s) it competes in than with the potential dangers of size itself.

The antitrust laws have been reasonably successful in preventing monopoly and monopolistic practices in particular markets, but they have done little to curb sheer size. Because of the antitrust laws, large firms have often chosen to grow by acquiring firms in different market areas. The result has been the creation of giant conglomerates operating in many different markets.

Bigness itself would be bad only if there were such insufficient social control that management could actually use its potential economic power in socially undesirable ways. The major system of control over business in our society has always been competition. There are two distinct areas in which competition places limits on the exercise of corporate power. The first is competition in the markets that the corporations serve. Giant corporations do not consider their fellows as allies but as rivals standing in the way of the achievement of corporate objectives. The second is competition to acquire the right to manage the corporation. Existing managers have to consider the possibility of being replaced by rivals who would like to have their jobs.

Let's first consider competition in the markets served by giant corporations. Has giant size insulated our largest corporations from the competitive acts of their rivals? It is one thing for a firm to grow with the economy. It is quite another to grow at the expense of its rivals. The increasing concentration of manufacturing assets in the hands of our largest corporations demonstrates that the giant corporation has grown at the expense of smaller firms. But the successful giants must also have grown at the expense of fellow giants.

The summit of corporate America is, in fact, a slippery place. A comparison list of the top 100 in 1977 reveals that 65 of the 100 on the list in 1917 are no longer there today. Armour (4th) and Swift (5th), both meatpackers, were among the top five corporations in 1917 and are not even in the top 100 today. Neither are some companies you may have heard about, such as Asarco (12th), Anaconda Copper (13th), Phelps-Dodge (15th), Singer (16th), B. F. Goodrich (23rd), or Pullman (26th), plus forty-seven others you probably haven't heard about.

Perhaps it would be more appropriate tò focus on the period following World War II. Even in this more recent period, a comparison of the top 100 in 1945 with the top 100 in 1977 would find forty-five firms that were on the 1945 list that are absent from the 1977 list. Among them would be Montgomery Ward, then a close competitor of Sears-Roebuck, and Curtiss-Wright, the largest manufacturer of airplanes in 1945. Replacing them, seemingly from out of nowhere, came companies such as Teneco, Litton, Xerox, Boeing, Monsanto, Caterpillar Tractor, and thirty-nine others.

The rise and fall of corporate giants can be ascribed to changes in technology, changes in consumer-spending patterns, to good and bad business decisions, but mostly to competition. This is not to suggest that giant companies are as vulnerable to misfortune as small firms; they are not. But they are far from invulnerable.

If competition places checks on the giant corporation in the marketplace, does it also place limits on the managers' use of the corporation's assets for its own economic and political ends? The management of a giant corporation with a compliant board of directors could, for example, grant to itself large salaries, attractive stock options, perquisites such as the use of company airplanes, fancy offices, extended paid vacations, liberal retirement plans. Such things do happen. The Internal Revenue Service on one occasion found more than seventy corporately owned jets parked at airports near the site of the Kentucky Derby on race day.

A management operating according to its own interests is from the point of view of the stockholder and society inefficient and perhaps dangerous. How can stockholders control the misuse of company assets? They can and have sued the management of companies for the use of company funds for personal purposes. Stockholder suits, however, are rare because they are expensive. A person owning 100 shares in a company with a management that is consciously or unconsciously misallocating the company's resources will probably not sue but will instead sell his or her shares. That is the easiest way out. If management, for one reason or another, performs inefficiently, the profits of the firm will decline and its stock price will fall as its stockholders attempt to get out. If the stock price falls below the level achievable by an efficiently managed firm, the stage is set for a takeover bid. The assets of a poorly run firm are now worth more to someone else, and the inefficient management should be concerned.

It is this concern that society ought to encourage because it promotes efficient management performance. The decline in stock prices that follows inefficient management is one part of the story. The second is the possibility of another, more efficiently managed firm acquiring the assets and profiting by making the assets more productive. An antimerger bill would reduce the potential number of acquiring firms, thus reducing the incentives for managements of giant corporations to operate efficiently.

Studies of recent mergers have found that the stock of firms that were acquired had fallen abnormally low prior to a takeover bid. The lower the price of the stock, the more likely that another corporation will attempt a takeover. The study also found that if the takeover was successful, shareholders of both firms benefited from higher stock prices. The only losers were the managers of the acquired firm, who were apt to lose their jobs. Furthermore, the study determined that the more incompetent the management, as reflected in abnormally low share prices, the more apt they were to resist the takeover. Approximately one-fourth of the firms subject to takeover bids resisted the attempt using the firm's resources to oppose the offer.

The most infamous examples of successful resistance occurred during 1978 when Mead, a forest products firm, resisted the offer of Occidental Petroleum and when McGraw-Hill resisted the attempt by American Express. In both cases the stockholders lost and management kept their jobs. An antimerger law would have the undesirable side effect of improving the job security of inept managements, who would have less to fear from the possibility of a takeover bid.

Furthermore, prohibiting mergers will not stop the growth of large firms, but it will stop some of them from growing in the most efficient manner. The markets of an inefficiently managed firm would still present an attractive target for more efficient firms. But instead of directly acquiring the firm's assets via a takeover bid, the more efficient firms would have to compete in the markets in which the inefficient firm sells. This would require the costly (from society's point of view) duplication of capital investment.

In most mergers it is bigger firms that acquire smaller ones. Therefore, it is the management of relatively small firms that must keep on their toes. But what about the largest companies, such as Exxon, General Motors, and IBM? What keeps their managements efficient? It is inconceivable that as long as the price of their stocks stay up, any other firm could raise the funds to buy any of the top ten. However, it can be argued that it is precisely because they are already efficiently managed that their stock prices stay up. Consider the plight of Chrysler, which in 1966 was the fourteenth largest industrial firm. In the 1970s Chrysler fell on hard times and lost hundreds of millions of dollars, slipping in size to eighteenth by 1977. The price of Chrysler stock fell below the book value of its remaining assets as stockholders attempted to sell out. Chrysler hired new management, which discovered that Volkswagen was secretly purchasing its stock. Chrysler was probably saved from a takeover by the action of the federal government guaranteeing over $1 billion in loans. Even the very large corporation's management is not isolated from competition. Management is secure only as long as it performs relatively efficiently.

This is not to suggest that bigness is good, and we should not be concerned with the continued accumulation of the nation's manufacturing assets in the hands of a relatively few persons. It may well be that giant corporations are inconsistent with democracy. Doubtless giant corporations can exert political power for their own ends. The federal government rescued Lockheed and Chrysler from bankruptcy because they were large employers whereas it did nothing for the thousands of smaller firms that were failing at the same time. Political power does count for some things.

But it would be costly to attempt to limit growth by prohibiting mergers because such a prohibition would reduce the incentives for corporate management to perform efficiently. Nor is a new merger law necessary to halt mergers pursued for purposes of obtaining a monopoly. The federal government already has that power. Section 7 of the Clayton Act allows the public and private prosecution of mergers if it can be demonstrated that there is a "a lessening of competition or a tendency to create monopoly in any line of commerce in any section of the country." So vigorously has this law been enforced that a shoe firm with only 4 percent of the market was prevented from acquiring a competitor one-eighth its size.

If bigness is bad per se, another way of taming the giant corporation other than by prohibiting large mergers should be found. Prohibiting mergers would have the undesirable side effect of reducing the discipline that competition imposes upon the managers of giant corporations. An antimerger law holds out the prospect for insulating incompetent executives from the rigors of the marketplace.

Additional Readings

Johnson, M. Bruce (ed). *The Attack on Corporate America.* McGraw-Hill, 1976.

Nader, Ralph, Mark Green, and Joel Seligman. *Taming the Giant Corporation.* Norton, 1976.

"Sixty Years of Corporate Ups, Downs, and Outs." *Forbes,* September 15, 1977.

Preview

There is a growing interest in tax reform in the United States. The objective of tax reform in this case is to create incentives for economic growth. A value-added tax has been proposed as an alternative to existing taxes, especially the payroll tax currently used to finance the social security program. According to the proponents, a value-added tax is a more effective tax because it creates incentives that promote economic growth whereas the payroll tax generates incentives to reduce the level of employment. This chapter explores the pros and cons of a value-added tax in comparison with the existing tax structure.

Key Economic Points

How would a value-added tax be collected?

Taxes in general, and the value-added tax in particular, will alter economic behavior.

Economic incentives created by a value-added tax are compared with the incentives generated by the existing payroll tax.

Proposed arguments against a value-added tax are weighed.

Is a value-added tax preferable to the payroll tax for financing social security?

8

Functions of Government: The Proposed Value-Added Tax

The major concern of tax reform for the past generation has been to use the tax system to achieve a more equitable distribution of income. There are signs that the times are changing, that concern has shifted to the effect of taxes upon economic incentives. Several years of relatively slow economic growth and lagging capital formation in the mid-1970s has increased interest in stimulating the level of investment and saving. The revenue bill of 1978, which cut the capital gains tax, was weighted toward the affluent, who are the large savers.

The same concern is behind the renewed interest in employing in the United States a value-added tax (or VAT), which is widely used in Europe. In the United States the Nixon administration proposed such a tax in 1972, first as a substitute for the corporate income tax and then as a replacement for the property tax. Neither proposal ever proceeded past the draft stage. In 1979 America's two most important congressmen involved in creating tax policy came out in favor of introducing a value-added tax in the United States: Senator Russell Long, chairman of the Senate Finance Committee, and Representative Al Ullman, chairman of the House Finance Committee. Both supported the VAT, which ensures that this proposed tax will be seriously considered as an alternative to our present tax system.

The current mood in the country, however, is to reduce taxes and government spending, not to introduce a new tax. This means that any proposal for a new tax would be coupled with promises and/or guarantees to eliminate or reduce other existing taxes. Senator Long suggested VAT as a replacement for the unpopular social security tax and/or as a means of reducing the income tax.

We shall consider the proposed value-added tax compared with the current system of taxation, especially the payroll tax. An economist comparing taxes is interested in the incidence of the tax (who actually pays the tax) and in the incentives the tax creates. Economists are also interested in determining whether the tax is progressive or regressive. A progressive tax is one that causes a person with a high income to pay a greater proportion of that income in taxes than a person with a lower income. A regressive tax is the reverse: it forces a person with a low income to pay a higher portion in taxes than a person with a higher income.

Almost all taxes cause some distortion of economic activity. That is, people will behave differently after the tax is imposed than they would in its absence. Most taxes change incentives in some way. It is important to understand the nature of the incentives that a tax creates in order to predict its overall effect upon economic activity.

A value-added tax is a tax on consumption rather than on income. It is a sales tax that is levied at each stage of production and distribution. Instead of a consumer paying a retail sales tax on each purchase, as is now done in many states, the tax is collected from each firm that had a hand in producing the good. Each company when figuring the tax it owes simply takes its gross receipts, subtracts its payments to other firms, and applies the tax rate to what is left. What is left is the value created, or added, by the company.

Let's consider an example. Suppose a bicycle manufacturer spends $30 to obtain the steel, handlebars, grips, pedals, chain, wheels, tires, and brake assembly that are then fashioned into a bicycle and sold to a dealer for $50. The value added is the difference between the revenues a firm receives when it sells the product ($50) and the payments it makes to other firms ($30). If the value-added tax is 10 percent, the bicycle manufacturer in our example must pay $2 (10 percent of $20) to the government. The manufacturer, of course, will add as much of the tax as possible to the price charged the dealer. The dealer, in turn, will be charged VAT on the difference between what he paid for the bicycle and what he sold it for, and will attempt to pass the tax on to the consumer. So VAT functions as a retail sales tax. The only substantive difference is that it is collected in many bits and pieces rather than all at once.

The value-added tax has been claimed to be a neutral tax, its supporters contending that it does not distort economic decisions, which supposedly gives it an advantage over existing taxes such as the payroll tax. The payroll tax, for example, drives a wedge between the cost of employing a worker and the amount the worker receives in take-home pay.

Because it costs more to hire a worker than the worker receives, employment suffers. The corporate income tax and personal income tax also distort economic decisions in similar ways.

The same is also true of the value-added tax, despite claims to the contrary. VAT taxes consumption but not saving, which is the alternative use consumers have for their income. Nor would the interest received from savings be taxed by a VAT. Consumption thus becomes more expensive than saving, so that consumers will consume less and save more than they would in the absence of a value-added tax. This distortion becomes a virtue for supporters of the tax because it encourages saving and investment, hence stimulates economic growth. Similarly, because households have savings as an alternative to consumption, the full cost of the value-added tax cannot be passed on to consumers. Some portion of the tax, probably a small part, will have to be absorbed by producers.

The value-added tax was first proposed in 1918 in Germany but was not introduced until after World War II. In France in the 1960s it was introduced as a tax on manufacturing. Denmark was actually the first European country to install a comprehensive VAT. Thereafter, VAT spread through Western Europe and currently accounts for a major portion of the tax receipts of many countries. VAT rates in Europe range from 8 to 12 percent in Britain to an average of 20 percent in Scandinavia. Value-added taxes account for 12 percent of total government revenues in Great Britain, 19 percent in Denmark, and 24 percent in France.

The proposals to introduce VAT into the U.S. tax system have not gone without criticism. Critics object that VAT is regressive, would be inflationary, would be widely evaded, would be expensive to collect, and would be hidden from consumers, thereby making it difficult for voters to determine the exact amount of taxes they pay.

There is little doubt that VAT, when considered by itself, is a regressive tax. Poorer people spend a higher proportion of their income on consumption than rich people; therefore they would be paying a high proportion of their income in taxes. This argument is somewhat muted if the value-added tax were used to replace payroll taxes, such as the social security tax, which is itself highly regressive. The social security tax rate is currently 11 percent of the national payroll. But this excise tax will have to increase to a hefty 24 percent of wage and salary income by the year 2030 just to support the current level of benefits. It would take a VAT tax rate of 13 percent in the United States to eliminate the payroll tax that supports the social security program. The 13 percent rate would raise sufficient revenues to replace the $130 billion a year payroll tax if it were to be used for that purpose.

The social security tax is highly regressive because it is charged only on a certain amount of income ($17,000 in 1979) and is not charged on incomes earned after that. Also, only wage and salary income is taxed; rental income, interest revenue, and profits are not taxed. VAT is probably less regressive than the social security tax because it taxes consumption, part of which is paid for by nonwage and salary incomes. Increasing the payroll tax to the proposed level would significantly alter economic behavior, discouraging employers from hiring workers and workers from seeking employment.

A value-added tax, if it were to be introduced in the United States, would almost certainly be used in conjunction with the existing personal income tax. This affords the opportunity to make the value-added tax as progressive as Americans desire by allowing the poor a tax credit on their income tax for the amount of the VAT paid yearly. A rebate of the VAT paid could be allowed the very poor, who would not ordinarily pay any income tax. So the potential problem of VAT being regressive could be overcome by a combination of tax credits and rebates.

The charge that VAT would be inflationary confuses a change in relative prices with a change in the absolute level of prices. Inflation is an increase in the absolute price level measured by the tendency for all prices in the economy to rise. A value-added tax would cause the prices of consumer goods that are taxed to rise relative to investment goods and to the consumer goods that would be exempted from the tax. The U.S. Treasury estimates that housing, banking, insurance, and charitable organizations, which account for about 20 percent of consumption expenditures, would be exempted from VAT. A value-added tax would cause the prices of the goods taxed to increase relative to goods and services that escape taxation, but relative price changes are not the same thing as inflation. Once the economy adjusted to the change in relative prices that a value-added tax would cause, no further price changes would be observed.

Another criticism of VAT is that the tax is apt to encourage widespread cheating. Visitors to several of the countries that employ a value-added tax soon discover that an underground economy which functions to avoid taxes does exist. Self-employed tradespeople and professionals often work only for cash and obviously do not pay the value-added tax. In Sweden, France, and Italy tax avoidance has become a serious problem to tax collectors. In Italy it is estimated that as much as one-quarter of the economic activities subject to VAT avoid payment by subterfuge and cheating.

But high tax rates are always an incentive to cheat, and in France and Italy avoiding taxes is considered by many a moral obligation. Even in the United States, where taxpayers readily consent to compute their own income taxes, a subterranean economy exists. Estimates of its size run as high as 10 percent of national income. Widespread tax evasion is more dependent upon the level of taxes than on how taxes are levied.

The proposal to levy VAT at every stage of the production process, rather than imposing a general sales tax, is designed to make it more difficult to evade the tax. The more stages involved, the easier it is for the tax collector to detect cheating by cross-checking. But collecting the tax from every producer is certainly more expensive than levying a sales tax on final consumption. It costs British companies about $1 billion a year to collect the tax, or 12 percent of the total VAT collections, considerably more than the United States spends to collect the income tax.

There are good political reasons to charge the tax at every stage of production. The tax becomes embedded in the price of the goods, and it becomes difficult for consumers to ascertain the total amount of taxes paid. Politicians since Colbert, the great French finance minister, have realized the political benefits of this strategy. Colbert thought the art of taxation lay in plucking the citizen's goose in a way that obtained the largest amount of feathers while provoking as little hissing as possible. Today this same approach is called the "political theory of the squawk."

The current social security tax, which accounts for 30 percent of government tax receipts, has begun to generate "squawks" from the taxpayer. The substantial deduction from each payroll check is painfully visible to the worker. Moreover, this forced contribution, as we saw above, is scheduled to go up substantially in the near future. It is no wonder that politicians are searching for a less visible way to meet the obligations of the social security system. VAT offers the opportunity to make the tax burden politically less visible, even if it is no less burdensome.

Also, the less visible the tax, the easier it is to raise its rates. For example, in 1978, West Germany increased its value-added tax from 12 to 13 percent with scarcely a murmur of protest. A tax with this kind of reception from taxpayers is very appealing to American politicians feeling the effects of the taxpayers' revolt.

VAT is receiving renewed attention by Congress because it appears to offer advantages over the present tax system, some economic, some political. The present tax system, it is widely acknowledged, discourages saving, investment, and employment. A value-added tax could be designed that would alter existing incentives in a way that would reduce consumption and encourage savings.

The value-added tax has been criticized because it is regressive, potentially inflationary, expensive to collect, would be widely evaded, and is a hidden tax. While in its pure form a value-added tax is regressive, it is no more regressive than present payroll taxes. VAT through income tax credits or rebates can be made as progressive as desired. As for inflation, we have seen that a value-added tax is not inflationary. Nor would it be easier to evade a value-added tax than other current taxes. It is true that VAT is less visible than either income or payroll taxes. A value-added tax is a shy tax, burying itself in the purchase price of goods and services, which does make it harder for consumers to determine their true tax bills. This fact alone makes it politically attractive to our elected representatives.

CHAPTER 8

Additional Readings

Hafer, R. W. and M. E. Trebing. "The Value Added Tax—A Review of the Issues." *Review*, Federal Reserve Bank of St. Louis, January 1980.

Lindholm, Richard W. *Value-Added Tax and Other Tax Reforms*. University of Oregon Press, 1978.

Sullivan, Clara K. *The Tax on Value Added*. Columbia University Press, 1966.

Surrey, Stanley S. "Value-Added Tax: The Case Against." *Harvard Business Review*, November 1970.

Ullman, A. "A Tax Policy for the 1980s." *Challenge*, March–April 1980.

II

MEASURING NATIONAL INCOME, INFLATION, AND UNEMPLOYMENT

Preview

Gross national product (GNP) is the most comprehensive and therefore the most important measure of the overall performance of the economy. This measure is available quarterly. These initial estimates are extremely important to economic decision makers in government and business. Unfortunately, GNP estimates are not written in stone, but are constantly being revised. The fact that GNP estimates are constantly revised raises the question of their reliability. This chapter explores why constant revision is necessary and assesses the reliability of the initially reported estimates in comparison with later revisions.

Key Economic Points

GNP can be calculated in two ways: either as the total value of all final goods and services produced or as the sum of the payments received by the factors of production.

How is reliability of the GNP initial estimates assessed?

Are the initial estimates of GNP reliable enough for employment by economic decision makers?

9

Measuring Gross National Product: Are Initial Estimates Reliable Enough?

Today's business people and economic policy makers require reliable, comprehensive, and timely data measuring the performance of the economy. The broadest measure of the level of overall economic activity of the economy is called gross national product, or GNP. GNP attempts to measure the total value of the final goods and services produced in the country during a single year. The Commerce Department's Bureau of Economic Analysis (BEA) is charged with the task of estimating GNP. Four times a year the BEA announces its estimates of the GNP registered by the economy during the previous quarter. This initial estimate is widely publicized by the nation's press and broadcasts.

A major difficulty with existing GNP statistics is that no single estimate is ever final. The BEA is constantly engaged in the process of revising its estimates. Consider the estimates for the first quarter of 1978. Real GNP was initially reported in April of that year to have fallen during the quarter by 0.6 of a percentage point, suggesting that the economy could have entered a recession. A recession is often defined as the fall in real GNP for two consecutive quarters. The May revision of the first quarter estimate reduced the decline to 0.4 of a percent. The June revision, however, eliminated the decline altogether, showing a slight increase over the quarter.

This wasn't the first time an initially reported decline in real GNP had been eliminated by subsequent revisions. The initial published estimate for the first quarter of 1967, for example, showed no decline, but a second look found that a decline of 1.2 percent had occurred. This estimate survived subsequent revisions for quite some time, and this period came to be known as the minirecession of 1967. But in January 1976, the BEA revised its past estimates of GNP once again and the minirecession was wiped off the books. Real GNP in the first quarter of 1967 is now shown to have increased by 0.7 percent.

Mark Twain was fond of quoting Disraeli to the point that there were "lies, damned lies and statistics." Perhaps the initial estimates of GNP are simply too gross to be useful to decision makers. It is certain that no GNP estimate is ever final; revisions are an inescapable fact of life. This chapter explores why constant revision is necessary, reviews the reliability of the initially reported estimates in comparison with later revisions, and answers the question: are the initial estimates of GNP reliable enough to use?

The main reasons for such extensive reevaluation is the immensity of the job of summing up the dollar values of individual economic activities to a total of over $2 trillion. The individual statistics themselves are in many cases initially collected for other purposes and do not meet the standards of accuracy required for calculating GNP. Furthermore, many statistics simply are not available on time, necessitating that the BEA rely initially upon preliminary estimates.

The Bureau is forced to update its estimates as new data become available. The first estimate, which is actually made 15 days before the end of every quarter, remains unpublished and is given only to the President and the Federal Reserve Board. The first published estimate appears only 15 days after the end of a quarter and is revised 60 days later when more reliable data are available. Thereafter, each GNP estimate is revised annually for 3 successive years. The availability of the Census Bureau 5-year economic census leads to further correction. For example, in 1977 the entire series going back to 1929 was revised.

Whereas increasing the accuracy of the series is valuable to economists and economic historians, it is the initial estimates that are important to decision makers. They need to know the current state of the economy. How reliable are the preliminary quarterly estimates?

The BEA, first of all, has an internal check to guide its calculations. It is constantly juggling two independent sets of numbers, both of which should add up to GNP. The first set is the product side, which states that GNP equals the sum of consumer purchases (C), business investment (I), government purchases (G), and the difference between exports and imports (X − M), or

$$GNP = C + I + G + (X - M)$$

But what is an expenditure for a buyer is income for the seller. Therefore,

GNP also equals the sum total of all the wages (W), rent (R), interest (i), and profits (P) in the economy, or

$$GNP = W + R + i + P$$

which is labeled the income side of GNP. The totals from both product and income sides ought to equal each other because they are merely two different ways to measure the same thing. However, they seldom match exactly because of measurement errors. The difference between the two is called the statistical discrepancy. The larger the statistical discrepancy, the more likely the initial estimate will be substantially revised later.

The BEA itself estimates that by the time the initial estimate for any quarter has gone through its first annual revision, nine times out of ten the revised number will be within a range of 3.9 percent. It could be as much as 2 percentage points higher or 1.9 percentage points lower. Suppose the initial estimate showed a growth of 4.0 percent. It is possible that the revised estimate could be as low as a slow 2.1 percent, or as high as an extremely rapid 6.0 percent. One time in ten the revision would be even more drastic. If such a wide variation between the initial estimate and its first annual revision occurred regularly, it would render the initial estimate of questionable use to economic decision makers. Fortunately, the difference is seldom this large.

The question remains: are the subsequent revisions of the initial quarterly estimates of GNP so large as to make these estimates misleading and perhaps useless to decision makers? There are three useful numerical measures of the reliability of initial GNP estimates that can be easily calculated. They are bias, dispersion, and the sign tests.

Bias, if present, means that the preliminary estimates are systematically too high or too low. It is calculated by comparing the average difference of the initial estimate with revised estimates. If, for example, the preliminary estimate in one quarter differs from the revised estimate by +2 percentage points, and in the next quarter by −1, then the bias is +1.5. In this case the initial estimates would be systematically too high.

The second measure of reliability is dispersion, which provides an indication of the accuracy of earlier estimates in comparison with later revisions. Dispersion is the average absolute difference between earlier and later estimates. Supposing in one quarter the initial estimate of GNP was +2 percentage points greater than the later revision and in the next −2 percent below its revision, then the dispersion is 2.

$$\frac{([+2] + [-2])}{2} = \frac{4}{2} = 2,$$

which suggests that the revised figure will on average be 2 percentage points more or less than the initial estimate.

The sign test measures the extent to which the direction signaled by the initial estimate of GNP (up or down) is confirmed by the revised estimate. If the initial estimate shows that GNP grew during the first quarter and again during the second, while the revision indicates that it grew during the first but fell during the second, the sign test reveals that initial estimates of GNP correctly indicate the direction the economy is taking 50 percent of the time.

The extent of bias and dispersion have been calculated for the period 1972–1978, along with a sign test for the period. This period includes a complete business cycle, featuring the most severe post–World War II recession, as well as a serious inflation. This period should provide a good test of the reliability of the initial GNP estimates when compared with the first annual revision.

During this testing period the initial estimates proved to be acceptably reliable. The initial estimates generally followed the path of the revisions within one quarter. The initial estimate correctly described the direction of the business cycle, when the economy went from expansion in the fourth quarter of 1973 to recession in the first quarter of 1974. When the resulting decline in economic growth stopped in the first quarter of 1975, the preliminary estimate narrowly missed the trough, which actually occurred in the second quarter, reporting it as occurring in the third quarter. Seventy-five percent of the time the initial estimate of GNP and the revision moved in the same direction. Thus three out of every four times the initial estimates suggested that GNP had expanded or contracted, the signaled direction of change stood up when the revised estimates appeared.

The measure of bias over the period was an acceptable –0.3, suggesting that the initial estimate systematically underestimated real GNP by a small amount. The measure of dispersion was somewhat greater, being 1.3. The initial estimate tended to differ from the revised estimate by 1.3 percentage points. That is, the initial estimate on average was 1.3 percentage points higher or lower than the revised estimate.

While this measure of dispersion may not appear very large, considering the enormous task of estimating GNP, it must be considered in relation to the normal real rate of growth of GNP. Between 1880 and 1970 the real rate of growth annually was 3.3 percent. The potential real rate of growth, the rate at which the economy's economic capacity was expanding, was until recently estimated at 4 percent a year. Thus, the average rate of dispersion was between 33 and 40 percent of the potential growth of real output.

The difference between the initial estimate and the annual revision can also prove misleading to decision makers. This occurred during the span of years considered in the statistical measures reported above. The rates of growth calculated from the initially reported quarterly estimates of GNP for 1973 were as follows:

I	II	III	IV
8.8	2.4	3.4	1.3

The economy during the first quarter was obviously growing at an extraordinary rate, much more rapidly than the economy's capacity to grow over a long period of time. It would be expected that the economy could not keep up this rate of increase. Therefore, it was no surprise that the rate of growth slowed during the second quarter. A fall of 6.4 percent between the two quarters was initially alarming, signaling, perhaps, that the economy was about to enter a recession. However, the rise during the third quarter to approximately the long-term rate of growth of the economy was reassuring. The fall during the fourth quarter, however, alerted government economists to the fact that the economy was entering a recession.

Consider now the picture that emerges from the revised estimates. The second quarter fall was substantially greater than initially reported, declining 8.6 percent as the economy almost stopped growing during the quarter, and the subsequent increase during the third quarter was not nearly as robust as initially reported, falling considerably short of the economy's potential for growth. The revised 1973 estimates were as follows:

I	II	III	IV
8.8	0.2	2.7	1.4

Had the initial estimates been as reliable as the subsequent revision, government economists probably would have recognized the danger of recession 3 to 6 months earlier, and corrective steps could have been taken that much sooner. Perhaps the social costs of the recession, which turned out to be the most severe since the Great Depression, would have been moderated by more timely government action.

Because GNP is the most comprehensive of all measures of economic activity, it is the most widely used by economic decision makers. The initial quarterly estimates receive the most attention. The timely character of the initial estimates, however, requires some sacrifice in reliability. Occasionally, subsequent revision of the quarterly real GNP estimates has shown the initial estimate to have been misleading.

However, an evaluation of the 6-year period from 1972 to 1978, which included a complete business cycle, suggests that the initial quarterly estimates of GNP do provide a generally reliable basis for assessing recent economic developments. The initial estimates, when tested for bias, dispersion, and with a sign test, performed adequately during that period. On the other hand, the statistical creation and disappearance of the minirecession of 1967, the misleading initial estimates of 1973, and the difficulties experienced with the first quarter estimate for 1978 should serve to warn the potential user of these estimates of the dangers of taking the initial estimates too seriously. The initial estimates are not carved in stone.

Additional Readings

Bechter, Dan M. and Steven P. Zell. "Preliminary Estimates of GNP: 1972–1978." *Economic Review,* Federal Reserve Bank of Kansas City, January 1979.

Malabre, Alfred L., Jr. *Understanding the Economy: For People Who Can't Stand Economics.* New American Library, 1976, Chap. 2.

Meadows, Edward. "Tracking the Ever-Elusive Gross National Product." *Fortune,* May 22, 1978.

Preview

Both economic theory and casual observation suggest that a subterranean economy exists in the United States that escapes detection and measurement by official government statistics. This subterranean or underground economy is composed of both legal and illegal activities that are carried on in ways designed to escape detection in order to avoid taxation. Recent estimates of the size of this underground economy suggest that it is both sizable and growing relative to measured economic activity. In this chapter the theoretical reasons that the presence of a subterranean economy should be suspected are explored. Then the recent estimates of the size of the underground economy are examined. Finally, the implications of the existence of an unmeasured, but sizable and growing, subterranean economy are considered for both the interpretation of official statistics and the determination of economic policy.

Key Economic Points

Why does economic theory suggest that an underground economy probably exists?

What conditions would lead to the creation and expansion of the subterranean economy?

The methods and reliability of indirect attempts to measure the extent of the underground economy are evaluated.

What are the implications of a large and growing subterranean economy for the reliability of official income, employment, and price statistics?

10

Reliability of Official Statistics: Impact of the Subterranean Economy

Not all economic activity is counted in the official national income statistics, much of it because it is carried on in such a way as to avoid official detection. For example, there is the small businessman who keeps two sets of books, one for himself and one for tax purposes, and the waitress who earns $200 a week but reports only $50 of it. Such persons, along with the plumbers, appliance repairers, mechanics, and physicians who prefer to be paid in cash, are members of what is probably the fastest growing segment of the U.S. economy: the subterranean, or underground, economy.

Some participants of the subterranean economy are engaged in illegal activities such as prostitution, drug sales, and gambling. The amount of these activities goes unreported for obvious reasons, secrecy being necessary to continue in business. By convention, such activities is excluded from the gross national product accounts. A far greater proportion of the participants of the underground economy perform legal activities, but much of what they do and earn goes unreported to government agencies, especially the Internal Revenue Service. The amount of these activities also is excluded from gross national income accounts, not because of convention, but because of the difficulty of estimating their value.

Although no one knows precisely how big the underground economy is, many economists now agree that it is large and growing. Existing estimates suggest that the underground economy may account for as much as 10 to 25 percent of measured gross national product. Although not everyone agrees that it is this large, if it is, then a covert, unrecorded economic sector larger than the agricultural sector of this country, and probably larger than the size of the entire economy of Canada, exists undetected and unmeasured within the U.S. economy.

The purpose of this chapter is to investigate the existence and extent of the underground economy in the United States. First, the reasons an underground economy is suspected to exist are explored; then the estimates that have been made of the extent of this sector are considered. Finally, the implications of these estimates for economics and economic policy are examined.

Economic theory suggests the probable existence of a growing underground economy. A person's willingness to participate in the subterranean economy and thereby engage in the illegal act of underreporting taxable income is based on personal perceptions of the benefits and costs of such an act. The benefits are obvious: a higher standard of living that results from a zero tax rate on the unreported income. The potential benefits of underpaying taxes grow as the tax rate increases. The cost of underpaying taxes is the probability of being caught and convicted multiplied by the actual punishment for violating the tax laws. Because much of the cost of being caught is the embarrassment of the arrest and trial, this cost is independent of the amount of tax underpayment. As a result, an increase in tax rates will increase the benefits of avoiding taxes much faster than it will raise costs.

The effect of the current inflation, which has increased for more than a decade, has been to move income earners into higher marginal tax brackets, thereby increasing the potential benefits of avoiding income taxes. Since the probability of being arrested for underreporting income has not changed appreciably with time, the rise in potential benefits would predictably result in increased underground activity. Economic theory thus suggests the strong possibility of a growing subterranean economy.

What evidence exists to support this prediction? The fact that participants in the underground economy are trying to escape detection means that directly measuring the income generated in this sector will be difficult. The IRS in 1976 attempted a "direct" estimation of unreported income through the use of the Taxpayer Compliance Audit, which is much more thorough than regular audits. The results indicate that the size of the underground economy was between $100 and $135 billion. These audits, however, cannot detect income for which there are no records, nor can audits reveal the income earned by nonfilers of income tax returns. Thus the IRS calculation is a low estimate of the size of the subterranean economy; the underground economy is at least this large.

Another way to arrive at an estimate of the size of the underground economy is to employ an indirect method. One way to do this is to measure the means of payment used by the underground economy—cash. Cash, unlike checks, does not leave a record, and the quantity of currency held by the American public is measurable. Today there is about $500 in cash for every man, woman, and child in the country. Why does the typical family of four need or want to hold $2,000 in cash? No doubt part of it is used to support transactions in the underground economy.

The most widely publicized estimate of the extent of the underground economy based on the amount of currency outstanding has been made by Peter Gutmann. Gutmann studied the historical relationship between cash and checking deposits. The proportion of cash to checking accounts fell between the turn of the century and World War II. In the period immediately preceding World War II, when tax rates were very low, currency amounted to about 22 percent of the total amount of checking accounts. During World War II, however, tax rates rose substantially, wage and price controls were imposed along with rationing, and black markets sprang up everywhere. An underground economy flourished, avoiding regulations and taxes. The public demanded more cash and the proportion of currency to checking accounts by 1945 had increased to 36 percent, making up for the decline of half a century in 4 years.

After the end of the war, the black markets disappeared along with price controls and rationing. The relative use of cash to checks declined. By 1961 the proportion of currency to checking accounts had fallen to 25 percent. During the 1960s and 1970s a number of financial innovations occurred that should have moved the economy toward a "cashless" society. Credit cards and bank cards, allowing the use of credit instead of cash to make trades, proliferated, creating accounts that are usually settled by check. Automatic debit cards were also introduced as was bill paying by telephone.

Despite these changes, the proportion of currency to checking accounts has risen since 1961. The advent of inflation began to move most income earners into higher marginal tax brackets, creating the incentive for the creation of an underground economy. By 1977, the proportion of currency to checking accounts was almost back to the black market level of 1945.

Professor Gutmann attributes the rise in the public's demand for cash to the needs of the subterranean economy. By assuming that the prewar low-tax period was a time when the underground economy did not exist, the difference between the $217 per $1,000 of checking account deposits in 1941 and the $344 per $1,000 in 1976 resulted from the needs of the underground economy. On this basis, of the $77.8 billion of currency in circulation in 1976, $28.7 billion was held for illegal purposes. This amounts to 9.4 percent of the total money supply (currency plus checking). Thus Gutmann reasoned that the size of the underground economy in that year amounted to a similar proportion of measured gross national product—or 9.4 percent of $1,693 billion, which is $176 billion.

This estimate has not been universally accepted. Some economists suggest that the increase in the amount of currency held by the public is for the purpose of hoarding money. These investigators point to the rise in the number of $100 bills outstanding; there is more money outstanding in this denomination than any other. Large bills would be chosen by the tax avoider to store the gains. Gutmann responds that during periods of rapid inflation and high interest rates, it would be irrational to hold money when interest paying securities are readily available. Such securities, however, often produce records that large participators in the underground economy would like to avoid. If a large part of the increased currency holdings are in fact hoarded and not used to facilitate underground transactions, then Gutmann's estimates are too high. All of this is, of course, conjecture; no one knows for sure.

Other economists have attempted to employ currency statistics to measure the extent of the subterranean economy in ways that overcome this objection. Generally, these latter estimates are even higher than the one Gutmann produced. One estimate, for example, found that the underground economy grew from 9 percent of reported GNP in 1970 to at least 15 percent in 1978. Still another estimate found that unmeasured output in 1976 was as high as 19 percent of total measured output and by 1978 had increased to 27 percent of total output. This procedure would yield even higher estimates for subsequent years.

Thus it is clear that no consensus exists as to the size of the underground economy. But these estimates do seem to suggest that Gutmann's initial estimate of the size of the underground economy, as approximately 10 percent of the size of the measured economy, was not too high and that the subterranean economy is growing relative to the legal measured economy.

The existence of a substantial and growing underground sector of the U.S. economy has substantial implications for the interpretation of official economic statistics. First, the actual national income statistics are larger than official statistics show. True national income may be as much as 10 to 25 percent greater than official estimates suggest. If the underground economy is growing more rapidly than the legal economy, the rate of growth of the actual economy is underestimated by the measured growth rates. The recent lagging growth rate reported by the official statistics may not be quite as serious as initially supposed.

Furthermore, the official unemployment statistics are clearly overstated. The high unemployment rates reported in ghetto areas, especially among the young, are unrealistic. Many are working in both illegal and legal (off-the-books) activities. Some workers who are collecting unemployment benefits are also working on the side. Gutmann has estimated that the official August 1979 unemployment rate of 6.0 percent was, in reality, only 4.5 percent. The extent of poverty in the country is also overestimated to the extent that some of the official poor are also working off the books.

In addition, the measured rate of inflation may be too high. If the rate of inflation is lower in the underground economy than it is in the legal economy, the true rate is lower than the measured rate.

Finally, the tax burden is disproportionately borne by those who are not engaged in the subterranean economy. If the underground economy had paid proportionately the same taxes that the legal economy paid, the recent federal budget deficits would have been substantially reduced, or even eliminated.

The effect of the underground economy is to create a bias in the official statistics. This would be extremely serious were the government to act as if the measured statistics accurately reflect the true situation. If the income and employment statistics understate the true level, then the government may adopt measures that are too stimulative. If the measured rate of economic growth is too low, then the government may take steps to stimulate growth that is thought to be missing but is merely unmeasured. Conversely, if the measured rate of inflation is actually higher than the true rate, deflationary policies may be too stringent, resulting in unnecessary, and unexpected, unemployment.

In conclusion, government economic policies are based on the reality suggested by official statistics. The presence of a large and growing underground economy may distort this view of reality. Where the perceptions of reality are mistaken, government policies are likely to be inappropriate, producing unexpected results. Especially if the size of the subterranean economy is growing as rapidly as some of its investigators suggest, then the continued disregard of the underground economy is likely to lead to serious misrepresentation of reality by the official statistics and to the possibility of the adoption of inappropriate public policies as a consequence.

Additional Readings

Feige, Edgar L. "How Big Is the Irregular Economy?" *Challenge*, November–December 1979.

Gutmann, Peter M. "Statistical Illusions, Mistaken Policies." *Challenge*, November–December 1979.

Gutmann, Peter M. "The Subterranean Economy." *Financial Analysts Journal*, November–December 1977.

Haulk, Charles J. "Thoughts On the Underground Economy." *Economic Review*, Federal Reserve Bank of Atlanta, March–April 1980.

Laurant, Robert D. "Currency and the Subterranean Economy." *Economic Perspectives*, Federal Reserve Bank of Chicago, March–April 1979.

Preview

The consumer price index is the most widely used measure of the rate of inflation. This index is frequently used as a cost-of-living index to link wage and retirement payments to the rate of inflation. It is now recognized that the CPI overstates the increase in the cost of living due to inflation, causing business and government to pay out more than would be required if a more accurate index were employed or if the consumer price index were modified. This chapter considers why the consumer price index overstates the rate of inflation and examines several proposed remedies for the situation.

Key Economic Points

The consumer price index is not a cost-of-living index.
Why does the consumer price index probably overstate the increase in the cost of
     living due to inflation?
Why is it difficult to improve the consumer price index?

11

Price Indexes:
The Consumer Price Index
Controversy

The consumer price index (CPI) is supposed to measure the extent of inflation, but according to many economists the CPI has itself become part of the problem. The incomes of millions of Americans are directly linked to the CPI. In an attempt to ensure that inflation does not erode the purchasing power of 7.7 million workers and 35 million retirees, their wages and social security checks have been indexed by the CPI. As the measured rate of inflation increases, the income of these people automatically increases. The problem arises because it is now widely believed that the consumer price index overstates the extent to which inflation has caused the cost of living to increase.

Each 1 percentage point rise in the CPI automatically triggers about $2 billion in increased federal transfer payments, and perhaps an equal amount of private spending increases. Thus, to the extent that the CPI overstates the actual increase in the cost of living of these persons, their real income rises in a way that was never intended. The unintended rise in government expenditures actually contributes to further increases in the overall level of prices, and the rise in labor costs distorts the efficient allocation of resources, increasing the costs that inflation imposes on society.

The main problem is that the consumer price index does not measure changes in the consumer's cost of living. When the index was first created in 1918 by the Bureau of Labor Statistics (BLS), it was called the cost-of-living index. Exactly the same problems arose during past periods of rapid inflation that have arisen today. People then as now questioned the accuracy of the index. The solution in 1945 was to maintain the index unchanged, but to change the name to warn of the problems that would be encountered in applying the index to wage agreements. The cost-of-living index became the consumer price index for moderate income families in large cities.

The warning proved insufficient. The CPI continued to be the most widely reported measure of inflation. It also continued to be the most widely used index to protect workers against general price increases. Even the federal government in 1972 chose to use the CPI to index social security benefits against loss from inflation.

Since the consumer price index continues to be employed as a cost-of-living index, this chapter explores the alleged defects of the CPI when used in this way and explores some of the current proposals for remedying these defects.

Currently the CPI is a measure of the change in prices of a market basket of goods and services actually purchased by a typical urban family in 1972 and 1973. The CPI measures how much it would cost to purchase these same goods and services in subsequent years. This market basket is deliberately held constant to hold the standard of living constant.

The cost of this market basket does not allow the consumer to substitute among goods. The prices of some goods will always rise more than the prices of others. Consumers will tend to buy relatively less of the goods that are rising more rapidly in price and relatively more of goods whose prices are rising less rapidly. It has been estimated, for example, that a consumer could have held household food costs in 1979 to their 1978 level, despite the fact that the CPI measured increase in food costs was 7.5 percent, by substituting in this manner.

The economists of the BLS know that consumers shift purchases in response to changes in relative prices, but they have no way of knowing whether these changes reflect a standard of living higher or lower than that of the base period. The purpose of the CPI is to determine the amount by which income must rise to maintain a constant standard of living. The only way this can be done is by ensuring that people can currently purchase the same bundle of goods and services they purchased during the base period. Thus, to the extent that consumers do substitute goods that rise less rapidly in price for goods that rise more rapidly without suffering a loss in their standard of living, the CPI has overstated the rise in the cost of living. Consumers sometimes are able to do this, but it is impossible to determine when and by how much.

In an index as comprehensive as the consumer price index, the weights of the base year will eventually become dated as consumers change their buying habits and will have to be changed periodically. The 1940 revision, for example, dropped the prices of barbershop shaves, high button shoes, and men's nightshirts for this reason. The 1953 revision eliminated salt pork, union suits, and laundry bar soap, and added television, frozen foods, and Coca Cola. The CPI was last revised in 1977, when weights from 1972 and 1973 surveys were substituted for weights that had been calculated in 1960–1961. There is no doubt that there have been substantial changes in consumer buying habits since 1972–1973 that should be recognized by the CPI. Consumers clearly purchase less gasoline and heating oil now than they did then because OPEC has substantially raised the price of crude oil. Using the 1972–1973 purchases of these goods as weights clearly overstates the rise in the consumer cost of living.

Most economists, including those at the BLS, agree that it would be a good idea to revise the market basket more frequently. According to the BLS, the problem is money. If Congress wants the CPI updated more frequently, it has to appropriate the money.

Some economists suggest that the problem could be solved if the CPI were calculated in the same way that the personal consumption expenditures (PCE) segment of the GNP deflator is obtained. The PCE each year measures the prices of the goods and services that consumers actually purchase. The PCE in effect changes weights each quarter without great difficulty. The BLS response to this suggestion is that the purposes of the PCE and the CPI are different. The purpose of the PCE is to measure the value of the economy's output. The purpose of the CPI is to measure constant purchasing power, and that cannot be done if the market basket is constantly revised. Constructing the consumer price index thus involves a continual compromise between the desire to hold the market basket constant, and the necessity to periodically eliminate items such as high button shoes and to add goods such as television sets.

The second major criticism of the CPI is less fundamental than the first, but may be even more important in generating the upward bias. This criticism regards the way the consumer price index calculates the cost of housing. The CPI treats the cost of housing basically the same way it treats the purchase of any other consumer durable bought on time payments, such as a refrigerator or an automobile, that is, so much down and so much a month. Because the CPI calculates the cost of a base period market basket in current prices, the prices for housing and the mortgage rate of interest listed are the current prices. During the rapid inflation of the late 1970s, the costs of both housing and borrowing money soared. Since the cost of home ownership represents more than one-fifth of the market basket used to calculate the CPI, the effect of the rapid increase in these two prices has been to cause the index to also rise rapidly.

Critics believe that the way the CPI handles the cost of housing overstates the effect rising housing costs have had on the cost of living of the typical urban consumer. More Americans bought homes several years ago (only 6 percent bought homes during the base year of 1972–1973), purchasing them at substantially lower prices and paying much lower rates of interest, than have purchased homes recently. Critics argue that while the

CPI measured the rate of inflation during 1979 at 13.2 percent, a consumer who purchased a house several years ago and spends 30 percent of the family income to make the mortgage payment, which did not change during the year, experienced a cost-of-living increase of 9.25 percent.

A variety of suggestions have been made as to how the CPI could be modified to handle housing costs more accurately. The most frequent suggestion is to stop measuring the price of purchasing a house and instead calculate what it would cost to rent a house. That is the way the personal consumption expenditure segment of the GNP deflator handles housing costs. Instead of directly measuring the price of new houses and the mortgage interest rate, the BLS should estimate what the typical consumer would have to pay to rent the house he or she owns.

The BLS has been sensitive to such suggestions and has been publishing several versions of the CPI using alternative measures for housing costs. During 1979, the difference in the rate of inflation between the official CPI and the CPI using a rental index for housing was more than 2 percentage points. The 13.2 percent increase in the CPI would have been about 11.0 percent if a rental index had been used instead.

When the BLS last revised the market basket in 1978, the staff recommended specific changes in the way housing costs were measured. These changes would have reduced the effect of soaring housing costs and interest rates on the CPI. However, the recommendation was not followed because the BLS will not change its methods of computing the index unless there is a consensus among its public advisors to do so. Representatives of organized labor vetoed the suggestion. It is not surprising that labor would object to a change that would reduce the measured rate of inflation, since 7.7 million workers have cost-of-living clauses in their contracts that are tied to the CPI.

A third major criticism of the CPI is that it overstates the rate of inflation because it does not adequately measure the improvements in the quality of the goods consumers purchase. Color televisions are of a much better quality today than they were in the 1972–1973 base period. Generally, higher quality items cost more. Consumers in the 1980s, therefore, are not buying the same television for a higher price; they are buying a better television at a higher price. Thus part of the measured increase in the price of television sets is due to the added costs of quality improvements. Because the CPI attributes the entire increase in the price of television sets to inflation, it overstates the real rate of inflation.

One study has attempted to construct a price index taking into account quality changes. The study tried to adjust for quality changes in the prices of the equipment that manufacturers use in producing products, measuring quality changes as the increase in energy efficiency and machine output per dollar of capital costs. The price index for manufacturers' equipment rose only one-tenth as much as the quality unadjusted price index for this commodity. Granted, consumer goods were not included in this study, but the findings suggest that quality changes could be an important source of upward bias in the CPI.

The BLS responded to this criticism by pointing out that whereas manufactured goods may have significantly improved in quality over time, services probably have deteriorated in quality. The quality change problem for the CPI may well be more apparent than real. The improvements in quality in some areas may be offset by the decline in quality in other areas, so that the net effect on the CPI may not be nearly as large as the measured effect on manufacturers' equipment.

Thus, although there is general agreement that the CPI probably overstates the effect of inflation on the cost of living, there is no general agreement about what should be done. There are two basic alternatives. The first would be to revise the CPI, changing weights regularly as is done in calculating the PCE, or at the very least using a rental index to measure the cost of housing. But the BLS won't go this route without the approval of its public advisory boards. If labor continues to object, this won't happen.

The second alternative would be to sever the link between the CPI and labor contracts and government transfer programs. Congress could, for example, repeal the 1972 law that indexes social security payments using the CPI, substituting another index instead. The BLS could be instructed to calculate a retiree's index that would more accurately reflect the cost of living of senior citizens. Another possibility would be to substitute the PCE for the CPI. Historically, the PCE has both risen less rapidly during inflationary periods and fallen more slowly when inflation moderates. The political possibilities of substituting some other index would appear remote indeed, since over 45 million Americans directly benefit from the use of the CPI.

Perhaps the only thing to be done about the upward bias of the CPI is be aware of it. The CPI overstates the rate of inflation for the typical urban consumer because it is a fixed weight index that does not allow for substitution, because of the way it treats housing costs, and because it does not adjust for quality improvements adequately. You can be fairly certain of one thing—the true rate of inflation is not greater than that reported by the CPI.

Additional Readings

Karnosky, Denis S. "A Primer on the Consumer Price Index." *Review*, Federal Reserve Bank of St. Louis, July 1974.

Levenson, Mark. "The CPI: Six Decades of Controversy—With No End in Sight." *Dun's Review*, May 1980.

Norwood, Janet L. "The Consumer Price Index Puzzle." *Challenge*, March–April 1980.

Rosen, Gerald R. "The CPI Controversy." *Dun's Review*, May 1980.

Preview

Since the middle of the 1960s the United States has attempted to eliminate poverty and increase the proportion of total income going to the poor. In order to do this, the government has transferred income from persons who are better off to the poor. Welfare expenditures have increased substantially, and currently more than 20 percent of GNP is now transferred. An effort this extensive should have substantially improved the economic condition of America's poor, and that improvement should show up in the official statistics. But it doesn't. Either the United States' antipoverty program has been a failure or the official statistics are woefully inadequate. This chapter explores the adequacy of the official income statistics in measuring the distribution of income and in determining the numbers of America's poor.

Key Economic Points

The proper measure of the distribution of income is total after-tax income.
Not all income is money income.
The adjustment of money income to exclude tax payments and to include in-kind transfers can alter the distribution of income statistics.
Why is it difficult to obtain a set of basic facts about the distribution of income that all economists will accept?

12

Distribution of Income: Trying to Determine the Extent of Poverty in the United States

Official statistics on the distribution of income show that income is and has been very unequally distributed in the United States. In 1962, for example, the lowest 20 percent of income earners received only 5 percent of total money income, while the top 20 percent received more than eight times as much, or over 40 percent of total money income. Since then the United States has undertaken extensive measures to redistribute income and combat poverty. Social welfare expenditures have increased during the period from less than $100 billion to almost $400 billion, or from 10 percent of GNP to almost 21 percent. Despite these efforts, the total money income received by the lowest 20 percent has not increased significantly. The share of the lowest 20 percent in 1977 was only 5.2 percent, or scarcely different than it was before the government began its "War on Poverty."

It is possible that these expenditures, although not altering the distribution of income, have succeeded in reducing the extent of poverty in the country. Poverty, unlike the distribution of income, is not a relative matter. Poverty exists when a person does not receive a sufficient income to purchase the goods and services that would allow a minimum standard of living. In 1965, the Social Security Administration estimated that an annual income of $3,165 was necessary to permit a family of four a nutritionally adequate diet and minimum standards of clothing and shelter. A family whose annual income was below this poverty level was defined as living in poverty. This minimum annual income had increased to $6,500 by 1979, basically because of inflation.

When President Lyndon Johnson started the War on Poverty, 33 million Americans had incomes below the poverty line. By 1977 there were still 25 million persons living in poverty in the United States. The percentage of Americans living in poverty had fallen from 22.4 percent to 12.6 percent in 1970, but because population has grown, the absolute numbers of the poor have not declined as much as would be expected. Moreover, since 1970 the percentage of poor Americans has not changed appreciably, despite the rapid growth in welfare expenditures.

These results, on the face of it, suggest to many that the antipoverty effort has been a failure. Despite the annual transfer of more than 20 percent of GNP to the poor, the relative position of the lowest 20 percent of money income earners has not improved. Nor has the percentage of our population living in poverty declined significantly since 1970.

Failure would be the inescapable conclusion if the official figures accurately reflect the situation. But not every economist agrees that they do. Recent research has cast doubt on the accuracy of the official statistics. In this chapter we first consider what information would be required to measure the ideal distribution of income and the extent of poverty in the United States, and the extent to which the official statistics meet the ideal. Then the results of several attempts to adjust the existing official statistics to more closely approximate the ideal are considered. Finally, it is noted that not all economists agree that these revisions are improvements on the official estimates.

The first step in evaluating the official estimates is to consider the appropriateness of money income as a measure of the total income received. First, the Census Bureau's money income statistics are before-tax figures. Thus, to the extent that higher income earners pay a larger proportion of their income in taxes than do lower income earners, the Census Bureau figures will overstate the extent of inequality in the society. The statistics that are more accurate are total income after taxes.

There is also a difference between total income and money income. We must take into account the production of goods and services by the household for its own consumption. In almost every family some food preparation, cleaning, and household maintenance takes place that could have been purchased but was domestically produced instead. Thus, to the extent that poorer families do relatively more of these activities, money income will not accurately represent the distribution of income.

Second, not all income is reported. There is a growing subterranean, or underground, economy whose transactions are designed to escape taxation. These activities take the form of either barter or nonreported cash transactions, as well as illegal activities, such as gambling, smuggling, prostitution, and drug sales. It has been estimated that the size of the underground economy has grown from 9 percent of GNP in 1970 to at least 15 percent of GNP in 1978. It is probable that proportionally more persons with low reported money incomes are engaged in these activities than persons with high reported money incomes. Therefore, to the extent that this is true, the money income statistics do not accurately reflect the distribution of income.

Finally, some income, particularly that of low-income earners, is received not as money but in kind. During the 1970s, when the percentage of families living in poverty was not declining significantly, the fastest growing transfer payments were in-kind transfers—Medicaid, food stamps, and public housing. In 1977, in-kind government transfers totaled $41.3 billion, which was $1685 per person for the officially poor. Transfers of these kinds are not reflected in the official poverty statistics.

In order to decide whether the distribution of income has equalized or not and to determine the extent of poverty that exists in the United States today, we need not the money income statistics that are officially used but the total income after taxes. Even if we had this information, some economists would argue that these statistics should be adjusted further. It has been argued that total after-tax income should be adjusted for the number of workers in the family. Increasingly, wives have joined the labor force; therefore, the distribution of income will be considerably different if we consider the income of households rather than the income of individuals. The same argument is made to justify the suggestion that size of family should be considered, as should number of families headed by a retired person, and that income should be adjusted for the age of the wage earner. Moreover, this is only a partial list of the adjustments that have been suggested, but it should be sufficient to demonstrate that it is a difficult, perhaps impossible, task to obtain all the information about the distribution of income and the extent of poverty that would settle the issue to the satisfaction of most economists.

Nevertheless, there have been several attempts to make some of these adjustments, the results of which are very instructive. One of the first economists to attempt some of these adjustments was Edgar Browning. Browning added the in-kind transfer, and subtracted income and social security taxes. By adjusting the data for family size, he measured the income per person. The effect of these adjustments on the distribution of income was striking. Instead of receiving 5.0 percent of income, the poorest 20 percent of wage earners in 1962 received 8.8 percent. Moreover, by 1972 the share of the lowest 20 percent of income earners had increased to 11.7 percent. Given the increase in in-kind transfers since 1972, it follows that this share has increased even more today.

The Congressional Budget Office (CBO) a few years later studied the effect the inclusion of in-kind transfers would have on the percent of the population living in poverty. The official poverty figures were adjusted for the benefits of food stamps, daycare service, public housing, school lunches, Medicaid, and Medicare. On the basis of these adjustments, the percentage of American families living below the official poverty level was less than half the official estimate, or 6 percent rather than 12 percent. The CBO concluded that "the nation has come a lot closer to eliminating poverty than most people realize."

In a still more recent study Morton Paglin refined the CBO estimates. Paglin calculated that only 3 percent of Americans were poor in 1976. He found that the size of the poverty population declined by 80 percent between 1959 and 1975. According to Paglin, economic growth and government programs have gone far toward winning the War on Poverty with only 6 million Americans still living in poverty.

Not everyone agrees with these estimates. Among the telling criticisms that have been made is the point that the studies count in-kind transfers as the equivalent of cash transfers. In-kind transfers do not allow individuals a choice as to how to spend the additional income. Valuing in-kind transfers as equal to cash is to make the unrealistic assumption that, if given money instead, each person would have chosen to purchase the goods and services that were transferred. As this is very unlikely, valuing in-kind transfers at their cost overstates the value of these transfers to the individuals. There have been several attempts to estimate how the poor value in-kind transfers. These estimates generally fall in the 50 to 75 percent range depending on the type of transfer. If the in-kind transfers are valued not at cost but at the estimated value the poor attach to them, the decline in the income equality and in the number of poor would not be as dramatic as the above studies report.

Other critics question whether Medicare and Medicaid benefits should be counted as income. The logical conclusion of counting these benefits as income is that the sicker a person becomes, the more medical benefits he or she receives, and the less poor the person becomes. If a person becomes sufficiently ill, the illness could even lift the person out of poverty altogether! It is ridiculous, according to these critics, to suggest that a serious illness could be a cure for poverty.

So where does this leave us? The critics of the official estimates clearly have a point, but so do the critics of the estimate revisions. Probably the official money income estimates overstate the degree of income inequality in the United States and the amount of poverty, but these overestimates are not as great as the critics reported above suggest. No one knows for sure. The extent of income inequality and poverty in the United States is one of the questions about basic facts on which economists disagree.

Additional Readings

Arnold, Mark R. "We're Winning the War on Poverty." *National Observer*, February 19, 1977.

Browning, Edgar K. "How Much More Equality Can We Afford?" *The Public Interest,* Spring 1976.

Browning, Edgar K. "The Trend Toward Equality in the Distribution of Net Income." *Southern Economic Journal,* July 1976.

Congressional Budget Office. *Poverty Status of Families Under Alternative Definitions of Income.* U.S. Superintendent of Documents, January 1977.

Paglin, Morton. "Poverty in the United States: A Re-evaluation." *Policy Review,* Spring 1979.

Preview

Both inflation and unemployment are considered to be social evils. Unfortunately, it may be necessary to increase one, at least temporarily, to reduce the other. Crucial to deciding whether it is wise, for example, to fight inflation at the cost of causing temporarily higher unemployment rates is an evaluation of the costs of inflation relative to the costs of unemployment. This chapter discusses how the social costs of unemployment and inflation can be evaluated in principle and in practice and why it is currently impossible to answer the question: which is worse socially, inflation or unemployment?

Key Economic Points

What is potential national income?

Potential national income is the bench mark from which the social costs of
    unemployment and inflation must be measured.

The social costs of unemployment differ fundamentally from the social costs of
    inflation.

13

Potential Income: The Social Costs of Unemployment and Inflation

There is widespread public agreement that high rates of inflation constitute a social evil and something must be done when inflation rates soar. There is a similar public consensus that excessive unemployment is also bad and should not be tolerated. These twin evils create a policy dilemma for economic decision makers whenever the economy is plagued, as it has been in recent years, with high rates of inflation. There is widespread agreement among economists that a trade-off exists, in the short run, between inflation and unemployment. The cost of permanently reducing the rate of inflation may be temporarily higher rates of unemployment. In order to suffer less from one evil, we may suffer, for a short time at least, from more of the other.

Whether it is a wise thing to fight inflation depends upon the relative cost of the two evils. It is conceivable that the social cost, in terms of unemployment, that must be paid to reduce the rate of inflation exceeds the benefits to be gained. Whether it is a wise policy to fight inflation by temporarily increasing unemployment depends upon determining the social cost of unemployment and the social cost of inflation.

This chapter explores the relative costs of each evil. But before we undertake this task, it is only fair to warn you that no definitive conclusions can be reached.

The social costs of unemployment are so obvious that it is a relatively easy task to calculate the losses involved. The social cost of unemployment is the value of the lost output the unemployed could have produced. The social costs of inflation, unfortunately, are much more difficult to determine. This does not mean that these costs are any less real, just that they are more difficult to conceptualize and measure. It is precisely our inability to calculate the costs of inflation that denies us the ability, at this time, to determine which of the twin evils is the least costly from society's point of view.

Let's examine first the more obvious of the two calculations. The social costs of unemployment can be readily determined in relation to the economy's potential gross national income. Potential national income is the value of gross national product that would be produced when the unemployment rate is equal to the "natural" or full employment rate of unemployment. Whenever the unemployment rate exceeds the full employment rate, the economy's output will fall below the potential possible. The relationship between the amount of excess unemployment and the decline in gross national product is known as Okun's law, after its originator, the late Arthur M. Okun. Professor Okun discovered statistically that there is roughly a 3 to 1 relationship between changes in national income and changes in the unemployment rate, that is, a 1 percentage point increase in the unemployment rate will result in a 3 percentage point fall in real national income.

The social costs resulting from excess unemployment can be and have been a source of substantial loss for the U.S. economy. There have been three lengthy periods in modern U.S. history during which actual GNP has remained below, sometimes substantially below, potential income: 1957–1964, 1969–1972, and 1974–present. During 1975, for example, the loss in income resulting from the increase in the unemployment rate to 8.5 percent was almost $100 billion. This translates into a loss of more than $467 for every person in the country.

The social costs of inflation are much more difficult to determine because there is no comparable direct loss of output as in the case of unemployment. When examining the social costs of inflation, it is necessary to distinguish between perfectly anticipated inflation which is taken into account in every economic transaction, and imperfectly anticipated inflation, which surprises economic decision makers.

Consider first the costs of inflation when the rate of inflation is perfectly anticipated. Suppose the economy had been experiencing a 5 percent rate of inflation for a long time and that people correctly expected the rate of inflation to continue at the 5 percent level. In that event all economic trades and transactions would take into account the expected 5 percent increase in prices. Borrowers and lenders would agree to add 5 percent to the rate of interest; employers and employees in negotiating would automatically agree to a 5 percent annual cost-of-living increase in addition to any productivity increase. The rate of inflation would also be taken into account in negotiating all long-term contracts, and even tax rates would eventually be indexed so that the real tax rates would remain the same.

In this case of steady-state inflation, all transactions would become indexed, so that the major costs associated with inflation would be the costs of changing prices more frequently than would be necessary if inflation did not exist. Such costs are often referred to as menu change costs, using the restaurant's costs of periodically reprinting menus to reflect symbolically similar costs borne by all businesses.

There is one cost that cannot be indexed to escape the problem of inflation and that is the cost of holding currency. A steady inflation rate of 5 percent makes it more expensive to possess cash, the value of which is steadily falling. Individuals will respond to this situation by conserving on the amount of cash they carry, substituting instead more frequent trips to the bank to cash smaller checks than they would in the absence of inflation. These costs are often called shoe leather costs in reference to the more frequent visits to the bank.

Both menu change costs and shoe leather costs are real social costs of inflation, costs that reduce the potential income of the country. But such costs are also clearly very low. So low, in fact, as to make the social costs of inflation, if this is all they amount to, a trivial social problem. Clearly, the finding that the social costs of a perfectly anticipated inflation are trivial does not square with the strong public aversion to inflation.

Inflation seldom, if ever, proceeds at a steady rate. The annual rate of inflation per year during the 1970s was 5.9, 4.3, 3.3, 6.2, 11.0, 9.1, 5.8, 6.5, 8.0, and 13.2, which was anything but steady and perhaps impossible to perfectly anticipate. The costs of an imperfectly anticipated rise are substantially different from the trivial costs of a perfectly anticipated inflation.

One of the most important effects of inflation is that it changes the real value of assets denominated in dollars. Between 1967 and 1977 the consumer price index roughly doubled. A person who bought a 10-year bond in 1967, expecting to have the real value of the money loaned returned in 1977, would have been sadly disappointed. The same number of dollars would buy only half as much as when they were loaned, the doubling of the price level thus reducing the value of money by one-half. Inflation had transferred one-half of the lender's wealth to the creditor. This effect operates on all assets fixed in dollar terms: money, bonds, savings accounts, insurance, pensions, and mortgages.

In 1975, the total value of the nation's assets fixed in terms of dollars was $5.1 trillion or about $24,000 per person. A 1 percentage point increase in the price level would reduce the real value of these assets by $51 billion, an amount equal to 3.5 percent of GNP. Inflation thus acts as a tax on assets fixed in money terms, reducing their real value to their owners.

These losses, while very real to creditors, are not social losses because what creditors lose, debtors gain. This wealth is transferred, without permission to be sure, to the persons to whom creditors loaned money, who can meet their obligations with dollars that are worth less. During 1975, the household sector was the major creditor in the economy to the extent of $1,130 billion, reflecting the degree to which households had lent more than they had borrowed. The other sectors of the economy—unincorporated business, corporations, and government—were debtors. The rate of inflation during 1975 was 9.1 percent, which translates into a transfer of $103 billion from the household sector to the business and government sectors.

It is clear from the above that the redistributive effects of unanticipated inflation can be large and that some groups can be severely harmed in the process. The social costs of these transfers is difficult to assess because there is a gainer for every loser. Persons aware of this fact compete to be gainers and avoid being losers, investing real resources in the attempt. Investors seek to acquire real assets such as real estate, precious metals, and gem stones, and avoid financial assets fixed in dollars. The consequence of these attempts during 1980 was record prices for real estate, gold, silver, and diamonds, and less resources available for capital investment, reducing the future potential income of the economy.

Another source of inflation costs is government regulations that did not anticipate inflation when they were enacted. Usury laws and the regulation of interest rates that financial institutions can pay are two examples. Many states have usury laws that set maximum rates of interest that lenders can charge. When these laws were passed, the high rates of inflation recorded during some years of the 1970s were not anticipated. As the rate of inflation accelerated, so did market interest rates. In state after state, market interest rates exceeded the usurious rate, and lending was severely curtailed. During 1980 it became necessary for the federal government to impose a temporary moratorium on state usury laws to allow some markets to continue to function.

The federal government has itself imposed restrictions on markets, impairing their operation as inflation proceeds. The Federal Reserve sets maximum rates that various financial institutions can pay on savings accounts. When rates paid by alternative investments rise above the legal maximums, the regulated financial institutions begin to lose funds, a process that is called disintermediation. Particularly hard hit in 1975 and 1979–1980 were savings and loan associations, a primary source of home mortgages. Less money was available for home purchases as a consequence.

Society as a whole is the loser when mutually beneficial transactions are prohibited by law and, as a consequence, houses go unbuilt or unsold, and when loans cannot be made for productive purposes. The tax system itself was not designed with inflation in mind. Tax regulations that require businesses to use historical cost instead of current value for purposes of depreciation raise the cost of capital and reduce the incentive for business to invest. As inflation proceeds, current tax laws can convert a nominal gain into a loss when figured in real terms.

Even if these legal institutions were modified to reduce the costs of inflation, some real social costs would remain. Uncertainty as to future rates of inflation impairs the willingness of buyers and sellers and lenders and borrowers to enter into long-term contracts. Uncertainty as to future rates of inflation discourages businesses from making the long-term commitments to acquire the plants and equipment upon which the future growth of potential income depends. It also discourages lenders from purchasing long-term equities such as bonds. The bond market almost disappeared in early 1980 when interest rates rose to record levels. As a consequence, some long-term capital investments will not be made that in the absence of inflation would have been made. The nation's capital stock is thus reduced from what it would have been in the absence of a high and variable rate of inflation, and with it the future potential income of the economy.

It is not yet possible to quantify the social costs of inflation with the same precision as the social costs of unemployment. No quantitative relationship does for the costs of inflation what Okun's law does for the costs of unemployment.

We have seen that there is a fundamental difference between the social costs of unemployment and of inflation. The costs of unemployment are short-term costs that can be readily measured by the extent that the economy fails to produce the potential national income it is capable of producing. In contrast, the social costs of inflation are long-term costs that show up in the reduction of future potential national income from what it would be in the absence of inflation. Given the current state of our knowledge, it is impossible to estimate the social costs of inflation, though doubtless such costs are real. Therefore, it is impossible to give a definitive answer to the question of which is socially more costly, unemployment or inflation. Yet that answer is crucial to deciding what action, if any, should be taken to fight inflation.

Additional Readings

Dornbusch, R. and S. Fischer, *Macroeconomics*. McGraw-Hill, 1978, Chap. 15.

Meyer, L. and R. Rasche. "On the Costs and Benefits of Anti-Inflation Policies." *Review*, Federal Reserve Bank of St. Louis, February 1980.

Okun, Arthur M. "Potential GNP: Its Measurement and Significance." Reprinted in *The Political Economy of Prosperity* by the same author. Norton, 1970.

III

INCOME, EXPENDITURES, AND FISCAL POLICY

Preview

The Great Depression was the worst and longest recorded economic contraction in American history. As a direct consequence of the misery the Depression created, the nation became interested for the first time in the performance of the overall economy. The national income and employment statistics were developed to keep track of the economy's performance and modern macroeconomic theory was invented to attempt to understand and to improve upon the economy's performance. One of the tasks of macroeconomics has been to produce an explanation for the causes of the Great Depression. There are two primary explanations—the "Keynesian" and the "monetarist"—both of which purport to explain the causes of the Depression as they contend to explain current macroeconomic problems. Thus an historical survey of the Great Depression and of its alternative interpretations is a good subject to introduce the study of macroeconomics.

Key Economic Points

The availability of national income statistics is important for measuring the performance of the economy.

It is necessary to adjust GNP estimates for changes in the price level to determine real changes in overall economic performance.

Two contending explanations exist for why the Great Depression occurred.

The two explanations emphasize deterrent causes of the Great Depression and suggest different possible remedies.

A preview of the two contending theories of macroeconomics is provided.

14

Introduction to Macroeconomics: The Great Depression

The Great Depression was for millions of Americans the major historical event of their lives. Many people lost everything and were reduced to dire circumstances. Even those who fared better lived in constant fear that it was merely a matter of time before they too would be impoverished. Certainly none who lived through it ever forgot it. There is no doubt that the Great Depression left deep scars on our nation's consciousness.

But could it happen again? Could history repeat itself? After all, it has been more than a half century since the Great Depression, and no business fluctuation of similar magnitude has occurred since then. It should be pointed out, however, that the second worst depression in our nation's history occurred approximately 60 years before the Great Depression of the 1930s. A half century of relative prosperity is no guarantee that another depression will not occur. The best way to answer the question is to explore what economists today know about the causes of the Great Depression. This chapter attempts to determine what happened and whether or not it can happen again in the light of current economic knowledge.

The severity of the economic decline in 1929 was not immediately apparent to contemporary observers because no statistics measuring the overall performance of the economy were at that time collected. The recognition that the contraction was no ordinary recession was significantly delayed by the lack of timely, reliable statistical information.

The Great Depression pointed up the need for statistical measures of the overall economy's performance. The development of the national income and employment accounts met this need. The concept of gross national product (GNP) allowed the total output of the economy's final goods and services to be summarized in one number. The comparison of GNP for one period with another reveals how the economy is performing. Had national income accounts been available during the Great Depression, no one would have failed to comprehend from the onset that the contraction was particularly severe; GNP fell by more than 12 percent between 1929 and 1930.

The national income accounts and employment statistics allow us in retrospect to measure the magnitude of the economic decline that took place. Gross national product fell by 46 percent between 1929 and 1933. However, prices also fell substantially, and when this is taken into account the real decline was 29 percent. Consumption expenditures in real terms fell by 18 percent and personal savings which had amounted to $4 billion in 1929 was actually a negative $0.75 billion in 1932. Gross investment declined from $16.2 billion in 1929 to practically zero in 1933. When the wear and tear in the nation's capital stock is taken into account, net investment was actually negative.

The nation's banking system collapsed under the strain; more than 5,000 banks failed between 1929 and 1932 and most of their customers' deposits were lost in the process. The nation's money supply declined by a third. The unemployment rate soared until one in every four workers was jobless. The situation improved somewhat after 1933, but even by the end of the 1930s the unemployment rate was still at 14.6 percent. In truth, the Great Depression finally ended when the Japanese bombed Pearl Harbor on December 7, 1941, and the nation converted to a wartime economy.

Clearly, the Great Depression was an extraordinary event bringing with it a collective misery that is usually only associated with war. The desire to avoid future recurrences requires that the causes of the Great Depression be identified.

There are two contending answers to the question, why did it happen? The first in the historical order in which the explanations appeared has been termed the spending hypothesis. This explanation is associated with the followers of the great English economist Lord John Maynard Keynes, the founder of Keynesian economics. The second explanation is the money hypothesis first suggested by the Nobel Prize-winning economist Milton Friedman. Both explanations see the decline in the economy as the result of a decline in aggregate demand. The Keynesians focus on the decline in investment and consumption spending whereas the monetarists see the contraction as the result of the significant decline in the amount of money in the economy.

According to the spending hypothesis, the Depression was generated by a sharp decline in private spending. For various reasons, the collective desire for consumption and investment fell after 1929. The two reasons most frequently mentioned by economists are the end of a construction boom and the stock market crash. Construction, which is a substantial component of investment, declined when the housing market became overbuilt and consumption fell sharply due to the loss of wealth resulting from the stock market crash. The fall in these components produced a fall in output and prices. The Depression was prolonged and severe because the fall in autonomous spending was large and sustained.

The decline in economic activity led to the banking crisis and to the formulation of adverse expectations that, when coupled with the collapse of the international economy, dragged the economy down to an under-full-employment equilibrium. The basic problem was the lack of sufficient aggregate demand. Once in this undesirable situation, recovery was slow because the fiscal policy of the government was not sufficiently expansionary, that is, the expansion of government spending was not sufficient to compensate for the decline in investment and consumption. The fiscal actions of government (spending and taxation) along with consumption and investment constitute aggregate demand. A substantial increase in any or all of these components of autonomous spending would drive the economy along the road to prosperity. Keynesian economists, however, point out that it is not to be expected that either consumption or investment would revive quickly in an underemployment situation like the one that existed in 1933. Business firms are not likely to invest in new plants or equipment as long as half the existing factories are shut down and the other half are operating at reduced rates. Nor are consumers likely to purchase a new home, car, or suit of clothes while they are jobless or fear they will be unemployed in the near future.

The only solution for such a situation is for the government to adopt an expansionary fiscal policy, to run a deficit by increasing expenditures or reducing taxes. During the early stages of the Great Depression the government did just the opposite, cutting expenditures and actually increasing taxes. When, after 1933, the budget of the federal government turned in an expansionary direction, this expansion was offset by the contraction of state and local government budgets. According to this interpretation, fiscal policy did not fail during the Great Depression because it was not even employed.

Once the economy was converted to fight World War II and the government budget registered sharp deficits, the economy moved quickly to full employment. According to the spending hypothesis, the Great Depression was so severe and lasted so long because the decline in two components of autonomous spending, consumption and investment, was large and fiscal policy was not employed.

The money hypothesis tells a different story. The decline in investment and consumption are seen as the result of the Great Depression, not as the cause. The money hypothesis views the Depression as a quite extraordinary event that common occurrences, such as a fall in stock prices or a decline in construction, are unlikely to have caused. This hypothesis suggests that such an uncommon event was most likely caused by unusual or nonrecurring forces. The monetarist explanation is that a normal business recession of the kind that regularly occurs every 3 to 7 years was converted into the Great Depression by the collapse of the banking system.

A bank serves the function of a financial intermediary. It collects the savings and deposits of its customers, providing check-cashing facilities and paying interest on savings deposits. In turn, it lends these funds to other customers in return for interest payments. As long as depositors retain confidence in the bank's solvency, the bank can retain only a small part of its deposits in cash to meet the depositor's normal requirements. It is free to lend the rest to earn the return necessary to pay the interest on savings deposits, to pay for servicing checking accounts, and to earn a profit for its stockholders.

However, if suddenly the depositors' confidence collapses, no bank can return all of every depositor's money instantly because it has loaned out most of it. Late in 1930, depositors began to worry that their money was no longer safe in the bank and rushed to take it out. The rush turned into a panic and many banks that were in ordinary times solvent could not meet their obligations and failed. The depositors lost their money in the process.

The failure of some banks in turn led to the failure of others. Individuals began to hold their money in cash and surviving banks sought to keep their deposits in assets that, unlike loans, could quickly be converted to cash. The result was a substantial reduction in the quantity of money in the economy. As people found themselves with less money, they spent less, which in time put downward pressures on output and prices.

The decline in national income and employment was severe and sustained because the decline in the quantity of money (25 percent between 1929 and 1933) was large and sustained. According to the money hypothesis, it was the collapse of the banking system that led to the drastic decline in the quantity of money that caused the Great Depression. Furthermore, it was all unnecessary. It happened because the Federal Reserve Bank, the institution that is in charge of the nation's banking system, failed to do its job. The Federal Reserve failed in two respects. First, it failed to solve the commercial bank's liquidity problems by exchanging cash for the loans the banks had made. As a result, 5,000 banks failed between 1929 and 1933 and depositors lost their money needlessly. Second, the Federal Reserve failed to offset (which it had the power to do) the decline in the quantity of money that resulted. The Great Depression, according to the money hypothesis, was the result of a great mistake made by the Federal Reserve Bank.

There are thus major differences between the two explanations. The spending hypothesis sees the Great Depression as the result of the decline in autonomous spending, and the collapse of the banking system as the result of the Great Depression. The money hypothesis sees the collapse of the banking system as the cause of the Great Depression, and the fall of autonomous spending as the result. The spending hypothesis explains the severity and prolonged duration of the Depression in terms of the drastic fall in consumption and investment, and the failure of government to adopt an expansionary fiscal policy. The money hypothesis focuses upon the prolonged decline of the money supply and faults the Federal Reserve Bank's policies. Keynesians who support the spending hypothesis believe the economy is basically unstable and requires the proper fiscal and monetary policy to ensure full employment. Monetarists, on the other hand, see the economy as basically stable, always tending toward full employment; it takes mistakes by policy makers to create economic disasters.

The answer to the third question—can it happen again?—thus crucially depends upon which of the contending hypotheses is believed to be the best explanation for the Great Depression. If the money hypothesis is selected, then the answer is that it would take another great mistake to generate another Great Depression because the economy is basically stable. In order to prevent this from happening again, monetarists suggest that the Federal Reserve adopt a monetary rule to require that the money supply grow at a constant low rate. If the spending hypothesis is accepted instead, the answer is different. Because the economy is believed to be unstable, another contraction potentially as bad as the Great Depression could start, but it need not be allowed to develop. The existence of the national income accounts and employment statistics would provide early warning of this development, in which case the proper fiscal and monetary policies could be instituted to quickly return the economy to prosperity.

The modern theory of macroeconomics developed out of the Great Depression in an attempt to analyze what happened and why. A series of national income accounts and employment statistics were developed to measure the aggregate performance of the economy. These statistics allow us to describe what happened during the Great Depression and what is happening to the economy today. Two schools of macroeconomic thought developed, both of which address why the Depression happened. The Keynesian school developed the spending hypothesis, and the monetarists, the money hypothesis. The former see the economy as basically unstable, and concentrate upon the behavior of real variables such as consumption and investment spending and place great faith in fiscal policy. The latter concentrate upon financial variables, in particular the quantity of money, to explain economic fluctuations, and believe that if the money supply did not fluctuate, neither would the economy. In order to prevent the recurrence of another Depression, Keynesians feel the government must adopt the proper fiscal and monetary policies, while the monetarists believe that if the government were to leave well enough alone, the economy would manage itself just fine.

Additional Readings

Friedman, Milton, and Anna J. Schwartz. *The Great Contraction, 1929-1933*. Princeton University Press, 1965.

Gunderson, Gerald. *A New Economic History of America*. McGraw-Hill, 1976.

Heller, W. W. "Can There Be Another Crash?" *Challenge*, March–April 1980.

Temin, Peter. *Did Monetary Forces Cause the Great Depression?* Norton, 1976.

Preview

The social security system as it exists today is a transfer program. Working persons pay taxes that are transferred to retired persons. Considered in the light of the standard Keynesian consumption function, the social security program would have no effect upon the amount of the nation's savings. But the Keynesian consumption function has been found inadequate in a number of ways. The life cycle theory of the consumption function has been demonstrated to be an improvement over the Keynesian consumption function. In this chapter the life cycle theory of the consumption function is used to explore the question of whether or not the social security system has affected the amount of saving in the economy. The nation's capital stock and national income are partially dependent upon the amount of saving.

Key Economic Points

The implications for the rate of saving from applying the standard Keynesian consumption function to a transfer program such as social security are determined.

The standard Keynesian consumption function is not able to account for some important economic observations.

How can the life cycle theory of the consumption function be employed as a means of determining the influence of the social security system on the rate of saving?

If the implications of the life cycle model are correct, social security has reduced both the nation's capital stock and the level of national income.

15

The Consumption Function: Has the Social Security System Reduced the Nation's Capital Stock?

The social security system is perhaps the main legacy of the New Deal. The main function of the system is to provide a supplemental retirement income for the working population. A majority of aged Americans today depend heavily upon social security benefits to support their retirement. As a consequence of the rapid rise in the number of retired persons, social security has become politically sacrosanct, while it has also become financially troubled. The social security crisis, amid predictions of impending bankruptcy, has led to a vigorous political debate over benefits and taxes. This debate has obscured the equally important question of the effects of social security on the nation's rate of saving and the size of the capital stock.

According to one estimate, the social security system has substantially reduced the national rate of saving. Because savings are the source of capital in the economy, the capital stock has been consequently reduced. The most often cited figure is that the nation's capital stock will eventually be reduced by almost 40 percent of what it would be in the absence of social security. A smaller capital stock means lower productivity, lower real wages, and a lower national income. According to this view, a major cost of the social security system is a substantially poorer America.

These findings have not been universally accepted. Other economists have examined the same problem and reached different conclusions. Some agree that social security reduces savings but by less than the above estimate. Others find that social security has not affected savings at all. The main difference between these estimates lies in the selection of the consumption function by the investigator. The consumption function, which is the relationship between income and other variables and current consumption, is the central idea in modern macroeconomic analysis.

The standard Keynesian consumption function, characterized by the assumption that the marginal propensity of consumption out of disposable income (the proportion of an additional dollar of income that will be spent on consumption) is the same for all age groups, predicts that social security will not affect aggregate savings at all. A dollar in social security taxes, which will reduce the consumption and savings of the taxpayer, will, when given to the recipient, increase consumption and savings by an equal amount. The reduction in savings by the taxpayer is just offset by the increase in savings by the recipient, so that the national rate of savings remains unchanged.

The standard Keynesian consumption function, however, has failed to account for two important economic observations. First, current consumption has been found to be more stable than current income. Individuals maintain their levels of consumption despite fluctuations in current income. When during a recession income falls, consumption expenditures do not fall proportionally. Conversely, during the recovery when income rises, consumption expenditures do not rise proportionally. Second, over short periods of time the marginal propensity to consume is significantly less than it is over longer periods of time. Another way to look at the same finding is that apparently people save a larger percentage of any additions to their incomes over short periods of time than they do when the increase in income persists over longer periods of time. The difference is important because the marginal propensity to consume figures prominently in the calculation of fiscal multipliers. Thus it is important to know which, the short or long run is the appropriate counterpart of our theoretical construction.

The solution was to recognize that current consumption depended upon a broader measure of income than just current disposable income, as the Keynesian formulation assumed. Consumption spending, it appears, depends not upon our earnings today but rather our average earnings over a longer period of time. The important question is, what do we mean by "average" in this situation? Two important hypotheses have been developed, the life cycle theory and the permanent income hypothesis, either of which is better able to explain the actual data than the standard Keynesian consumption function. In this chapter we apply the life cycle theory to explore the effect that social security has upon the nation's savings.

The life cycle theory of consumption and savings is the central idea of our current understanding of the determinants of consumption and saving in the economy. In contrast to the standard Keynesian consumption function, the life cycle model views individuals as planning their consumption and savings so as to provide an even flow of consumption throughout their entire lifetimes. During the working years current consumption is less than current income, so savings are positive. During retirement, since working income ceases, consumption must be financed from the savings accumulated during the working years. Thus individuals save during their working years to provide an even flow of consumption for their retirement years. The life cycle theory predicts that an individual's savings or assets will rise during the working years and decline as they are used to finance continued consumption during a person's retirement years.

Therefore, in addition to current income, a person has assets (accumulated savings) with which to finance his or her lifetime consumption. The closer the individual is to the end of a lifetime, the higher the marginal propensity to consume. An additional dollar received by a person expecting to live 2 years will be spread equally over the 2 years while an additional dollar received by a person expecting to live 40 more years will be spread evenly over that longer period. An additional dollar will cause both individuals' current consumption to increase, but the older person's will increase more. Similarly, increasing the age of retirement, say from 65 to 70, would increase current consumption since less would have to be saved over a lifetime to finance consumption during the fewer remaining retirement years.

The creation of a social security program that provides a guaranteed income after retirement will thus reduce the overall savings in the economy because a person will have to save less to finance an even flow of consumption over a lifetime. A dollar of guaranteed social security income will simply replace a dollar of savings. Suppose that during retirement social security benefits exactly replace a person's wage income. Then there would be no need to save while young to finance consumption during retirement. Individual savings would be zero. Currently social security benefits for most people are less than their earnings from work, so some saving exists, but the total is reduced by the existence of social security benefits.

The social security system is often mistakenly considered to be a national version of private retirement plans. It is not. A private retirement program collects from the worker periodic payments that are invested in financial assets. Upon retirement the individual collects both the principal paid in and the interest earned. The individual's savings add to the economy's capital stock, and the increased productivity of the additional capital pays the interest payments. Social security, in contrast, is not voluntary, nor are an individual's tax payments invested. Instead, the receipts of the social security tax are directly transferred to retired workers. No capital is created in the process. The social security system effects a transfer from the working population to the retired population.

Contributors are guaranteed that upon retirement they will be able to participate as recipients in this transfer. Individuals treat these guaranteed benefits as if their wealth had increased by the amount that would finance the consumption benefits social security will supply. This perceived increase in wealth reduces current savings and stimulates current consumption. It is no longer necessary to save out of current income while working the amount that social security will provide. But there has been no increase in the society's total wealth that corresponds with the individual's perception of increased personal wealth. The taxes that workers pay in to social security are immediately paid out again to retired persons, who mainly spend this income on consumption. Little or none of this income is saved because retired workers are all nearing the end of their lifetimes. Thus no saving exists to supply the additional capital to enhance the productivity and income of the economy in order to pay for the retirements of currently working persons. The life cycle theory predicts that because individuals believe themselves to be wealthier than they really are, the total savings in the society will be reduced. Therefore, the size of the nation's capital stock and national income is lower than it would be in the absence of the program. This is called the savings replacement effect.

There is, however, a mitigating factor at work that is reducing the savings loss and perhaps overcoming it entirely. Suppose the existence of social security induces people to retire earlier than they would if the program did not exist. There is some evidence that this happens. In 1900, prior to social security, only 37 percent of men over age 65 were retired; by 1971, 74 percent of those benefiting from social security were retired. The effect of reducing working years (the induced retirement effect) and extending the period of retirement is to increase personal savings because more assets will be required to finance consumption over the longer retirement period. The net effect of social security on the savings of the working population becomes indeterminant, depending upon the relative impact of the savings replacement effect and the induced retirement effect. Thus the overall impact of social security upon savings becomes an empirical problem.

The most frequently publicized estimate is that the total effect of social security on savings is substantial, reportedly reducing personal saving in 1971 by half, which implies a reduction in total private saving of 38 percent.

This result would have been considered encouraging by Keynesian economists at the time the social security system was being created. At that time the Great Depression was in full swing. Economists stressed that it would continue as long as the full-employment rate of savings remained greater than the rate of investment. By providing an illusionary substitute for private savings, social security could reduce the savings rate and help to promote the recovery to full employment.

Economic conditions today are very different. It has been a half century since the Great Depression. Today the major economic problems are not caused by a lack of aggregate demand. A program that discourages private savings and encourages early retirement no longer serves a useful social function in comparison with a retirement system that does not produce these incentives.

The social security system is in need of reform, as almost everyone agrees. Unfortunately, the debate about the reforms required has almost exclusively focused upon benefits versus taxes. The nature of the system itself, existing as a transfer program rather than as an investment-financed retirement system, has not been widely debated. The application of the life cycle theory of the consumption function to social security as it exists today suggests that the system may well have had expensive side effects, significantly reducing the nation's capital stock. Surely this effect should be included in any discussion of social security reform.

Additional Readings

Feldstein, Martin S. "Seven Principles of Social Insurance." *Challenge,* November–December, 1976.

Feldstein, Martin S. "Social Security and Saving: The Extended Life Cycle Theory." *American Economic Review,* May 1976.

Preview

When President John F. Kennedy took office, he inherited an economy in a recession. During the campaign, he had promised to "get the economy moving again." In order to deliver on this promise, Kennedy adopted the "new economics," which sought to apply the principles of modern macroeconomics to economic policy making. The most important contribution of the new economics was to employ the fiscal multiplier to guide the 1964 tax cut. The best known fact about the 1964 tax cut was that the economy, soon after it was enacted, reached full employment, an occasion that had not occurred for more than a decade. In this chapter the fiscal policy of the Kennedy administration and the role modern macroeconomic analysis played are examined.

Key Economic Points

The concepts of potential national income, the GNP gap, and the full-employment budget played a role in economic policy making during the Kennedy administration.

The concept of the fiscal multiplier can be used for calculating the amount of fiscal stimulus required to eliminate a GNP gap.

Okun's law can be applied as a means of calculating how much the unemployment rate will fall as GNP increases.

16

Fiscal Multiplier: The Magnificent Tax Cut of 1964

When President John F. Kennedy took office in 1961, the economy was in the throes of a classic recession. The unemployment rate was at the then unacceptable level of 6.7 percent, almost 3 percent above the full-employment level. Inflation was not a problem; prices were barely increasing at the rate of 1 percent a year. President Kennedy had promised during the election campaign to "get the economy moving again." The immediate economic goal of the Kennedy administration was for the economy to attain full employment. In order to deliver on this promise, Kennedy adopted the recommendations of the "new economics." The new economics, which was in reality the economics of most professional economists, advocated the active use of fiscal policy to manage the economy.

The administration chose to enact a series of tax cuts to stimulate aggregate demand. The first tax cut was the passage of the investment tax credit in October 1972. This tax reduction provided a sizable incentive for business to undertake new investment. The second tax cut was a large permanent reduction in both personal and corporate income tax rates that took place in 1964. Personal taxes were cut 20 percent and corporate taxes by about 8 percent. The 1964 reduction in taxes stimulated aggregate demand via the fiscal multiplier and appears in retrospect to have provided the stimulus that drove the economy to full employment. The unemployment rate fell from 5.2 percent in 1964 to 4.5 percent in 1965 and to 3.8 percent in 1966. The economy, after more than a decade of high unemployment, finally was operating at capacity. The 1964 tax cut has been widely credited with bringing about this achievement and is now referred to as the "magnificent tax cut."

In this chapter, the fiscal policy of the Kennedy administration is examined. The Kennedy administration was the first to be guided by modern macroeconomic analysis. Below we shall consider how modern macroeconomics was employed and evaluate what effects that had on the economy. In particular, the role of the fiscal multiplier, which lies at the heart of the 1964 tax cut, will be studied.

President Kennedy relied heavily for economic advice upon his Council of Economic Advisors (CEA), a body of professional economists that advises the President on economic policy. The chairperson of the CEA, during the Kennedy years, was Walter Heller. Heller was the person who most of all was responsible for introducing Keynesian economics to policy making.

It was clear to Heller that the economy needed a substantial dose of fiscal stimulus if it was to operate at full employment. His most difficult task was to convince first the President and then the Congress to adopt this view at a time when the federal government budget was already running a deficit. The conventional view at the time was that prudent fiscal policy required the government always to attempt to balance the budget. Heller had to convince the political decision makers that cutting taxes when the budget was in deficit was not an irresponsible action.

In order to do this, the CEA introduced several new concepts into policy discussions. The council stressed the concept of potential, not actual, national income to focus attention on the social costs of unemployment. The novel idea of the full-employment budget as a better guide to fiscal policy than the current budget was introduced to stress the notion that there was nothing particularly desirable about a balanced budget. Finally, the concept of the fiscal multiplier was employed to calculate the amount of fiscal stimulus required to achieve the goal of full employment.

The tools and concepts the council employed were the standard tools of macroeconomics. The CEA did not invent these tools. However, the CEA did, under the leadership of Walter Heller, innovate the use of modern macroeconomics into the realm of policy making. What was new about the new economics was not the analysis, but the active and successful employment of modern economic concepts to guide fiscal policy.

The CEA stressed the concept of potential output, which measured the national income the economy would produce when operating at full employment. Along with the idea of potential output went the notion of the GNP gap. The GNP gap is the difference between the actual and the potential national income at full employment. When President Kennedy took office the GNP gap was about $60 billion or nearly 8 percent of GNP. A gap of that size served to illustrate the significant waste of economic resources that was occurring. A GNP gap of that size clearly called for expansionary fiscal policy.

The CEA also employed the concept of the full-employment budget surplus. The full-employment budget surplus is the surplus, or deficit, that would occur if the economy were operating at its potential income. This concept was used to direct attention away from the actual budget surplus or deficit, which is a misleading indicator of fiscal policy. An actual budget deficit can change for reasons that have nothing to do with fiscal policy. During a recession, for example, the budget deficit will increase because tax collections fall along with national income, but this certainly does not mean that fiscal policy, by design, has become more expansionary. The full-employment budget overcomes this deficiency.

It was important to focus the President's and Congress's attention on the full-employment budget rather than the actual budget because the actual budget in 1961 was running a deficit of $3.5 billion. This deficit was the direct result of the high unemployment created by the recession and not because of attempts to stimulate the economy. The actual deficit during that year was clearly a misleading indicator of fiscal policy. The full-employment budget for the same year revealed a surplus of $8.8 billion, clearly indicating that fiscal policy was contractionary at a time when it should have been expansionary.

It took some time for the council's economic crusade to bear fruit. The Kennedy administration had taken office in 1961, but it wasn't until June of 1962 that the administration developed a strong commitment to fiscal action. The first step was the investment tax credit of October 1962. The purpose of this measure was to raise the profitability of investment and thus stimulate aggregate demand. In January 1963, with the economy's recovery flagging, the Kennedy administration asked for a major change in the tax structure. It proposed a permanent reduction in income tax rates. This proposal was the basis of the Revenue Act of 1964, enacted in February of that year.

A tax cut was selected instead of an increase in government spending for two reasons. A tax cut could be effected quickly in comparison with increasing government expenditures, and a tax cut at that time was considered more politically acceptable than a spending increase. The size of the tax cut required to drive the economy to full employment was determined by first establishing the size of the GNP gap. The gap between potential and actual GNP had been reduced by the investment tax credit but still totaled $30 billion during 1962, and remained about the same during 1963.

Given the size of the GNP gap the calculation of the size of the tax cut necessary to close the gap is an exercise in multiplier analysis. The fiscal multiplier is the relationship between the amount of fiscal stimulus (positive or negative) and the multiplied increase or decrease in national income. Most studies of the fiscal multiplier place its value between 2 and 3.

Thus to close a GNP gap of $30 billion required a political fiscal stimulus of between $10 and $15 billion. Walter Heller later stated that the rationale for the 1964 tax cut came straight out of economics textbooks. In turn, the tax cut would repay its debt to the textbooks by supplying "the classic example of modern fiscal policy and multiplier economics at work."

The Revenue Act of 1964 provided the needed fiscal stimulus. This act reduced the marginal tax rates for individuals, which had ranged from 20–91 percent, to 14–70 percent. The corporate income tax was reduced at the same time from 52 to 48 percent. It was estimated that the reduction in personal income taxes would amount to $10 billion and for corporations to $3 billion. This suggests that the Kennedy administration believed that the total long-term tax cut multiplier was about 2.3 ($30 billion GNP gap ÷ $13 billion tax cut). They expected that reducing taxes by $13 billion would eventually have a multiplied effect upon GNP sufficient to eliminate the GNP gap.

What effect did the tax cut actually have on economic activity? The best known fact about the Revenue Act of 1964 is that in the year and a half after the tax cut took effect the output of the economy grew at a rate not previously recorded during peacetime. This rapid growth had, by 1966, completely eliminated the GNP gap, an event that had not occurred since 1955. The tax cut then began to be called the magnificent tax cut of 1964.

But was the tax cut responsible for the elimination of the GNP gap? After all, many things happened during 1964 besides the tax cut. The University of Illinois won the Rose Bowl, and Senator Barry Goldwater decided to run for President. Arthur Okun, a member of the CEA at that time, undertook, during the summer of 1965, to empirically examine the effects of the tax cut. Okun recalculated the multiplier for the reduction in both personal income taxes and the corporate income tax. He calculated the multiplier for personal income tax cuts to have been 2.59 and for the corporate tax cut to be 3.45. Thus the long-term effect upon GNP from reducing personal tax by $10 billion was to increase national income by $25.9 billion. The $3 billion corporate tax reduction raised GNP by another $10.4 billion. The combined effect of the tax cut was to increase GNP by $36.3 billion, or more than enough to eliminate the GNP gap.

The multiplier effect of the tax cut upon national income would also have substantially reduced the unemployment rate. The gain in employment resulting from increases in GNP can be estimated by employing Okun's law. Okun's law states that the unemployment rate is reduced by 1 percent for every 3.2 percent increase in GNP. The extra GNP, attributed above to the tax cut, would have reduced the unemployment rate, according to this relationship, from the 1963 average of 5.7 percent to around 4.3 percent by the end of 1965. The unemployment rate at the end of 1965 actually stood at 4.1 percent, so the effects of the tax cut could account for most of the decline in the unemployment rate.

Okun's analysis clearly attributes the recovery of the economy to the

1964 tax reduction. Most economists at that time would have agreed with Okun's analysis. Belief in the effectiveness of fiscal policy to deal with an economy operating below its potential reached its zenith in the wake of the 1964 tax cut. Economics textbooks now had a real-world example of the workings of the fiscal multiplier.

Additional Readings

Dornbusch, R., and S. Fischer, *Macroeconomics,* McGraw-Hill, 1978, Chap. 10.

Okun, Arthur M. "Measuring the Impact of the 1964 Tax Reduction." *Perspectives on Economic Growth,* Walter W. Heller, ed. Random House, 1968.

Preview

The current inflation, which has plagued the economy for well over a decade, began in 1965. Initially, it was generated by the growth of government expenditures and financed by deficit spending, at a time when the economy was already at full employment. The principles of fiscal finance called for a tax increase to reduce the inflationary pressure during 1966. This increase for political reasons was delayed until 1968. Meanwhile inflation had worsened substantially. When the tax increase was finally enacted, it was expected that it would work exactly like the 1964 tax cut, only in reverse, reducing aggregate demand until the economy was just operating at its potential national income with a stable price level. It did not work that way. This chapter applies the modern theory of the permanent income hypothesis to explain the failure of the 1968 tax surcharge to curb inflation.

Key Economic Points

Time lags between the decision to employ fiscal policy and the time it is implemented affect its outcome.

Temporary changes in income, whether caused by fiscal policy or not, have only minor influences on the level of consumption.

The permanent income hypothesis can be applied to evaluate the effectiveness of the tax surcharge in reducing the level of aggregate demand.

17

Fiscal Policy: The Failure of the 1968 Tax Surcharge to Curb Inflation

The seeds of our current inflation were sown and germinated more than a decade ago during the Vietnam War. Between 1965 and 1968 government spending increased substantially to finance both the expanding Vietnam War and the social programs that constituted President Johnson's "Great Society." The growth in government expenditures during this period absorbed almost one-third of the entire growth of GNP. The budget of the federal government slipped sharply into a deficit at the same time the unemployment rate actually fell below the full-employment level. The result, as would be expected, was that aggregate demand exceeded the productive capacity of the economy and the consumer price index (CPI) began to rise. The CPI, which had increased on average a little more than 1 percent during the first half of the 1960s, grew at the rate of 3.4 percent during 1966, 3.0 percent during 1967, and 4.7 percent during 1968.

The Revenue and Expenditure Control Act of 1968 was passed in June 1978, raising taxes to reduce aggregate demand and inflationary pressures. Despite the increased taxes, aggregate demand did not decline but increased, causing prices to rise by 6.4 percent, at that time the highest rate of inflation since World War II. Since then the economy has not returned to the relative price stability experienced during the first half of the 1960s.

The beginnings of inflation did not go unrecognized by government economists. The Economic Report of the President for 1966 called for tax action to moderate the growth of private spending. President Johnson was advised by his economists to ask Congress for a general increase in income taxes to prevent aggregate demand from exceeding the economy's productive capacity. President Johnson did not believe an income tax increase would at that time pass the Congress. He therefore delayed for an entire year before asking Congress to increase taxes. Then he requested not a permanent income tax increase, but a temporary tax surcharge of 10 percent. A tax surcharge is a proportional increase above existing rates. Individuals calculated their taxes according to the old rates and added 10 percent to the amount. Congress during 1967 remained reluctant to pass this tax request, delaying passage until June 1968, 2½ years after the Council of Economic Advisors had first recommended it. Meanwhile, the rate of inflation had increased to nearly 5 percent per year.

The government expected that this restrictive fiscal action would affect the economy in a way exactly the reverse of the successful 1964 tax cut. The surcharge was expected to reduce consumption expenditures directly and, through the fiscal multiplier, reduce GNP by even more.

The results were not as expected. Aggregate demand did not decline and the rate of inflation actually worsened after the tax increase was enacted. Either the tax increase was not large enough or it did not have the expected effect upon consumer spending. There are good theoretical and empirical reasons to expect that it was the latter reason rather than the former that lies at the heart of the fiscal failure of the tax surcharge.

There was an important difference between the 1964 tax cut and the 1968 tax increase that was ignored by government economists. The 1964 cut was a permanent reduction in taxes while the 1968 surcharge was clearly recognized to be temporary, expiring in June 1969.

The modern theory of the consumption function suggests that people plan their consumption over a period longer than 1 year. For example, people get paid relatively infrequently, say each Friday, but they do not concentrate their week's consumption expenditures on payday. Instead, individuals seem to prefer a smooth consumption flow, consuming some every day. Similarly, there is nothing special about the length of one year. There are no forces that cause an individual to plan consumption within the year solely on the basis of the income received during that year. Consumption expenditures are planned over a longer period of time.

This view lead to the development of the permanent income hypothesis, which, like the life cycle theory, stresses that a person's consumption behavior is geared to long-term consumption opportunities. Consumption spending is not governed by what we earn today, but by what we earn on average over a longer period of time. According to the permanent income hypothesis, consumption expenditures are linked to average or permanent, not to current, level of income.

People calculate their permanent level of income from their past earning experiences. Permanent income is calculated as a weighted average of current and past income, with current and immediate past earnings being weighted more heavily than earnings in the more distant past. Changes in current income affect consumption expenditures only through their effect upon permanent income.

If current income goes up this year, permanent income will obviously also increase but by less. Since consumption is influenced by the level of permanent income, predicted consumption will increase less than if it depended only upon current income. Thus the permanent income hypothesis accounts for the historical observation that consumption expenditures are much less variable than income.

No individual can be certain that a change in income is temporary or permanent. Thus if current income increases, the individual does not immediately increase his or her consumption. Instead, the full increase will be added to savings. If in the future the higher income is maintained, then consumption will also increase as the individual realizes that the increase is permanent. Thus consumption depends entirely upon the individual's perception of his or her permanent income. Temporary or transitory increases in income will be saved, not spent. The same is true for declines in current income. The permanent income hypothesis predicts that transitory fluctuations in income will affect only savings, not consumption expenditures.

The 1968 tax surcharge was quite explicitly recognized as temporary This means that individuals viewed the tax as a temporary, or transitory, decline in income. The additional taxes due would then be financed mainly out of savings, and consumption expenditures that depend upon permanent income would be little affected. The evidence was in accord with these theoretical expectations. Taxes in 1968 rose by $11 billion and savings fell by $9 billion. Consumption spending actually increased along with personal income.

The rate of saving out of personal income, which prior to the surcharge averaged over 7 percent annually, fell to 5.7 percent during the year the tax was in effect. When the surcharge expired, the rate of saving revived, climbing within three-quarters to almost 8.0 percent. It is quite evident that most of the increased tax payments, in accordance with theoretical expectations, were financed by reduction in personal savings.

These impressions are supported by the econometric investigations of economists. Professor Robert Eisner stated that "the tax surcharge should never on basic theoretical grounds have been considered an effective anti-inflationary device. ... The basic error ... may be charged to failure to take into account the implications of the permanent income hypothesis." (*American Economic Review*, p. 898.) Eisner has estimated that the marginal propensity to spend out of transitory income, the income generated by a temporary tax increase, is between 0.1 and 0.3, which is close to the zero predicted by the permanent income hypothesis.

More recently, William Springer, senior economist for Data Resources, Inc., has investigated the question of whether the 1968 surcharge really worked. He concluded that "the evidence of the 1968 surcharge period, far from confirming the general efficiency of temporary changes in income taxes, leads me to be pessimistic regarding the use of flexible tax policy to regulate aggregate demand." (p. 658) It appears that in order to have significant effect on consumption expenditures, a tax change must be permanent.

The evidence suggests quite strongly that the 1968 tax surcharge had, at best, a minor influence on consumption spending. Both the modern theory of consumption (either the life cycle or permanent income hypothesis) and the experience of the tax surcharge of 1968 suggest that temporary or transitory tax changes will have little impact on consumption spending. Temporary tax changes are not a very useful tool for managing aggregate demand in the economy.

Additional Readings

Dornbusch, R., and S. Fischer, *Macroeconomics,* McGraw-Hill, 1978, Chap. 10.

Eisner, R. "Fiscal and Monetary Policy Reconsidered." *American Economic Review,* December 1969.

Eisner, R. "What Went Wrong?" *Journal of Political Economy,* May–June 1971.

Okun, A. "The Personal Tax Surcharge and Consumer Demand." *Brookings Papers on Economic Activity,* Brookings Institution, 1971.

Springer, W. L. "Did the 1968 Surcharge Really Work?" *American Economic Review,* September 1975; see also the March 1977 issue for a follow-up article.

Preview

The taxpayers of the United States are in revolt. Inspired by the success in obtaining constitutional amendments to limit both taxes and expenditures in California, a national movement to amend the Constitution of the United States seeks to require an annually balanced federal budget. The goal of such an amendment is both to limit the growth of the federal government and to reduce inflation, which the amendment supporters feel is caused by federal budget deficits. Despite the widespread popularity of this proposed amendment among voters, few economists are in favor of the proposal. This chapter explores the reasons the economics profession has not endorsed a balanced budget amendment, examining in turn the basic contentions of the amendment's supporters.

Key Economic Points

There is a difference between requiring each member of society to balance a personal budget and requiring the federal government to do so.

There is no necessary link between inflation and federal budget deficits.

A constitutional amendment requiring an annually balanced budget would effectively eliminate fiscal policy as a countercyclical tool that could be used to stabilize the economy.

18

Fiscal Policy: The Constitutional Amendment to Require an Annually Balanced Budget

There is a movement throughout the United States to amend the Constitution to require the federal government to balance its budget annually. Such an amendment would require that all federal expenditures be financed by an equivalent amount of tax revenues. Recent polls have shown that an overwhelming proportion of the nation's voters (between two-thirds and three-fourths), favor such an amendment. Reasons for such popular support are not hard to find. Between 1969 and 1979, personal income in the United States rose 158 percent, while total federal government expenditures rose 263 percent, consuming 21 percent of gross national product. Federal tax receipts rose significantly less than expenditures. The result was a successive series of deficits that have occurred during every year since 1969.

The result of this fiscal performance is the widespread belief that federal government finances are out of control. That at least is the position of the National Taxpayers Union, which maintains that "deficit spending has helped erode the value of the dollar and decrease the spendable income of virtually every American. . . . What's more, inflation, caused largely by deficit spending, has pushed Americans into higher tax brackets, dramatically increasing the tax burden on you and other citizens." The National Taxpayers Union is the main advocate of the drive to call a constitutional convention for the purpose of adopting a balanced budget amendment. Thirty-four of the fifty states must pass such a resolution before Congress could call a convention for this purpose. By 1980, thirty states had approved a convention, testifying to the momentum of the amendment.

The argument in favor of a constitutional amendment rests on three major contentions. First, since all voters, in conducting their personal financial affairs, and the state and local governments must balance their budgets, why shouldn't Uncle Sam? Second, the growth of government spending in general and federal deficits in particular are the main causes of inflation. Three, a constitutional requirement for a federal balanced budget would be a simple, sure-fire way to limit government spending that is currently out of control.

Despite the widespread political support for such an amendment, few, if any, professional economists support the drive for a balanced budget amendment. The reasons for this opposition will become clear as each of the three contentions of the supporters of the amendment are considered.

The first contention made by supporters of the balanced budget amendment is that since individuals, business firms, and state and local governments must balance their budgets, there is no reason that the federal government should be any different. This contention ignores the fact that individuals and businesses often do not balance their budgets annually. Sometimes they too run deficits—often huge deficits—in relation to their annual incomes. This often takes place when a family buys a house, incurring a debt several times their annual income, or when business firms sell bonds or borrow from financial institutions to finance their business activities or capital acquisitions. State and local governments also can and do borrow to finance capital constructions.

If the federal government separated operating expenses from capital outlays in the same way that individuals, businesses, and state and local governments do, then the recent federal deficits would disappear. One estimate for 1979 states that approximately $120 billion of the $494 billion in federal expenditures could properly be considered capital outlays. Since the deficit during that year was $28 billion, separating capital outlays from operating expenses would show the federal government operating with a substantial surplus rather than a deficit.

There is, moreover, a decisive difference between the impact state and local government budgets have on the economy and the impact of the federal budget. A state or local budget can be balanced by tax increases or spending cuts without influencing the entire economy; the federal budget cannot.

When the economy moves into a recession, the rate of unemployment rises, income and profits fall, and consequently federal tax receipts fall, expenditures rise, and the budget deficit increases. All of this happens automatically. Currently, a decline in GNP of 3 percent, which roughly corresponds to a 1 percent increase in the unemployment rate, produces a $20 to $25 billion increase in the budget deficit. Most of this increase (80 percent) is the result of the decline in tax revenues, but 20 percent is the result of increased expenditures for unemployment compensation and public assistance benefits. Thus the federal budget, without the necessity of political action, automatically adopts the appropriate fiscal action to limit the severity of the recession.

A balanced budget requirement would require the federal government to cut expenditures or raise taxes when a recession arises—just the opposite of the appropriate countercyclical actions that modern economic theory suggests as appropriate. Consider the 1974–1975 recession, the most severe the economy has suffered since the Great Depression. The unemployment rate averaged 8.5 percent, and 7.8 million persons were out of work. The deficit in 1974 was only $4.7 billion, or less than 1 percent of government spending. The severity of the recession caused the deficit to swell to $45.2 billion, or 14 percent of expenditures. The chairman of the Council of Economic Advisors estimated that to balance the budget in 1975 would have required Congress to cut spending or increase taxes by $90 billion. The result of such an action, according to the income-expenditures theory, would have made an already severe recession even more costly to American society.

Nobel Prize-winning economist Paul Samuelson has pointed out that during the great Depression the federal government did follow this strategy. When the budget fell out of balance, President Hoover and the Congress raised taxes in a vain attempt to balance the budget. Professor Samuelson suggests that the "rash attempt did most definitely worsen the state of bankruptcy of the economic system. How much worse would have been the pressure on Congress and the executive to perpetuate these follies if the Constitution itself called for such suicidal policies." (p. 6)

The second contention of the supporters of the balanced budget amendment is that federal deficits have been the main cause of our recent inflation. Both economic analysis and historical evidence cast doubt on this contention. Deficits do not always fuel inflation. When the economy is in a recession, deficits increase aggregate demand, which helps to reemploy idle workers and machinery and to revive the economy. The years 1919–1920 saw one of the most rapid inflations in U.S. history while the budget was running a large surplus. Between 1959 and 1965 the federal budget was in deficit, and yet the rate of inflation was about 1 percent per year. During 1974 inflation was running over 12 percent a year, but dropped to less than 6 percent in 1976 despite huge deficits.

There are also many times in U.S. history when federal deficits have been unnecessarily incurred, fueling inflation. When federal deficits increase aggregate demand in an already prosperous economy, they fuel inflation. The failure to eliminate a deficit to finance the Vietnam War contributed greatly to the inflation problem of the last decade. Wise fiscal management requires a budget surplus during inflationary periods just as it calls for a deficit during a recession.

Those economists who believe that inflation is purely a monetary phenomenon do not blame inflation directly for federal deficits. Budget deficits are inflationary, according to this view, only to the extent that deficits prompt the Federal Reserve to finance the deficits by creating new money. This could occur if government borrowing caused interest rates to rise significantly, inducing the Federal Reserve to increase the money supply to drive interest rates back down. Economists disagree about the extent to which this has happened.

In summary, there is no necessary relation between federal budget deficits and inflation. There is, however, no doubt that deficits incurred unwisely have in the past added to the inflation problem. There have been both destructive and constructive deficits. There is also little doubt that inflation could have been controlled by monetary policy despite the existence of these deficits.

The final contention made by supporters of a balanced budget amendment is that such an amendment would be a sure-fire way to limit spending by the federal government, which is currently out of control. On the face of it, there is nothing in the proposed amendment that would limit spending. All that would be required is for expenditures to be covered by tax revenues. The most rapid rate of growth in government expenditures has taken place not at the federal level, but at the state and local levels, which are covered by a balance of budget requirement. In California, the rapid growth in state expenditures and taxes eventually led in 1978 to Proposition 13, which reduced property taxes by 57 percent and limited future increases to 2 percent a year. The success of Proposition 13 led California voters to overwhelmingly approve Proposition 4 the next year. Proposition 4 limited state and local government spending to the 1978–1979 level except for adjustments for inflation and population growth. The experience in California suggests that a balanced budget amendment would not limit federal spending. A spending limitation, such as Proposition 4, would be required for that.

The attempt by the Carter administration to balance the budget for 1981 is further evidence that a balanced budget does not in itself limit spending. The 1981 federal budget projects an increase in expenditures of 16 percent over the previous year. This budget is only balanced by increased tax receipts due to inflation and increased taxes on crude oil. This is not to suggest that federal government expenditures are currently out of control. As a proportion of a gross national product, the expenditures of the federal government have remained constant for several years. The proportion of GNP absorbed by the federal budget has actually fallen slightly from 22.6 percent in 1976 to less than 22 percent in 1981. The federal government thus has been growing at about the same rate as gross national product.

In summary, most economists feel that the dangers associated with a constitutionally mandated annually balanced budget outweigh the possible benefits. Such an amendment would reduce future inflationary pressures by eliminating the possibility that a deficit would occur during times of full employment, which would be inflationary to the extent that the Federal Reserve finances the new debt by increasing the money supply. Greater than offsetting this possible benefit is the loss of fiscal policy as a countercyclical tool that can be used to stabilize the economy. Furthermore, a balanced budget amendment will not necessarily limit future government expenditures; only a ceiling on actual expenditures, such as the experience in California testifies, could do that.

Additional Readings

Brimmer, Andrew F. "The Political Economy of Limitations on Federal Spending." *Challenge,* March–April 1980.

Burns, Arthur F. and Paul A. Samuelson. "Two Views on the Balanced Budget Amendment." *AEI Economist,* April 1979.

Cox, William N. "Constitutional Limitation of the Federal Budget." *Economic Review,* Federal Reserve Bank of Atlanta, May–June 1979.

Heller, Walter W. "Balanced Budget Fallacies." *Wall Street Journal,* March 16, 1979.

Stein, Herbert. "To Balance or Not to Balance." *Wall Street Journal,* March 12, 1979.

Preview

Traditional Keynesian economics has concentrated upon aggregate demand to regulate the overall level of economic activity. Recently, an increasing number of economists have recognized that fiscal decisions, especially tax policy, also influence aggregate supply. These economists have found supporters in the halls of Congress, who have proposed tax cuts to fight inflation. This recommendation is precisely the opposite of what Keynesian analysis suggests as the appropriate fiscal policy for dealing with inflation. This chapter explores the economic arguments of the supply side fiscalists and compares these arguments with those of Keynesian analysis.

Key Economic Points

The supply side of macroeconomics has until recently been ignored in macroeconomics.

The heart of supply side economics is an analysis of the limitations that taxes create.

The fiscal policy of supply side fiscalists is compared with that of traditional macroeconomics for dealing with inflation.

Is there evidence to support the supply side view that tax rates are so high in the United States that they substantially discourage economic activity?

19

Criticisms of Keynesian Economics: Supply Side Effects of Fiscal Policy

It looked like the height of the silly season. There were 151 members of Congress during the summer of 1978 introducing a bill to cut taxes by almost one-third over the next 3 years. It might appear that there is nothing unusual about Congresspersons proposing to cut taxes just prior to an election. After all, being in favor of lower taxes has in the past proven to be good politics. But inflation was at that time the number one political problem, and the federal government's budget had a deficit of more than $40 billion. Moreover, most of these congresspersons were Republicans to whom a stable price level and a balanced budget were commandments written in stone.

According to conventional economic wisdom, a tax cut at that time would have been the height of fiscal irresponsibility, stimulating aggregate demand when the problem was that there was already too much aggregate demand. The Congress was warned by many economists that a tax cut of that magnitude at that time would almost certainly push the economy into a runaway inflation. Evidently a majority of Congress agreed and the proposed tax cut legislation was defeated.

The defeated tax cut was not a political ploy designed to win votes by proposing legislation that had no chance of passage. Those who proposed it were serious. They wanted to pass a massive tax cut. Furthermore, they wanted to pass the tax cut because they desired to reduce inflation and balance the federal budget. They believed that, contrary to traditional economic thought, a tax cut would accomplish both. A few unkind critics also suggested that these persons must also still believe in Santa Claus and the Easter Bunny.

What the proponents of a tax cut actually believed in was the "supply side of economics." According to this view, the causes of the current inflation, the slow rate of economic growth, and even the federal budget deficit are to be found among the forces that limit aggregate supply. The appropriate role for government in this situation is to attempt to stimulate aggregate supply by adopting policies that will encourage employment, stimulate increases in productivity, increase the rate of capital formation, and foster technological change. They believed that a massive tax cut would do all of these things.

Historically, ever since the U.S. government assumed the responsibility for managing the economy, policy makers have focused almost exclusively upon demand management. When the economy moved toward recession, the government sought to stimulate aggregate demand by increasing government spending and/or reducing taxes. When inflation threatened, the proper strategy was to cut spending and/or increase taxes. The underlying assumption in all this was that aggregate supply would passively respond to changes in aggregate demand.

A decade of soaring inflation, anemic economic growth, and massive budget deficits have caused some economists, journalists, and members of Congress to increasingly question this assumption. A *Wall Street Journal* editorial (February 27, 1979) illustrates this view:

The problem, we believe, is that the conventional wisdom confuses the growth in aggregate demand with the growth of the economy. Restraining inflation does require a slower growth in demand, but the economy could actually grow faster as a consequence. There is, after all, a supply side to the economy, and aggregate demand is not the only factor to which supply responds. Supply is also influenced by production incentives and expectations about the future. Both have been adversely affected by the excessive demand stimulation that the economy has experienced for over a decade.

The editorial goes on to attribute the economy's current economic problems to the "tired and worn-out Keynesian doctrine" that adequate demand will in itself be sufficient to generate adequate supply, "but it hasn't worked out that way."

Economists concerned about the supply side of macroeconomics see the causes of the current inflation to be in large measure the failure of aggregate supply to keep pace with the growth in aggregate demand. As a consequence, instead of a period of rapid economic growth with relatively stable prices, the U.S. economy during the 1970s experienced stagflation—slow economic growth and rapid inflation.

The recent slow rate of American economic growth according to the economists investigating the supply side results from the negative effects of current tax rates upon the incentives to allocate resources efficiently. These economists, known as supply side fiscalists, emphasize that changes in tax rates not only affect disposable income (altering aggregate demand), but induce changes in aggregate supply. This occurs because tax rates change the relative prices of goods and resources, and therefore directly affect the allocation of resources.

As the theory goes, any tax drives a "wedge" equal to the amount of the tax between the price the buyer must pay and the price the seller receives. The bigger the wedge, the less incentive there is to work, save, or invest. In the labor market, for example, there is a substantial tax wedge, as the deductions from your paychecks readily testify. This wedge is composed of the income tax, social security tax, plus the employer's contributions for unemployment compensation and the workmen's compensation tax. Thus it currently costs an employer substantially more to hire a worker than the worker receives as take-home pay. The effect of this wedge is to reduce both the quantity of labor demanded by business firms and the quantity of labor supplied by workers, reducing the total output of the private sector accordingly. A reduction in tax rates would, by reducing the size of the wedge, increase the quantity of labor supplied and demanded by the private sector, thus increasing the total output of the economy. A similar wedge exists when households decide how much of their income to save. The bigger the bite taxes take, the less the incentive to save and to invest. Consumers can either spend or save the income they receive. The proportion of income devoted to savings depends in part upon the rate of return savings earn. If that rate of return is taxed while consumption is not, then households will save less and consume more out of current income. The amount of savings out of which the nation generates its capital will be smaller, the larger the tax wedge.

The size of the tax wedge also affects the amount of economic activity that is carried on in the nation's marketplaces. The recent rise in the underground economy is often explained with reference to existing tax rates. Market activity is taxed while nonmarket activity escapes taxation. For example, a physician may decide to paint his or her house instead of treating patients and hiring a painter because the earnings of doctors are taxed at a high rate but efforts spent painting a house are not taxed at all. The higher the tax rates, the more that economic activities will be carried on outside existing markets. As a consequence, society loses some of the gains from specialization and trade that organizing economic activities via the market creates.

The inevitable consequence of most taxes is to create a wedge that discourages economic activity, but this is not to suggest that the optimum tax rate would be zero, the only tax rate that does not create a wedge. The optimum tax rate is not zero because tax revenues are used to finance public services that are necessary if a market economy is to function at all.

These essential services are national defense, the establishment and maintenance of a system of secure property rights, the provision of justice, and so on, without which a market economy simply could not operate. If tax rates were zero, then these essential services could not be provided, and the nation's output would be very low, perhaps even zero.

If the resources of the private sector are to be efficiently employed in a market economy, it is therefore necessary that some public goods be provided. Thus taxes are required to finance the provision of these essential public services. As tax rates rise from zero, these essential public goods can be provided in increasing amounts, which contributes to rapid increases in the efficiency of employing labor and capital in market activities. The resulting increases in the nation's output more than compensate for whatever disincentive effects the higher tax rates might create.

However, as tax rates rise, the disincentive effects of higher tax rates grow more important, and the after-tax rewards for working, saving and investing decline. At the same time, the productivity-increasing effect from providing additional public goods also declines as increasingly less essential services are provided. Eventually, at some tax rate, the disincentive effects suffered by the private sector equals the productivity increases from the increased availability of public goods. The economy's output is maximized at this tax rate. Thereafter, if tax rates continue to increase, the nation's output will actually decline as the disincentive effects overwhelm the productivity increases generated by more public goods. Owners of the factors of production will, after this point as tax rates rise further, increasingly withdraw their factors from the market economy. When an effective tax rate of 100 percent is imposed, no factors will be supplied and no production will take place in the market economy. There therefore exists an optimum tax rate, the tax rate that maximizes the nation's market output. A tax rate below the optimum would reduce output below the economy's potential because too few public goods are available. A tax rate above the optimum will also reduce output because sufficient incentives (after-tax income) no longer exist to allocate resources effectively.

The optimum tax rate has another important implication for tax policy. The optimum tax rate also maximizes the tax revenues the government receives. The government has every incentive to discover and establish the optimum tax rate because it will maximize the resources available. The taxpayers, as a group, would also desire to pay this tax rate because the public services that would be financed by their tax payments would allow them to maximize the output of the private sector.

Most economists would agree with the analysis up to this point. The disagreement begins when an attempt is made to compare existing tax rates with the theoretical optimum rate. Many supply side fiscalists, and certainly the 151 members of Congress who proposed to slash taxes drastically, believe that existing tax rates are substantially higher than the optimum rate. They cite as evidence studies that have found that social security taxes may have reduced the nation's capital stock by 40 percent and a more recent study showing that the current tax wedge reduces the nation's savings by 20 percent. Although comparable studies on the effects of the tax wedge in the labor market still remain to be done, the supply side fiscalists are not ready to admit that it is savings that are most affected by existing tax rates. The rapid rise of the underground economy is also viewed as supporting evidence for the proposition that current tax rates exceed the optimum rate.

Other economists remain skeptical or unconcerned. Many do not feel that the current tax structure—where the highest tax rate on earned income is 50 percent—has such an adverse affect upon incentives that a reduction in tax rates would actually increase economic output and tax revenues. Moreover, many feel that the effects of taxes on the supply side are long term in nature. The positive stimulus to supply from a tax cut may require several years to take effect. As a consequence, these economists warn against the dangers of a massive tax cut such as that proposed by the members of Congress. The effect of such a tax cut would be to stimulate demand immediately, fueling the fires of inflation, while the positive effect upon aggregate supply, even if it would be substantial (which many doubt), would not be felt for several years.

Recently, the Congressional Joint Economic Committee of the U. S. Congress adopted supply side economics. Both Democrats and Republicans united in this panel to urge that the solution to the problem of inflation is to promote private investment and economic growth. The joint economic committee urged that the government stop using monetary and fiscal policy to solve the short-run problem of unemployment and instead use both to promote long-term economic growth. The panel hired an economic forecasting firm, Data Resources, Inc., to test the validity of its supply side philosophy. Data Resources found that a $10 billion tax cut would, by promoting output, reduce the rate of inflation by 1 percent without changing the unemployment rate at all, but to accomplish the same effect on inflation by conventional fiscal policies would significantly increase the rate of unemployment. The committee concluded that to employ traditional fiscal policy to fight inflation would be "inefficient and inhumane."

Most economists would concur that the supply side effects of fiscal policy have been too long ignored. Moreover, the theory of supply side effects does not in itself elicit much disagreement. Many economists, however, would disagree that substantial evidence exists that current tax rates are higher than the optimum rate, and many, perhaps most, do not feel that the evidence is substantial enough to support the proposed reduction of taxes.

CHAPTER 19

Additional Readings

Evans, Michael K. "The Bankruptcy of Keynesian Econometric Models." *Challenge*, January–February 1980.

Kelcher, R. E. "Fiscal Effects On Potential Output." *Economic Review*, September–October 1979.

Miller, P. J. "The Tax-cut Illusion." In *Federal Reserve of Minneapolis 1979 Annual Report*, Federal Reserve Bank of Minneapolis, 1979.

Roberts, Paul Craig. "The Breakdown of the Keynesian Model." *The Public Interest*, Summer 1978.

Wanniski, Jude. *The Way the World Works: How Economics Fail and Succeed*. Basic Books, 1978.

IV

MONEY AND
MONETARY POLICY

Preview

During the second half of the 1970s, the formerly stable relationship between the amount of reserves created by the Federal Reserve and the amount of money created by the nation's banking system collapsed. The banking system no longer created as much money out of every dollar of new reserves as it had in the past. This situation became known as "the case of the missing money." This mystery was easily solved: the missing money had found its way into the new interest-paying accounts recently created by the nation's banking system. Because the deposits held in these types of accounts were not included in the operational definitions of money, their existence was not included in the measures of the money supply. The solution was to redefine money to take into account the effects of these financial innovations. This chapter explores the criteria the new definitions of money must meet and discusses the difficulties of putting a new definition into practice.

Key Economic Points

The factors that led to the attempts to redefine money are identified.

Different approaches to defining money are compared.

The usefulness of old definitions are compared with the new ones according to the differing approaches.

The response of the Federal Reserve to the need for a new definition of money is evaluated.

20

Redefining Money: Solving the Case of the Missing Money

In 1974 a large part of the nation's money supply was missing and the monetary authorities became appropriately alarmed. In subsequent years the shortage worsened. By 1979, more than $50 billion, or 15 percent of the nation's money supply, was missing from the monetary statistics. The problem was quickly diagnosed. The nation's banking system was not creating as much money out of the reserves supplied by the Federal Reserve Bank as it had in the past. Prior to 1974, a regular and predictable relationship, known as the money multiplier, had existed between the amount of monetary reserves created by the central bank and the total amount of money, defined as currency plus demand deposits, in circulation. The Federal Reserve Bank had in the past relied heavily upon this relationship to conduct monetary policy.

The inability to accurately predict the quantity of money a given expansion of reserves would create obviously complicated further the already difficult business of conducting monetary policy. The Federal Reserve's concern was shared by a host of economists and financial analysts known as "Fed watchers." During the 1970s it had been increasingly recognized that the money supply was an important determinant of the behavior of the economy. The Fed watchers closely monitored the latest monetary statistics in an attempt to divine in them the future course of the economy. The peculiar behavior of the money supply did not make their task any easier.

Almost as soon as the problem was recognized, a number of economists, inside and outside the Federal Reserve, began to search for the missing money. The cause of the problem, it was quickly identified, was to be found in the recent innovations occurring in the nation's financial sector. The financial system during the past decades had been particularly inventive in creating new alternatives to the traditional checking account. A depositor could choose the place to temporarily deposit money from automatic transfer services, negotiated orders of withdrawal accounts, share drafts, repurchase agreements, and money market mutual funds, to name just a few. The advantage of these alternatives is that each pays the depositor interest on the funds deposited, which the traditional checking account, known as demand deposit, did not. These new accounts allowed the customer the opportunity to earn interest and still have the funds readily available to spend.

Prior to the development of these new accounts, whenever the Federal Reserve created new monetary reserves, the banking system used these reserves to make loans, creating demand deposits in the process. Thus the money stock, calculated as the amount of currency and demand deposits held by the public, increased in a predictable fashion. However, once the public had interest-paying alternatives to noninterest-paying demand deposits, part of the funds created from the reserves were deposited in these new types of accounts. Therefore demand deposits did not expand as rapidly as they should have on the basis of past experience. Consequently, the money stock, of which demand deposits are the largest part, also did not grow as rapidly as expected. Part of the expected money supply was missing, being held instead in new types of accounts that were not included in the calculation of the money supply.

Thus it was a relatively easy matter to find the missing money. It was, however, considerably more difficult to decide what should be done about the situation. The problem, in view of many economists, was that the operable definition of money as currency and demand deposits held by the public was no longer appropriate. The difficulty was to find a new operable definition to solve the problems created by the innovations in the financial sector.

Economists have never defined money by what it is, choosing instead to define money by what it does. There are three widely used approaches to defining money in this way. The first approach is to define money as a "medium of exchange." Money in this case is composed of those assets that can be used to purchase goods and services or to pay debts. Because until recently only currency and checks could be so employed, the operable definition of money was confined to the total amount of cash and demand deposits held by the public. The Federal Reserve called this the money stock, or M_1.

The second approach views money as the "temporary abode of purchasing power." Money in this case is composed of those assets held for brief periods of time when receipts exceed expenditures. Thus to the components of M_1 (cash and demand deposits) must be added part of the nation's savings accounts, known to economists as time deposits. The Federal Reserve also recognized this approach and published a statistical series known as M_2, calculated by adding the time deposits of small savers to M_1.

The third approach to defining money is more pragmatic. Rather than defining money theoretically, make money that combination of financial elements that works best. What works best is an empirical problem. It is the combination of financial elements that is most highly correlated with other macroeconomic measures of economic activity, such as gross national product, the price level, etc. Economists in the past have been divided over whether M_1 or M_2 better meets this criterion.

The financial innovations that have taken place in the banking sector made both M_1 and M_2 obsolete by the criteria of all three approaches. It is now possible to make payments directly from accounts other than demand deposits. Automatic transfer services (ATS) allow a customer of a bank to make payments directly from savings accounts, earning interest of deposits in the meantime. Negotiated orders of withdrawal accounts (NOW) and share drafts allow the customers of savings and loans, mutual savings banks, and credit unions to do the same thing. The old definition of money M_1, according to the medium of exchange approach, is now clearly too narrow.

It is also now possible to temporarily hold money in deposits other than checking accounts. Besides ATS and NOW accounts, repurchase agreements provide the large customers of financial institutions with a way to convert a demand deposit to an interest-bearing asset. Furthermore, most money market mutual funds allow investors the opportunity to write checks against their holdings in these funds. Thus the old operable definitions of money do not include all the current opportunities that provide a temporary abode of purchasing power.

It was also clear that neither M_1 nor M_2 any longer performed very well according to the "what-works-best" approach. The past stable relationship between the monetary aggregates and national income, the rate of interest and the price level, no longer hold.

The opportunity to make payments directly from interest-paying accounts made the existing operable definition of the money stock (M_1) obsolete according to the medium-of-exchange criteria. The combination of these accounts coupled with the spreading practice of repurchase agreement did the same thing to M_2 as defined by the temporary abode of purchasing power criteria. The failure of either M_1 or M_2 to correlate as well with other macroeconomic measures as they had in the past created doubts as to the continuing usefulness of either definition for the what-works-best school. The need, by whatever criteria money is defined, was for a new operable definition.

The difficulty was in finding a better definition, given the existing available components. The Federal Reserve responded to this problem early in 1980 in a novel and interesting manner. It decided to revise the several definitions of money it uses to calculate the monetary aggregates, the individual series that purport to measure the amount of money in the economy. The Federal Reserve Bank also decided to publish a do-it-yourself list of the components of the money stock, along with revisions of the old monetary aggregates of M_1 and M_2. M_1 is to be split into M_{1A} and M_{1B}. M_{1A} is the old M_1 whereas M_{1B} adds to M_{1A} the new interest-paying accounts available at banks, savings and loans, and credit unions. The problem with M_{1B} is that some of the funds deposited in these new accounts came from savings accounts, not demand deposits, and should not be counted according to the medium-of-exchange criteria. Part of these funds are held not for the purpose of making immediate future purchases, but to obtain interest. Thus if M_{1A} understates the true quantity of money, M_{1B} is apt to overstate it.

The biggest revision is in M_2. M_2 was expanded to include the deposits of savings and loans and other thrift institutions, such as credit unions, as well as assets held by money market mutual funds and approximately half of the amount of deposits held as repurchase agreements. Even some Eurodollars held at offshore banking centers, such as the Cayman Islands, will be included. The difficulty with this revision is the same as with M_{1B}. Some of these deposits, prior to the financial innovations, were held as nonmonetary assets. Therefore if the old M_2 was too narrow according to the temporary abode of purchasing power approach, the new M_2 is apt to be too broad.

But to forestall such criticism, the Federal Reserve has also decided to publish the separate components that make up a money supply. Thus if a Fed watcher, or economist, does not like the new definitions, he or she will be free, in the words of one Federal Reserve governor, "to roll your own."

If all this sounds too complicated to be useful, there is another alternative. Forget all the above and concentrate instead upon the raw materials out of which the quantity of money, however defined, is fashioned. The raw material is called the monetary base and is primarily composed of the deposits of member banks held at the Federal Reserve banks along with the amount of currency in circulation. The monetary base, during this time of definitional turmoil, is thought by some economists to be a better guide to monetary policy than any money stock definition that can be currently fashioned out of the available monetary components.

The case of the missing money was easily solved. Some of the funds that would have shown up in the past as demand deposits now are deposited in the new types of interest-paying accounts. This fact led many persons to question the continued usefulness of existing definitions of money. The Federal Reserve Bank responded to this problem by redefining money to include the previously missing money in the new definitions. The problem with the new definitions is that they are apt to be overinclusive, counting as money assets that should not be counted. Until a consensus view develops about a new appropriate definition of money, the Federal Reserve will make available the statistics necessary to "roll your own."

Additional Readings

Burke, W. "Measuring M." *Business and Financial Letter,* Federal Reserve Bank of San Francisco, June 25, 1976.

"Fed Redefines Monetary Aggregates." *Voice,* Federal Reserve Bank of Dallas, March 1980.

Hafer, R. W. "The New Monetary Aggregates." *Review,* Federal Reserve Bank of St. Louis, February 1980.

Judd, J. P. and G. C. Zimmerman. "Monetary Aggregates—Redefined." *Weekly Letter,* Federal Reserve Bank of San Francisco, February 29, 1980.

Wenninger, J. and C. M. Sivesind. "Defining Money For a Changing Financial System." *Quarterly Review,* Federal Reserve Bank of New York, Spring 1979.

Wilson, R. "Why Redefine the M's?" *Weekly Letter,* Federal Reserve Bank of San Francisco, April 20, 1979.

Preview

Recently, a significant financial innovation has been increasingly used by the commercial banks to legally evade both the prohibition on the paying of interest on demand deposits and the reserve requirements on part of their demand deposits. This financial innovation is called a repurchase agreement. This chapter explores the reasons commercial banks have increasingly chosen to use such an agreement and the implications of this agreement for the ability of the Federal Reserve to control the money supply.

Key Economic Points

Why do commercial banks choose to use repurchase agreements?

How do repurchase agreements allow banks to legally evade the reserve requirement?

The use of repurchase agreements affects the quantity of money in the economy.

21

The Reserve Requirement: How Banks Legally Evaded the Reserve Requirement

Among the significant innovations that have occurred in the financial sector is the development of the repurchase agreement (RP). The amount of funds subject to this agreement has increased from less than $3 billion in 1970, to almost $50 billion by the end of the decade. The significance of the repurchase agreement is that it allowed commercial banks to legally evade, for a portion of their demand deposits, the reserve requirement. Thus, by 1980, between 10 and 20 percent of the demand deposits held by commercial banks legally evaded the reserve requirement, which is a crucial element in the Federal Reserve's ability to control the money supply. In this chapter we investigate the rise of the repurchase agreement and explore the effect of RPs upon the ability of the Federal Reserve to control the money supply.

A repurchase agreement is the acquisition of funds by a commercial bank, reportedly through the sale of government securities to a customer, with a simultaneous agreement by the seller to repurchase them at a later date, usually the next day. Such a buy-tonight, sell-back-tomorrow transaction is clearly unusual; in fact, it is not a trade at all, but rather a disguised loan. The bank merely borrows a customer's demand deposit overnight, pledges government securities for the loan, pays the customer interest, and returns the deposit the next day.

In order to understand why the practice of borrowing demand deposits overnight developed, it is necessary to consider the regulations that govern the U.S. banking system. The Federal Reserve system is set up as a fractional reserve system. Each member bank is required by the Federal Reserve to maintain as reserves a certain fraction of its deposits. Cash held by the banks and member bank deposits held with the Federal Reserve Bank (FRB) count as reserves. Currently, the reserve requirement for large banks on demand deposits is 16.25 percent and on time deposits 3 percent. The required reserves are calculated at the end of the business day. Neither cash nor deposits with the FRB earn interest, so that reserves constitute a substantial drain on the earnings of member banks, which are, after all, profit-making institutions. Each bank, therefore, has an incentive to minimize the amount of noninterest earning reserves that must be maintained. Reserves serve the function of maintaining the solvency of the individual banks and of providing one of the FRB's tools for controlling the money supply. The Federal Reserve, in conducting monetary policy, generally requires member banks to maintain more reserves than they would wish in the absence of the reserve requirement.

The second regulation prohibits banks from paying interest on demand deposits (checking accounts). The banks feel that this prohibition places them at a competitive disadvantage in attempting to attract deposits. Potential depositors often have alternatives such as money market funds, certificates of deposit, and the like, which provide many of the advantages of demand deposits and simultaneously accrue interest. In the absence of a repurchase agreement, banks feel they would lose funds to other nonbank rivals seeking short-term loans.

The prohibition from paying interest on demand deposits, and monetary reserve requirements that earn no interest, created the conditions that made repurchase agreements a profitable financial practice for a commercial bank. Because reserve deposits maintained at the Federal Reserve earn no interest, individual banks have a strong incentive to minimize the amount required. However, it is inevitable that on any given day some banks will not be fully loaned up and have excess reserves, while others will find themselves temporarily short. The federal funds market developed initially to facilitate the exchange of reserves from banks with an excess to banks with a shortage. Initially the participants in this market were solely commercial banks. These loans are of very short duration, often just overnight, and the rate of interest paid (figured on an annual basis) is known as the federal funds rate. There are no reserve requirements for federal funds because, initially at least, these funds were themselves reserves.

But then a clever banker made a simple innovation that substantially changed the nature of this practice. This banker reasoned that if his bank could buy overnight funds to cover its reserve requirements from another bank, why not purchase some of the demand deposits of its larger customers for the same purpose? Its customers would benefit from the interest payments and the bank would have a ready source of funds to meet its reserve requirements. Thus the prohibition of paying interest on checking accounts is circumvented for corporations, state and local governments, and wealthy individuals whose deposits any bank would like to attract.

It was not long before bankers discovered that by borrowing customers' demand deposits overnight and calling them federal funds, they could legally reduce their required reserves and consequently expand their loans. Let us examine the situation of a large fully loaned-up bank with assets of $1.5 billion. The deposits of such a bank are typically composed of one-third demand deposits and two-thirds time deposits. This bank is thus required to keep $111.25 million in reserves: $81.25 million in reserves for its demand deposits (0.1625 × $500 million) and $30 million as reserves against its time deposits (0.03 × $1,000 million). It is free to loan and invest the rest as can be seen from its balance sheet reproduced in Table 1.

Consider now how the bank can profit from as simple an innovation as purchasing its customers' demand deposits rather than the excess reserves of another bank. Suppose the bank purchases overnight 20 percent or $100 million of its demand deposits. The balance sheet (Table 2, act one) on the liabilities side now shows demand deposits of $400 million instead of $500 million and federal funds purchased of $100 million. No reserves are required against federal funds purchased, so that the bank now has excess reserves of $16.25 million. By purchasing overnight 20 percent of its demand deposits, it has reduced its required reserves by 15 percent.

The bank can then lend the $100 million it borrowed to another customer, creating a demand deposit of that amount using the excess

TABLE 1

BALANCE SHEET

Bank Assets and Liabilities Before Repurchase Agreements

Assets (In $ Millions)		Liabilities	
Loans	1,125.00	Demand deposits	500.00
Gov't securities	150.00	Time deposits	1,000.00
Other investments	113.75	Federal funds purchased	0
Required reserves:			
Demand deposits 81.25	111.25		
Time deposits 30.00			
Total Excess reserves	0		
TOTAL	1,500.00		1,500.00

reserves to satisfy the 16.25 percent reserve requirement. The balance sheet (Table 2, act two) now shows on the asset side loans up by $100 million and on the liabilities side demand deposits up by $100 million. Consequently, total assets and liabilities also rises by $100 million, from $1,500 million to $1,600 million.

During the middle of the business day the bank would be short of the required reserves, having returned the borrowed demand deposits to its customers, but at the end of the business day the bank will simply repurchase the $100 million for the night. Repurchase agreements are generally negotiated in advance as part of a prearranged package of banking services offered to large customers. The bank can then borrow the demand deposits overnight whenever needed. The bank's holdings of government securities are used as collateral for these overnight loans. The customer benefits from the interest paid, and the bank legally evades both the prohibition on paying interest on demand deposits and the reserve requirement that applies to funds were held overnight as demand deposits.

TABLE 2

Bank Assets and Liabilities After Repurchase Agreements

Assets (In $ Millions)			Liabilities	
Act One				
Loans		1,125.00	Demand deposits	400.00
Gov't securities		150.00	Time deposits	1,000.00
Other investments		113.75	Federal funds purchased	100.00
Required reserves:				
Demand deposits	65.00			
Time deposits	30.00			
Total		95.00		
Excess reserves		16.25		
TOTAL		1,500.00		1,500.00
Act Two				
Loans		1,225.00	Demand deposits	500.00
Gov't securities		150.00	Time deposits	1,000.00
Other investments		113.75	Federal funds purchased	100.00
Required reserves:				
Demand deposits	81.25			
Time deposits	30.00			
Total		111.25		
Excess reserves		0		
TOTAL		1,600.00		1,600.00

Use of repurchase agreements has increased rapidly during the last decade. The largest banks in the country currently finance 12 to 14 percent of their loans using federal funds borrowed, a substantial portion of which are actually repurchase agreements, demand deposits by day masquerading as federal funds at night.

The spread of repurchase agreements affected the calculation of the money supply. Because the statistics used to calculate the money supply are those existing at the close of the business day, the demand deposits absorbed by repurchase agreements previously were not counted as part of the money supply. By the beginning of the 1980s, more than $50 billion in daytime money thus escaped being counted. Because the use of repurchase agreements was increasing, the extent of underreporting of the true money supply was also increasing. The Federal Reserve responded to this problem by redefining one of the monetary aggregates—M_{2B}—to include the federal funds created by repurchase agreements.

There are several options open to the Federal Reserve to directly deal with repurchase agreements. The most straightforward would be to simply require member banks to hold the same amount of reserves against nonbank federal funds as they do for demand deposits. This action would, in one fell swoop, eliminate the financial advantages of using repurchase agreements that banks currently enjoy. The Federal Reserve has been hesitant to take this step, which would reduce the profitability of member banks at a time when increasing numbers of individual banks are choosing to withdraw from the system.

The Federal Reserve chose late in 1979 to go part way in this direction, when a marginal reserve requirement was placed in managed liabilities. An 8 percent reserve requirement was imposed on new bank repurchase agreements in excess of the amounts agreed upon in September of that year. Thus any growth of repurchase agreements will carry a reserve requirement of less than half that on demand deposits and more than twice that imposed on time deposits. A reserve requirement of this size on repurchase agreements would slow down the rate of growth of this type of practice.

Repurchase agreements have, prior to the setting of a reserve requirement, grown rapidly in recent years, attaining the status of a major financial instrument. RPs have allowed commercial banks to legally avoid the prohibition on the payment of interest on demand deposits and, at the same time, evade the reserve requirements placed on demand deposits. These agreements have proved beneficial to both the commercial banks and to their large customers. The rapid spread of repurchase agreements have made the problems of controlling the money supply more difficult for the Federal Reserve. The Federal Reserve Board has responded to this threat by imposing a reserve requirement on any additional repurchase agreements.

CHAPTER 21

Additional Readings

Bowshaw, Norman N. "Repurchase Agreements." *Review*, Federal Reserve Bank of St. Louis, September 1979.

Garcia, Gillian. "The Money Puzzle." *The Collegiate Forum*, Dow Jones and Company, Fall 1978.

Knight, R. E. "Guidelines For Efficient Reserve Management." *Monthly Review*, Federal Reserve Bank of Kansas City, November 1977.

Lucas, C., M. Jones, and T. Thurston. "Federal Funds and Repurchase Agreements." *Quarterly Review*, Federal Reserve Bank of New York, Summer 1977.

Preview

The Federal Reserve has always attempted to cloak its actual decision-making procedures in secrecy. The complete minutes of the Open Market Committee are not available to the public until 5 years have past. Recently, a study of how the Open Market Committee went about the business of actually determining monetary policy, based upon the actual minutes, was completed. The findings of this study are very revealing and often in sharp contrast with the traditional textbook account of how monetary policy is made. This chapter reveals how, according to this study and other related information, monetary policy was actually formulated during 1970–1973.

Key Economic Points

How, in theory, does the Federal Open Market Committee decide monetary policy?

What is the role played by the staff, in theory and practice, in creating monetary policy.

How, in practice, and in contrast with theory, does the Federal Open Market Committee actually set monetary policy?

It may sometimes be impossible to devise a policy that both ensures a stable economy and maximizes the safety of the banking system.

22

Monetary Policy: Past Decision Making by the Federal Open Market Committee

The actual decision-making procedures of the Federal Reserve have always been cloaked in secrecy. It required an act of Congress to prod the Board of Governors to merely announce their yearly targets for monetary growth. The minutes of the Federal Open Market Committee (FOMC), the prime architect of monetary policy, are available a month after the meetings, but only in a sharply edited version. In the words of a former governor of the system, "the Fed has always resisted being too specific about its methods and its goals, clothing its operations in a kind of mystique that left it more freedom to maneuver."

The Federal Reserve insists that the detailed minutes of the Federal Reserve Open Market Committee be kept secret for 5 years. Therefore, based on these records, any study of how this committee sets monetary policy becomes more of an exercise in economic history than a study of contemporary policy making. This did not deter a pair of economists—Raymond Lambra and Michael Moran—from doing just that. They studied the operations of the Federal Open Market Committee for the period 1970–1973, using information previously unavailable to economists. They were able to reconstruct how the FOMC went about making monetary policy during those years. This chapter draws heavily from this pioneering study as it explores how, in the past, the Federal Open Market Committee actually formulated monetary policy.

The Federal Open Market Committee is composed of the seven governors of the Federal Reserve and five of the twelve presidents of the district Federal Reserve Banks. The president of the New York bank is a permanent member; therefore, four of the remaining district presidents serve on a rotating basis. The FOMC is aided in their deliberations by a staff of more than 150 economists. The senior staff is charged with the responsibility of developing an overall, integrated assessment of the economic and financial situation, of laying out feasible policy alternatives for the committee's consideration, and of making specific policy recommendations.

The FOMC employs a two-stage approach to policy making, a long-run or strategy stage, and a short-run or tactical stage. At the long-run stage the committee considers and determines the long-run targets for the monetary aggregates, which in practice breaks down to selecting the desired rate of growth of each aggregate for the next year. Then the FOMC considers at the second stage how best to meet these targets during the next 2 months. The committee will choose, at this tactical stage, the appropriate "operating handle" that they believe will lead to the attainment of the long-run monetary targets. The operating handle is the method, either by controlling reserves or by setting the federal funds rate of interest, that will be used to conduct monetary policy.

The FOMC meets monthly to review the long-term monetary targets in the light of revised forecasts of economic conditions prepared by the staff. The committee can decide at this time to set new goals or continue the existing targets. At that point the FOMC will, in the light of prospective economic and financial developments, adopt a set of short-run goals for the monetary targets and the federal funds rate that are thought to be consistent with the ultimate achievement of the long-run targets.

The process that led to the development of the staff's revised forecasts began weeks before the meeting. The staff is continuously updating its forecasts on the basis of new economic and financial developments. It employs an econometric model of the economy but modifies its predictions with personal judgmental projections to obtain the book's predictions. The staff produces two forecasts. The green book, named because of its green cover, contains a description of current economic conditions. The blue book, again known for the color of its cover, deals with monetary aggregates and money market conditions.

The blue book contains the staff's best estimates of the short-run alternatives available to the FOMC that are consistent with meeting the long-term objectives it has set. The alternatives are presented in terms of the trade-off between interest rates and rates of increase in the monetary aggregates. A certain interest rate is consistent with a particular rate of growth of the money stock, a slightly higher rate of interest with a slightly lower expansion of the money supply, or a slightly lower rate of interest with a slightly higher rate of monetary expansion. These alternatives thus traced out the staff's estimate of the nation's demand for money.

At its meeting, the FOMC debates the various alternatives and then in theory selects the alternative that in its collective judgment best meets the economic conditions reflected in the green book. The FOMC then instructs the Open Market desk at the New York Federal Reserve Bank as to which monetary tool, amount of total reserves or the interest rate, to control. In practice, until October 6, 1979, the interest rate was generally chosen.

The remarkable thing is that the FOMC generally did not follow the alternatives presented by the staff during the period 1971–1973. In only six of the thirty-seven meetings did the FOMC select one of the staff's alternatives. In the vast majority of cases, the FOMC adjusted the staff's menu of choices before making its selection. Sometimes the committee selected a rate of interest from one alternative and a rate of monetary growth from another. This process became known among the staff as the Chinese menu approach. The FOMC would generally ignore the staff's recommendations and substitute their own collective judgment.

It may have been that the analysis submitted by the staff was recognized by the committee to be of dubious quality and that the FOMC felt it possessed superior analytical ability, an ability it had not succeeded in transferring to the staff. An evaluation of the predictions contained in the blue and green books, however, casts doubt on this possibility. The staff's nonfinancial green book forecasts, when compared with other economic forecasts, were as good and often better than any available. The monetary forecasts in the blue book were, as the staff readily admitted, less reliable than those in the green book. However, it is not clear that a better approach was available. The staff's monetary forecasts were strictly Keynesian by design, and focused entirely on the demand for money. These forecasts ignored the effects of the supply, thought to be very important by economists of the monetarist persuasion. The monetarists believed they would have done better, but not all economists would agree.

The important question is that if the FOMC thought the staff produced poor analyses, what were the methods they used for improving the forecasts so that they could make the appropriate policy decisions? Another way of asking the same question is, what economic theory did the committee use in formulating policy? An economist who interviewed members of the FOMC regarding their views about monetary theory was not able to discover a consistent, widely held view. This finding was supported from the complete minutes of the FOMC itself. One member of the committee, during the April 17, 1970 meeting, said that "it would be difficult for members of the FOMC to agree on a specific theory of monetary policy." Another member stated 3 years later that "the basic problem . . . was a consequence of the fact that the committee as a whole did not have such a theory, although individual members might" (December 17, 1973). The FOMC, as a body, did not have a basic theory of monetary policy.

Neither did the committee, as a whole, have a set of stabilization goals. Although individual members probably had desired objectives for the level of national income, prices, and employment, the group as a whole did not have a set of ultimate objectives. The detailed minutes of committee meetings often revealed the members to be poles apart in their policy views. One group, which was concerned with fighting inflation, persistently urged tighter monetary policy. This group was, equally persistently, opposed by another group that was more concerned with unemployment and therefore argued for easier monetary policy.

When faced with such conflicts, the energies of the FOMC were usually devoted to attempting to find a policy that could win unanimous or near-unanimous approval. Achieving a clear consensus was always the prime consideration of the committee's chairperson. The formulation of monetary policy appears to have often been a seat-of-the-pants operation. The indications are that the committee often operated strictly by guess, attempting to achieve a consensus among its members without regard to any formal economic analysis.

This ad hoc approach of the FOMC certainly did not produce superior monetary policy. The only possible advantage of such an approach was that the committee's work could proceed even though it was impossible for the FOMC to reach internal agreement about the ultimate goals of monetary policy or the means of achieving the goals. Even if this approach allowed the committee to proceed, it is unlikely that the results would prove acceptable either to the individual FOMC members themselves or to the nation. Common sense suggests that the first thing that policy makers must determine is what they are trying to do before they attempt to do it. Disregarding this fundamental premise is to risk ending up where no one wanted to go.

There is substantial evidence that the FOMC was often able to agree in one area. The committee was predominantly concerned with moderating interest rate changes; more than any other issue, the "appropriate setting" of the federal funds rate dominated discussions at FOMC meetings. Furthermore, the Federal Reserve proved to be very good at hitting the interest rate targets and much less adept at hitting its goals for the monetary aggregates. The primacy of the Federal Reserve Bank concern with interest rates during this period could be due to a number of factors. Setting the federal funds rate is relatively easy. All the Open Market desk has to do is add or subtract reserves by buying or selling government securities until the desired interest rate exists. Setting an interest rate target has the great advantage of being relatively easy to accomplish. This task becomes much more difficult when the Federal Reserve must simultaneously hit both an interest rate target and goals for the monetary aggregates. If the FOMC with its ad hoc methods was correctly estimating the demand for money, the setting of the appropriate interest rate would automatically create the desired expansion of the money supply. The demonstrated inability of the Federal Reserve to hit simultaneously both the interest rate and the monetary growth rate suggests that their collective theory was not very good.

The second influence operating on the Open Market Committee was their responsibility to ensure the stability and safety of the nation's banking system. Widely fluctuating interest rates increase the possibility that individual banks and financial institutions might get into trouble. By ensuring that interest rates changed only moderately, the Federal Reserve Bank reduced this possibility.

A third influence that operated during this period, which reinforced the FOMC concern about the level of interest rates, was generated by the government's wage and price control program. The potential existed that a confrontation with Congress would be created if interest rates rose significantly when other prices and wages were subject to some control. The danger of such a confrontation was that the Federal Reserve's cherished independence might be threatened.

Another factor influencing the FOMC's ability to agree to stabilize interest rate fluctuations revolved around the unwillingness of several of the more experienced members of the committee to commit themselves to developing precise guides for monetary policy. One member stated, during a meeting held in 1972, that he could recall the time when committee members felt they could describe their policy preferences simply by choosing from terms such as "tighter," "easier," "unchanged." On that basis he would on that occasion place himself in the "easier" or "somewhat easier" category. Later in the same year, another member stated that "he would favor an effort to snug up a bit on short-term interest rates, while keeping an eye cocked on long-term interest rates." He would not try to translate that into a choice between the alternatives presented by the staff. It would be difficult for the committee to seriously pursue monetary policy in terms of setting targets if many members insisted on following this approach.

Finally, despite the setting of long-range goals for the monetary aggregates, the FOMC during its meetings was preoccupied with the present economic situation. Although frequent references were made to forecasts and future prospects, most comments were focused on the current situation. Even though the staff frequently pointed out the long and indeterminate lags between a change in the money stock and its effect upon other macroeconomic variables, the FOMC did not spend a great deal of time concerned about the future. Dealing with the future is risky for all policy makers, and the FOMC recognized their predicament. Suppose the economy is expanding rapidly but analysis predicts a future downturn. If the FOMC were to ease up on monetary policy and the expansion became more rapid, the cost in terms of higher inflation rates to the economy and to the policy maker would be very high. The Federal Reserve is an independent agency but it is not immune to criticism. The FOMC intended to wait until a future situation materialized before acting. The problems associated with this response pattern is that, given the lags involved, attempts by the Federal Reserve to stabilize the business cycle might well result in the opposite effect.

The picture that has emerged from the detailed study of the actual operation of the Open Market Committee is quite different from the usual textbook presentation. At least during the years 1970–1973, the FOMC consistently ignored the advice of its professional staff, substituting its own impressionistic beliefs despite the fact that the staff's predictions were as good as any others available. Besides keeping its own council, the FOMC went about its monthly meetings without agreeing on the long-run goals of monetary policy, nor on a specific theory of the effects of monetary policy upon the macroeconomy. However, the Open Market Committee was able to agree that interest rate changes should be moderated and stuck to this policy at the cost of letting the growth rate of the monetary aggregates get out of hand. Furthermore, despite the fact it was widely recognized that changes in the money supply affect the economy only after a long and indeterminate lag, the committee was preoccupied with current, not future, economic conditions. Certainly this picture of the actual past operations of the Federal Open Market Committee is not one to justify placing great confidence that the Federal Reserve will generally adopt the proper monetary policies to ensure the stability of the economy.

It must be pointed out that the membership of the Open Market Committee has changed substantially since 1970–1973; therefore, the way it conducts monetary policy may also have changed substantially. What has not changed is the cloak of secrecy that surrounds the policy actions of this important body. It is as difficult as ever to follow closely the actions of the Open Market Committee.

Additional Readings

Lombra, R., and M. Moran. "Policy Advice and Policy Making at the Federal Reserve." *Preprint,* Pennsylvania State University, 1979.

Poole, William. "The Making of Monetary Policy: Description and Analysis." *Economic Inquiry,* June 1975, pp. 253–265.

Weintraub, Robert. *Report on Federal Reserve Policy and Inflation and High Interest Rates,* U.S. Congress, House Committee on Banking and Currency, 93rd Congress, July–August 1978, pp. 31–76.

Preview

Suddenly, late in 1979, the Federal Reserve Board drastically changed its approach to the conduct of monetary policy. Prior to this change, the Federal Reserve had concentrated its attentions on regulating interest rates, apparently in the belief that the level of interest rates was a good guide to monetary policy. High interest rates signaled tight monetary conditions, low interest rates the reverse. During the second half of the 1970s this approach proved misleading and resulted in high rates of inflation. As a consequence, the Federal Reserve abandoned its attempt to control interest rates precisely, choosing instead to concentrate upon the strict control of the monetary aggregates. This chapter explores the reasons that focusing upon interest rates proved an unreliable guide to monetary policy.

Key Economic Points

Under what conditions would the precise control of interest rates also precisely control the money supply?

Why was the Federal Reserve unable to control the money supply by controlling interest rates?

Why the Federal Reserve Board preferred to control interest rates rather than to try to precisely control reserves.

How Gibson's paradox can be resolved.

23

Monetary Policy:
Why the Federal Reserve
Changed Its Approach

During an unusual evening news conference on Saturday, October 6, 1979, the Federal Reserve Board announced the most important policy decision the board had taken since the 1950s. The financial press later referred to this decision as the "Saturday Night Special." The Chairman of the Federal Reserve, Paul Volcker, that night stated that the FRB was adopting a tougher monetary policy to combat inflation, then raging at a 13 percent annual rate and threatening to increase to still higher levels. The board stated that it was immediately raising the rediscount rate and increasing some reserve requirements. Furthermore, in future the Board would pay less attention to interest rates in setting monetary policy and more to the increase in the quantity of money.

The increase in the rediscount rate and reserve requirements received most of the attention from the nation's press, but it was the change in how monetary policy would be conducted in the future that captured the attention of economists. This chapter reviews the methods used by the Federal Reserve, prior to its October announcement, to conduct monetary policy and provides an explanation as to why this approach led to double-digit inflation.

Prior to Saturday night the Federal Reserve had, in its conduct of monetary policy, concentrated upon setting the interest rate for federal funds. Federal funds are the monetary reserves that banks lend one another for short periods of time. Banks that were members of the Federal Reserve were required to hold reserves (mostly in the form of deposits with the Federal Reserve Bank) equal to a specified percentage of their total deposits. Some banks at any point in time will have excess reserves while others will be short. Banks with a surplus lend their excess reserves for short periods (often just overnight) to banks with a deficit so that the latter can meet their reserve requirements. The federal funds rate is the annual rate of interest charged for these short-term loans.

The U.S. banking system, as a whole, does not maintain substantial excess reserves; banks earn profits mainly from making loans and tend to quickly use any excess reserves for that purpose. Consequently, substantial changes in total deposits, hence in the money supply, can occur only if the Federal Reserve supplies additional reserves. There are three ways the FRB can do this: through open market operations, the buying or selling of government securities; through loans to banks at the Federal Reserve rediscount window; or through changes in the reserve requirements. Reserve requirements are not frequently used to effect reserve availability, nor is the rediscount rate frequently changed. Therefore, when both occur at once, it is a newsworthy action. That is why the change in reserve requirements, simultaneously coupled with an increase in the rediscount rate announced that Saturday night in October received the primary attention of the media.

In practice, the principal tool of money management is open market operations—the buying and selling by the Federal Reserve of government securities. The Federal Open Market Committee of the Federal Reserve regularly meets monthly, and more often if the situation warrants. During 1978, for example, the Open Market Committee met nineteen times. At each meeting, the committee by majority vote establishes two primary targets for monetary policy: a range for the federal funds interest rate and a growth rate for the money supply, the latter taking the form of a specific range for the various money aggregates.

The difficulty with this approach is that the Federal Reserve may be attempting too much if they try to control both the price of credit (the interest rate) and the quantity of money (the rate of monetary growth). The FRB does not have the tools to independently set both the interest rate and the quantity of money. It can set one and the demand schedule for money will set the other. In order to specify and achieve both targets, the Open Market Committee must be able to predict the actual demand schedule for money. To guide in the selection of consistent targets, the Federal Reserve employs a staff of economists and an econometric model to attempt to predict the federal funds rate that is compatible with its monetary growth targets. The Open Market Committee then selects the goals of monetary policy for the next 2 months and sends a directive to that effect to the Open Market trading desk at the Federal Reserve Bank of

New York. It falls to the Open Market trading desk to actually implement open market policy by buying or selling government securities.

Because of the difficulty of establishing accurately in advance the rate of interest that will result from a particular rate of increase of the money supply, these directives have in the past specified a fairly wide range for the monetary targets. The federal funds interest rate in contrast was specified within a very narrow span. The targets set at the July 18, 1978, meeting, for example, ordered the trading desk to maintain during July and August the rate on federal funds between 7¾ and 8 percent and the rate of growth of the money supply (M_1) of between 4 and 8 percent.

If, for example, market forces threaten to move the federal funds rate above the upper limit of the target range, the trading desk will purchase securities in the market, supplying additional reserves to the banking system, which eventually expands the money supply. The increase in reserves initially drives down the interest rate on federal funds. Conversely, if the rate of growth of monetary aggregates threatens to exceed the upper limit of the range selected by the Open Market Committee, the Open Market desk will sell securities, reducing reserves and the quantity of money. Selling securities also effects the federal funds rate, causing it to rise as available reserves decline.

A problem arises when the two objectives are not mutually consistent. This occurs when both the federal funds rate and monetary aggregates simultaneously reach the upper or lower limits of their prescribed ranges. When this happens, as it did, for instance, during July and August 1978, the Fed must choose whether to maintain interest rates and let the monetary aggregates exceed their objectives, or maintain the monetary aggregates and let the interest rate rise above the target rate.

The Federal Reserve at that time chose to meet the interest rate target, maintaining the federal funds rate at 7⅞ percent. In order to keep the interest rate at this level, it was necessary to supply more reserves to the banking system than the Open Market Committee had thought necessary. As a consequence, the growth of the money stock increased at the annual rate of 11.2 percent, or 3.2 percent over the target limit set by the Open Market Committee. The decision to sacrifice the goals set for the monetary aggregates to achieve the interest rate target was not unusual. An examination of the 47 months that followed the Federal Reserve's public announcement of its monetary and interest rate targets shows that the federal funds rate only five times fell outside the narrow target range prescribed by the Open Market Committee. But over the same period the money supply fell outside the target range on twenty-three occasions, or roughly half the time. It is fair to conclude that in the past the Federal Reserve, when faced with a choice between the two objectives, has sacrificed the target rates of growth of the money supply to achieve its interest rate targets.

Apparently, within the Federal Reserve the view prevailed that it was extremely important to maintain stable interest rates, allowing the federal funds rate to change only slowly with time in response to changes in financial markets. There were three reasons for this approach. First, the FRB felt that highly volatile interest rates would disrupt financial markets. This in turn would increase the instability of prices, employment, and output. Focusing primarily on the money supply, and allowing the interest rate to fluctuate widely, would be to invite disaster. Second was the view that interest rates were the best guide to monetary policy. High interest rates signaled tight monetary policy and low interest rates indicated the reverse.

Third, the Federal Reserve found it easy to set the federal funds rate and technically much more difficult to control monetary aggregates. Therefore, if interest rates are a good guide to monetary policy and widely fluctuating interest rates would prove destabilizing to the economy, there is no reason to be overly concerned if the monetary targets are not achieved as long as the interest rate target is met. These views had prevailed at the Federal Reserve since the mid-1960s.

Thus the Saturday night announcement that the Federal Reserve was going to pay more attention to monetary aggregates, even if it meant that interest rates would fluctuate more, astonished economists. It suggested a complete policy reversal. Moreover, the decision was made by unanimous vote of the board members. Previously unanimous decisions among the board members had been the exception, certainly not the rule.

What caused the board to suddenly change its views remains a mystery. It is, however, always possible to speculate. It is possible to argue that the extremely poor policy results during the last decade demanded a change. The rate of inflation at the time the Federal Reserve acted was 13 percent. The prime rate of interest was also 13 percent and would shortly rise to over 16 percent. Despite the efforts of the Federal Reserve to hold down the federal funds rates, interest rates roughly doubled during the 18 months prior to the abrupt policy switch.

The reason the Federal Reserve's policy of setting interest rates did not work is that market interest rates are sometimes a poor guide to monetary policy. Consider what happens when the Federal Reserve attempts to hold down interest rates by the only means at its disposal, that is, increasing reserves. An increase in reserves increases the money supply, which, with a lag, results in higher prices. But the increase in the quantity of money should also drive down the interest rate. Therefore, an observor could expect to find high rates of inflation associated with low interest rates and vice versa. Consequently, if during an inflation interest rates are high, it shows that the FRB is following a tight money policy.

Around the turn of the century an English statistician named Gibson observed that in fact exactly the opposite relationship was observed. High rates of inflation were associated with high, not low, rates of interest. This observation came to be known as Gibson's paradox. Gibson's paradox was later resolved by the famous economist Irving Fisher. Fisher pointed out that Gibson was observing nominal, or market interest, rates rather than the real rate of interest. During periods of rapid money supply growth, prices will begin to rise and people will come to expect more inflation in the future. Lenders will only make loans if the real value of the money lent will be returned along with a real rate of return. Market interest rates will rise to adjust to the expected rate of inflation. Thus the nominal interest rate established on loans contains a component for the decline in the value of money and a component for a real return on the loan. During periods of rapid inflation, the inflation component is the larger of the two.

When the Fed reversed its policy, market rates of interest were then at an all-time high, 13 percent, but the rate of inflation was also 13 percent, so that the real rate of return was for all practical purposes zero. Clearly, the record high rate of interest did not signal tight money but just the opposite.

The Fed's concentration upon stabilizing interest rates also explains how the rate of inflation got out of hand during the second half of the 1970s. The FRB consistently tried to maintain a lower interest rate than a growing money supply would allow. The federal funds target could only be maintained by consistently exceeding the monetary growth targets. The rapidly growing money supply increased aggregate demand in the economy, causing prices to rise. As inflationary expectations increased, so did interest rates. The FRB was eventually forced to increase interest rates in the face of increasing inflationary expectations, but the attempt to maintain a smooth, slow adjustment in the interest rates meant that the FRB consistently supplied too many reserves, overshooting its targets for the money aggregates. Thus the money supply and inflation got out of hand.

Finally, recognizing the folly of attempting to control interest rates the Fed changed its tactics, concentrating more on hitting its targets for the monetary aggregates and allowing, if necessary, interest rates to fluctuate more.

Market rates of interest are sometimes a poor guide to the true state of monetary policy. The reason is found in the solution to Gibson's paradox, which was the discovery that market rates of interest include an inflation premium that varies with the rate of inflation. When the rate of inflation is rising, so too will the interest rate. This rise in the interest rate does not reflect tight monetary policy but its opposite. Monetary authorities who ignore Gibson's paradox may be misled as a result, believing that monetary policy is tight when it is not. This potential mistake is avoided if the Federal Reserve Board concentrates instead upon hitting its targets for the monetary aggregates.

CHAPTER 23

Additional Readings

"Announcements: Monetary Policy Actions." *Federal Reserve Bulletin,* October 1979.

Clark, L. H., Jr. "A Cynical View." *Wall Street Journal,* November 13, 1979.

Clark, L. H., Jr. "The Bingo Approach." *Wall Street Journal,* November 27, 1979.

Judd, J. P. and J. L. Scadding. "The Fed Crosses the Rubicon." *Weekly Letter,* Federal Reserve Bank of San Francisco, October 19, 1979.

Lang, Richard W. "The FOMC in 1979: Introducing Reserve Targeting." *Review,* Federal Reserve Bank of St. Louis, March 1980.

Preview

The Federal Reserve Board of Governors announced late in 1979 that the board was giving up its attempts to conduct monetary policy by the precise control of interest rates. Thereafter, the board stated, it would pay a great deal more attention to the rate of growth of the money supply than it had in the past. Furthermore, the board would focus on controlling the amount of bank reserves as the means of regulating the rate of growth of the money supply. This chapter explores how the Federal Reserve can control the money supply by the indirect means of regulating the amount of bank reserves. The difficulties involved in employing this method are also considered.

Key Economic Points

What conditions must be met to control the supply of money?

Can the Federal Reserve meet these conditions?

The link between the amount of bank reserves and the amount of money in existence makes regulation possible.

How can we recognize some of the practical difficulties the Federal Reserve encounters in managing the amount of bank reserves?

24

Federal Reserve Operations: Controlling the Money Supply by Controlling Reserves

The Federal Reserve Board announced on October 6, 1979 that thereafter it would seek to control the money supply by regulating the amount of bank reserves directly rather than by maintaining a precise interest rate target, as it had in the past. The board had for a number of years set targets both for the growth rate of the money supply and for the federal funds interest rate. The Federal Reserve proved able with great consistency to achieve its interest rate goal and with equal, but deplorable, consistency to miss the monetary growth targets. While there is theoretically, at any moment, a rate of monetary growth that is consistent with a given federal funds rate, the FRB in practice was unable to discover it on a regular basis. The Federal Reserve prior to its October announcement had been reluctant to drastically change the federal funds rate in order to slow the rate of monetary growth. As a result, the growth of the money supply consistently exceeded the targeted rate, and consequently the rate of inflation rapidly got out of control.

The Federal Reserve Board, frustrated in its efforts to halt inflation, decided under the leadership of a new chairman to radically alter its policy-making process. The board decided to foresake the precise management of interest rates and to concentrate upon controlling monetary reserves. The board was not unprepared to implement this decision. Controlling the money supply by regulating total bank reserves has a long history of research, discussion, and experimentation both inside and outside the Federal Reserve. This chapter explores how, in principle, the Federal Reserve can control the money supply by regulating the total amount of bank reserves. Controlling reserves, as we shall see, is in many ways much more difficult to implement than the direct regulation of interest rates.

Money is a peculiar commodity in several respects. Among them is the fact that virtually everyone feels its production must be controlled. This task by law belongs to the Federal Reserve. The FRB regulates the stock of money by controlling the production of one element of the money supply—the deposits held by commercial banks. Deposits are the main component of any practical definition of the money supply; thus to control the amount of deposits is to control the money supply itself.

To understand the system the FRB uses to control total bank deposits, forget for a moment that we are concerned about money and consider how the government could control the production of some other good. Suppose the government wished to limit the output of this good to 1 million a month. First, the government would issue production permits, each of which allowed the holder to produce, say, five units of the good. No one could legally produce the good without a permit. Then the government would distribute 200,000 permits among the producers of the good. Since each permit would allow five units of the good to be produced, an output limit of 1 million per month would be established.

In order for the control system to work, three conditions would have to be satisfied. First, no one but the government would be able to issue permits; counterfeiting would obviously destroy the system. Second, the government would have to be able to enforce the five-for-one ratio between the units of the good produced and the number of permits held. Finally, the government would have to rely on the profit motive to ensure that actual output did not fall below the production limit. Unless it was profitable to produce 1 million units of the good, the permit system would merely impose a meaningless production ceiling without controlling output.

The above output-limiting scheme parallels the system used by the Federal Reserve. Bank deposits are the good to be controlled, commercial banks are the producers of the good, and bank reserves are the production permits. Bank reserves are the required proportion of a commercial bank's deposits that must be held as deposits with the Federal Reserve itself. Bank reserves are for the most part checking account balances held by commercial banks at their regional Federal Reserve Banks. Since the FRB keeps the books, there is no way to counterfeit the permits.

The second requirement for the permit system to work is that the required ratio between reserves and deposits be enforced. Enforcement in this case is assured by the Federal Reserve's surveillance and examination of commercial bank activities. It is a relatively easy matter for the monetary authorities to determine the amount of reserves by calculating the amount of a commercial bank's deposits held at the Federal Reserve and to require a commercial bank to report the total amount of bank deposits held by the public. The Federal Reserve, therefore, can readily enforce the reserve ratio.

Since the first two conditions for a production ceiling to be effective in limiting the expansion of demand deposits exist, whether the production ceiling is in fact effective depends upon whether the third condition also holds. In practice, it does. When the Federal Reserve increases the amount of reserves by buying government securities from the public, it pays for the securities with checks that are deposited in a commercial bank. The banks then have more money to lend. Because banks earn most of their profits from making loans, the desire to maximize profits ensures that banks will attempt to lend to customers the newly acquired reserves. The profit motive combined with existing competition between banks ensures that demand deposits will expand to the production limit. Historically, this has been the case; the nation's banking system has generally operated with few excess reserves.

Basically, then, the FRB can limit the amount of bank deposits by setting the reserve requirement and by controlling the total amount of reserves available to the banking system. The profit motive and competition among the banks serves to keep the total deposits close to the reserve ratio. The power to limit total reserves is, in practice, the power to control the total amount of deposits.

The Federal Reserve system for employing bank reserves to control total bank deposits, hence the money supply, though simple in concept encounters some frustrating complications in practice. One problem is that not all bank deposits are treated alike. Not all deposits carry the same deposit-to-reserve ratio. Checking accounts (demand deposits) require the largest reserves; savings accounts (time deposits) require considerably less; and some deposits, such as some repurchase agreements, carry no reserve requirements at all. Over time the competition between banks has resulted in a shift away from demand deposits to other types of deposits that carry lower or no reserve requirements. Current regulations also require larger banks to maintain more reserves per dollar of deposits than smaller banks. The proliferation of deposit types with different reserve-to-deposit ratios complicates the reserve control system in practice.

Perhaps the biggest problem for the Federal Reserve in the daily operations is called the Fed float. The Federal Reserve is used by the banks to clear checks. Suppose a person pays a bill by a check to a business in a faraway state. The business deposits the check with its bank, which in turn sends the check to its regional Federal Reserve Bank for collection. The regional Federal Reserve Bank credits the commercial bank's reserve account with the amount of the check and sends it to the regional Federal Reserve Bank where the check was initially written. There the individual's commercial bank's reserve account is debited by the amount of the check and the check sent to the bank, which in turn debits the customer's account and sends the check back to the customer with his or her monthly statement. There is some delay between the time one bank account is credited and another account debited. Thus, for a period of time, total reserve accounts are swollen by the amount of the nation's checks that have not totally cleared. This is known as the Fed float. Delays in the physical shipment of checks from a major city due to a strike or storm, for example, will delay the final collection of these checks. As the Fed float varies, so does the total reserve in the system. This compels the Federal Reserve to engage in open market operations on a daily basis to try to affect variations in total reserves resulting from Fed float.

We have seen that it is possible for the Federal Reserve to control the money supply by managing the amount of reserves available to the banking system. In terms of the FRB's daily operations, it is more difficult to manage reserves than to manage interest rates. In order to hit its interest rate target, all the Federal Reserve must do is add or subtract reserves by buying or selling government securities until the federal funds rate is within its interest rate target. But if the Federal Reserve is unable, as it proved to be, to select the interest rate that is consistent with the desired rate of growth of the money supply, this simple approach to conducting monetary policy is doomed to fail.

The Federal Reserve announced on October 6, 1979 that it was thereafter going to concentrate upon reserves rather than rate of interest in conducting monetary policy. The practical difficulties of this new approach soon became evident when a large commercial bank made a mistake in calculating the required deposit information, causing the money supply to be understated by $2 billion for 1 month. Because bank data must be collected and it takes time to reach the Federal Reserve, it is simply easier for a mistake to be made, based upon incomplete information, than if interest rates are used as the guide to monetary policy.

Despite the practical problems the shift to reserves could create, such a shift would nevertheless give the Federal Reserve better control over the money supply, something the central bank believes it needs to curb inflation.

Additional Readings

Cacy, J. A. "Reserve Requirements and Monetary Control." *Monthly Review*, Federal Reserve Bank of Kansas City, May 1976.

Cox, W. N. "Controlling Money With Bank Reserves." *Economic Review*, Federal Reserve Bank of Atlanta, November–December 1979.

McDonough, William R. "Effectiveness of Alternative Approaches to Monetary Control." *Business Review*, Federal Reserve Bank of Dallas, August 1976.

Preview

The Federal Reserve system has been losing members at an increasing rate. The problem is purely economic, as it has become increasingly expensive to remain a member of the system. The main cost is the implicit tax that members must pay by maintaining reserve deposits with the Federal Reserve that earn no interest. Nonmember banks escape this tax. The Federal Reserve Board of Governors feels that should the rate of member bank withdrawals continue, the Federal Reserve system will not be able to perform the tasks assigned it by Congress. This chapter examines the reasons banks left the system and reviews the Federal Reserve's proposed solutions as well as the arguments of its critics. Finally, the chapter details the plan Congress has prepared to deal with the problem.

Key Economic Points

The reserve requirement imposes a tax on member banks.

How much will the abilities of the Federal Reserve to perform the tasks assigned it by Congress be impaired by further declines in system membership?

The arguments for and against mandatory uniform reserve requirements for the banking systems are weighed.

How well will the new congressional plan meet the needs of both the Federal Reserve system and the nation's banking sector?

25

The Federal Reserve System: Problems Created by the Exodus of Member Banks

The Federal Reserve System (FRS) has been experiencing the painful process of change. This independent agency, created by Congress to regulate the nation's banking system, control the money supply, and ensure the stability of the financial sector, in the opinion of the Federal Reserve Board of Governors soon may no longer be able to perform these tasks. The basic problem is that membership in the FRS is declining. Commercial banks in increasing numbers are deciding to withdraw from the system. The reason is purely economic. Many banks are finding it too expensive to remain members of the Federal Reserve system.

During 1979, for example, Seattle Trust and Savings Bank, the 301st largest financial institution in the country, found a way to substantially increase its profits: the bank withdrew from the Federal Reserve system. Seattle Trust, in this action, was not unique; it was following the lead of hundreds of banks that in the past few years withdrew from membership in the Federal Reserve. During the last few years of the 1970s more than 200 banks voluntarily left the system, and the departing banks were getting larger. More than twenty-five of these banks had deposits of $100 million or more. The largest bank to withdraw so far is Bay Banks, a Boston bank-owning company, which pulled out five of its eleven banks in 1977. These five banks held deposits totaling $1.5 billion.

Banks in the United States are legally incorporated either as national banks or as state banks. National banks are required to be members of the Federal Reserve system, whereas membership for state banks is voluntary. The state banks are increasingly questioning whether they should belong to the system. As a consequence, by the end of the 1970s more than three-fifths of all banks did not belong and more than one-fourth of all commercial bank deposits were outside the direct control of the Federal Reserve.

The membership decline has been going on for some time. Almost 50 percent of all banks were members of the Federal Reserve at the end of World War II. These banks held 85 percent of all commercial deposits. By 1967, less than 45 percent of all banks belonged to the FRS, and the percentage of deposits held by member banks had declined to 82.5 percent. Thereafter, the rate of decline in membership increased substantially. Furthermore, the percentage of deposits held by member banks declined even more rapidly as larger banks such as Seattle Trust and Bay Banks began withdrawing from the system.

Should the trend in membership attrition continue, the board feared that it would undermine the reserve's ability to conduct monetary policy. In particular, the accuracy of collecting money supply statistics, the power of the reserve requirement in controlling the money supply, and the ability of the Federal Reserve to serve as the lender of last resort were all threatened by the membership decline.

The Federal Reserve was established by Congress in 1913 after an epidemic of bank failures demonstrated the need for an agency that could bail out financially troubled banks. The system was overhauled in 1933 when it failed to do precisely that, allowing thousands of banks to fail during the Great Depression. Should the decline in membership continue, the ability of the Federal Reserve to carry out the role intended by Congress to be the lender of last resort would be jeopardized. When a member bank finds itself short of cash, known as a liquidity crisis, it can within a few hours obtain a loan, at the rediscount rate, from the Federal Reserve.

Once outside the system, a bank with a liquidity problem is not able to turn to the FRS for a quick loan. The nonmember bank must instead either approach another bank, or apply to the Federal Reserve for an emergency loan. Neither alternative is guaranteed. Other banks, for instance, especially if the liquidity crisis reflects the state of the entire economy, might not have the funds available to provide the necessary amount in time. An application to the Federal Reserve for an emergency loan is currently a complicated process that can take a long time, especially if many nonmember banks are seeking help at the same time.

The Federal Reserve Board is also concerned that the decline in membership will threaten the effectiveness of the reserve requirement as a tool of monetary policy. One of the major functions of the Federal Reserve system is to regulate the nation's money supply. Fewer banks within the Federal Reserve means that fewer financial institutions can be affected by changes in the reserve requirements. Controlling the reserve requirements, the percentage of deposits that must be held as reserves, is one of the ways the Federal Reserve can control the amount of money in the economy. The largest member banks are currently required to set aside as reserves 16.25 percent of their customers' demand deposits (checking accounts) and 3 percent of their savings deposits. The smaller banks' requirements are 7 percent for checking and 3 percent for savings accounts. By changing the reserve requirements within the range set by law, the Federal Reserve can expand or contract the nation's money supply.

Ironically, it is the reserve requirement that is the major cause for the defection of hundreds of banks from the Federal Reserve system. The reserve requirements established by the Federal Reserve Board have to be met by holding cash or deposits with the Federal Reserve Bank. Neither cash nor reserve deposits earn interest. Member banks are in effect taxed by the FRS by being required to forego the interest they could earn on the reserves they are forced to maintain against their deposits.

Instead of paying interest the FRS offers certain "free" services to member banks in order to make membership attractive. The Federal Reserve provides its members with free check-processing services, free security safekeeping and transfers, and ready access to emergency loans. Nonmember banks have to purchase these services from a correspondent bank. Generally, a large national bank is a member of the Federal Reserve system.

In the long gone days of low interest rates, many banks were content to maintain reserves that earned no interest in return for the package of free services offered by the Federal Reserve. But now that banks can earn more than 10 percent on their deposits, many banks that have the alternative of withdrawing from the system are looking wistfully at the nonearning reserves tied up by the Federal Reserve.

The alternative available to state banks is to withdraw from the Federal Reserve and escape from the increasingly costly reserve requirements. State banks generally must also maintain reserves but state requirements are generally much lower than those of the Federal Reserve. Furthermore, most states allow the banks to count interest-earning government securities (treasury bonds and notes) as part of their reserves. Thus state reserve requirements are often less costly than those of the Federal Reserve.

The decision to belong, or not, to the Federal Reserve is complicated by the difficulty of valuing the free services offered by the Federal Reserve. Generally most studies find that the value of these services is equal to an implicit return of about 1 percent on the reserves member banks are required to hold. The sacrifice of a potential 10 or more percent interest that could be earned on the required reserves for a 1 percent implicit return from free services is more than many banks have been willing to pay.

That was certainly the reason Seattle Trust left the Federal Reserve. According to Seattle Trust's president William P. Riley, "It's too damn expensive. Our money can do more for us if we leave the Federal Reserve." In the case of Bay Banks, leaving the Federal Reserve system immediately added 9 percent to its total profits. Citibank, the second largest bank in the country, has estimated that it would add $100 million to its gross profits if it left the system.

The desire of commercial banks to see their reserves earning interest has also increased as a result of the increased competition from other depository institutions, such as savings and loan associations. These so-called thrift institutions, which are not subject to the FRS reserve requirements, have recently begun to offer negotiated orders of withdrawal accounts (NOW accounts). These accounts allow depositors to keep their money in interest-earning savings accounts and at the same time write checks against their savings deposits. Commercial banks have countered this innovation by offering automatic transfer accounts that do the same thing.

The consequence of this development is that commercial banks must now pay interest on deposits that used to not earn interest. The profit margin of commercial banks has fallen as a result, causing many bankers to seriously review the costs and benefits of continued membership in the Federal Reserve system. Even the Federal Reserve admits that member banks are now at a competitive disadvantage relative to other depository institutions, referring to the current system as legislated inequity.

The Federal Reserve proposed to Congress a remedy for this situation: subject all depository institutions to universal reserve requirements set by the Federal Reserve and allow all banks access to the services of the FRS. In short, legislate compulsory membership. Should Congress pass uniform reserve requirements, all depository institutions would compete for customers' accounts on an equal basis. Furthermore, the Federal Reserve would be better able to implement monetary policy. Also, if all banks, not just the declining membership, had to report to the Federal Reserve and maintain reserves, the reliability of monetary statistics would be vastly improved.

The Federal Reserve's proposals met with less than unanimous support in Congress. The state-chartered banks and thrift institutions naturally oppose mandatory reserve requirements that would reduce their current competitive advantage, hence their profits. Instead of universal reserve requirements, the American Bankers Association wanted reserves to be lowered in amount and to earn interest. A number of economists do not see the decline in membership as an important problem. They note that changes in reserve requirements are rarely used to conduct monetary policy. In any event, open market operations are a much more useful tool, the efficiency of which is not threatened by the exodus from the Federal Reserve system. This view stresses that to revitalize the reserve requirement is to add one more tool to the Federal Reserve's tool box than is needed to do the job of controlling the money supply. The impaired ability of the Federal Reserve to act as a lender of last resort could be better corrected by directly authorizing the Federal Reserve to be available to all depository institutions, a change that would not require universal reserve requirements.

After debating for several years the problems that a declining membership posed for the Federal Reserve system, the two houses of Congress approved a plan that would greatly increase the authority of the Federal Reserve. This plan would bring the estimated 8,913 nonmember banks under the reserve requirement. The plan would require all banks to set aside reserves equal to 3 percent of the first $25 million of demand deposits and, initially, 12 percent of demand deposits greater than this amount. The Federal Reserve Board will have the authority to vary the reserve requirement in larger banks between the range of 8 and 14 percent. The board will also have the authority to set and vary, within limits, the reserve requirements on other types of deposits. These new reserve requirements will be phased in over a period of 8 years.

The Federal Reserve system thus finally won the day in Congress, obtaining the authority it desired to stem the decline in system membership. The major reason for withdrawal has been eliminated. The Federal Reserve thus begins the 1980s a different, more powerful institution than it had been in the 1970s.

Additional Readings

"Banking Act—A New World." *Economic Review*, Federal Reserve Bank of Atlanta, March–April 1980.

Gambs, Carl M. "Federal Reserve Membership and the Role of Nonmember Bank Reserve Requirements." *Economic Review*, Federal Reserve Bank of Kansas City, February 1979.

Johnston, Verle. "Historic Legislation." *Weekly Letter*, Federal Reserve Bank of San Francisco, April 4, 1980.

Laporte, Anne Marie. "Competitive Equality and Federal Reserve Membership— The Board of Governors' Proposal." *Economic Perspectives*, Federal Reserve Bank of Chicago, July–August 1978.

Lynch, Mitchell C. "Federal Reserve Frets About Increasing Loss of Its Member Banks." *Wall Street Journal*, April 9, 1979.

Preview

The great German inflation that occurred between 1919 and 1923 destroyed millions of Germans financially and led to the rise of the Nazi party and World War II. This inflation is of historical interest because of the severity of the inflation rather than the uniqueness of underlying causes. The inflation stemmed from causes that were easily understandable at that time and should have been apparent to the German leaders. This German tragedy is testimony to the danger of ignoring economic theory and past historical experience.

Key Economic Points

The cause of the German hyperinflation is identified.
The social and economic costs of a runaway inflation are determined.
The quantity theory of money is employed to explain the German hyperinflation.

26

Quantity Theory of Money: The Great German Hyperinflation

The upward trend in the rate of inflation in the United States began during the Vietnam War but has increased steadily since the end of that war. Recessions, it appears, have brought only temporary periods of respite to the upward spiral in the rate of price increases. Should this trend continue or accelerate, it would paint a grim picture of America by the end of the century. Inflation and war have always been bedfellows, but normally when the war ends, the rate of inflation declines. This has not happened recently in the United States, nor did it happen in Germany during the early 1920s; instead, hyperinflation broke out. Given the current fears about the increasing rate of inflation in the United States and the similarity between the early stages of the German hyperinflation and the current situation in the United States, it is instructive to review the causes and consequences of the great German inflation.

The great German inflation began during World War I, accelerated during 1919, became a hyperinflation during 1922, and ended in 1923 with a currency reform that amounted to the confiscation of all outstanding currency. During this inflation the price index rose from 8 in 1919 to 1 ½ trillion in 1922. Production declined and unemployment reached depression levels as the German people refused to accept the now worthless national currency. The combination of hyperinflation and consequent depression ruined millions of German families financially and has been causally linked to the fall of democracy and the rise of fascism, Adolf Hitler, and World War II.

The great German inflation is of interest more because of the extravagance of the historical facts than the nature of its causes. Nothing that happened could not have been predicted by existing theory and past historical experience. In this chapter we first trace the development and impact of the German inflation between 1919 and 1923. We then explore the theoretical reasons for the inflation and draw certain conclusions from this tragedy that are relevant to today's economy.

The German economy began to experience inflation during World War I when the price level increased two and one-half times. In retrospect this appears to have been a minor inflation when compared with what was to come. Beginning in 1919 the rate of inflation increased as the price level more than tripled during the year. The rate of inflation slowed during 1920 when prices did not quite double, but the next year prices increased almost two and one-half times. The rate of inflation exploded into a hyperinflation during 1922, increasing over 1,400 times, which was followed during 1923 by an increase of over a billion times, which made the currency worthless.

As might now be expected, inflation initially stimulated production and employment. Unemployment among trade union members fell from 2.9 percent at the beginning of 1919 to less than 1 percent during much of 1922. As the hyperinflation took hold, however, the rate of unemployment among union members increased to depression levels. At times during 1922, the rate of unemployment reached 23 percent and by the end of 1923 almost one-third of all union members were unemployed. National output followed the same pattern. In 1919 real national income was only 90 percent of the 1913 level. The index rose to 92 percent during 1921, but fell drastically to only 65 percent in 1923.

The main reason for the decline in both employment and production was that the hyperinflation impaired the functioning of the market economy, eventually leading to its breakdown and forcing many people to resort to barter. A highly specialized industrial economy simply cannot function as a barter economy.

In order to avoid a total collapse, some larger German businesses began to issue their own money, called "notgeld," or to use foreign currency. The U.S. dollar was particularly prized at this time. Such desperate measures, as the production and unemployment figures testify, were only partially successful, but they did keep the German economy from a total collapse.

The German inflation, because its severity was totally unexpected, drastically reduced and redistributed income within the German economy. Wages did not keep pace with rising prices and, when coupled with the decline in employment, drastically reduced the standard of living of German labor. Aggregate real wages, which initially rose from 81 in 1919 to 89 in 1921, fell to 68 in 1922 and 65 in 1923. The hyperinflation lowered the German laborers' standard of living by 20 percent.

Nor did the salaried middle class fare better. The real wages of high-level civil servants fell by over 60 percent while those of lower levels fell somewhat less. This reflected a general narrowing of the pay differentials between high- and low-skilled workers. Professionals such as doctors and lawyers suffered even more drastic declines in income. The runaway inflation absolutely destroyed those economic groups, such as retired persons and bond owners, whose incomes were fixed in money terms. Debtors actively pursued creditors attempting to pay debts in the now much depreciated currency. It is perhaps not too far from the truth to state that the middle class was financially destroyed by the great inflation and was forced into drastic financial straits.

The great industrialists, whose main assets were invested in capital goods, prospered initially. Their books showed huge paper profits, which turned out to be more illusion than reality when the economy collapsed during 1923.

The great German inflation ended late in 1923 when the existing currency was called in and exchanged for newly issued rentermarks. The rate of exchange was 1 trillion paper marks for one rentermark, a rate that was tantamount to the expropriation of the old currency. The new currency held its value and the economy quickly recovered, but for millions of Germans it meant starting over, their life savings having been wiped out by the great inflation.

The tragedy of the German inflation is that the persons in charge of the government and the central bank should have known better. A basic knowledge of economics as it existed at that time or an acquaintance with the historical past would have prohibited the actions that caused the inflation. The fundamental cause of the German inflation, as it is of any inflation, was the excessive creation of money. This relationship had been known for centuries. Copernicus, writing in 1596 to the King of Poland, stated: "Money loses in value when it has become too much multiplied." This view was amplified during subsequent centuries and became known as the quantity theory of money.

The quantity theory of money holds that the stock of money (M) times the number of times a unit of money circulates each year, which is known as the velocity of circulation (V), must equal the output of the economy (Q) times the price of this output (P). Thus:

$$MV = PQ$$

which states that the volume of expenditures of the economy (MV) must equal the value of the purchases (PQ). If the stock of money is greatly multiplied, expanding the volume of expenditures, the value of purchases must increase equally. Since the output of the economy cannot rapidly expand, price must rise.

The German authorities ignored this theory, and between the end of 1919 and the end of 1923 the volume of paper marks in circulation increased from 35.7 billion to 180,000,000,000 billion. As a direct consequence, the economy experienced the hyperinflation known as the great German inflation.

The rate of increase in the price level was boosted by two subsequent developments: (1) the velocity of circulation (V) increased dramatically as people came to expect further inflation and (2) the output of the economy fell as people resisted accepting paper marks in trade. As the inflation progressed, workers who had previously been paid weekly first insisted on being paid daily, and then every hour. Workers' wives waited at the factory gates for the hourly pay and rushed to spend the rapidly depreciating currency before it lost even more value. Shopkeepers began to make daily and then hourly price changes. Finally, both workers and shopkeepers refused to accept German paper marks at all. Output and employment fell as the market mechanism failed to function because of the lack of a stable currency.

The rapid multiplication of the currency in circulation came about as a direct result of the government's reliance upon deficit financing to obtain resources for the public sector. The Weimar Republic was the constitutional democracy that governed Germany during this period. It had replaced the monarchy, which collapsed late in 1918 amid political turmoil that approached anarchy. The political parties that undertook to govern were never able to give Germany a stable government. One of the areas in which this instability affected the economy was in taxation policies. The early leaders of the Weimar Republic were simply politically unwilling to impose direct taxation upon its citizens.

Instead, the government resorted to issuing treasury bills, which were sold to the Reichbank, Germany's central bank. The Reichbank immediately issued paper marks with the treasury bills as backing. Thus each treasury bill issued produced an equivalent increase in the amount of currency in circulation. The size of the budget deficits increased after 1920 as Germany was called upon to make reparation payments to the victorious allies to pay for the cost of World War I. By 1922 the Weimar Republic was issuing treasury notes for 75 percent of its expenditures, and by 1923 for 95 percent. Currency in circulation increased by the same amount as the treasury bills outstanding. The great German inflation was the consequence.

The lessons of this hyperinflation are clear. Unrestrained note issue by a government or central bank will inevitably lead to a rapidly rising price level. Increases in the money supply alone are not responsible for the entire rise in the price level. Expectations for future inflation led to increases in the velocity of circulation, which led to further price increases. The effect of runaway inflation was to impair the workings of the price system itself, leading to a decline in output, which added to the upward pressure on prices. According to the quantity theory, an increase in the price level can result from an increase in the money supply, an increase in the velocity of circulation, or a decline in output. Although the great German hyperinflation was initiated by the unrestrained issuance of money, it was the product of all three factors acting together that led to the complete breakdown of the German economy.

Additional Readings

Bresciani-Turroni, C. *The Economics of Inflation.* George Allen and Unwin, 1937.

Graham, Frank D. *Exchange, Prices, and Production in Hyperinflation Germany,* Princeton University Press, 1935.

Hill, L., C. Butler, and S. Lorenzen. "Inflation and the Destruction of Democracy: The Case of the Weimar Republic." *Journal of Economic Issues,* June 1977.

V

CURRENT
MACROECONOMIC
PROBLEMS

Preview

During the 1970s the economy experienced two inflationary recessions. During these recessions the price level continued to rise, albeit at a reduced rate, as the rate of unemployment increased. Inflation was thus combined with unemployment to create a situation that was called stagflation and represented the worst of all macroeconomic situations. It was widely believed that stagflation was a novel occurrence and that its appearance contradicted the laws of macroeconomics. In particular, the inflation-unemployment trade-off, known as the Phillips curve, was believed to have been invalidated, its predictions repudiated by the inflationary recessions. This chapter examines the dilemma. The concept of expectations-augmented Phillips curve and the natural rate of unemployment hypothesis are applied to resolve the dilemma and to explain how inflationary recessions can occur not as violations of laws of economics, but as a consequence of them.

Key Economic Points

The occurrence of an inflationary recession contradicts the implications of the traditional Phillips curve.

An inflationary recession can occur by applying the expectations-augmented Phillips curve and the natural rate of unemployment hypothesis.

The policy of gradualism is derived from the expectations-augmented Phillips curve.

The possibilities of success are weighed from employing gradualism to fight inflation.

27

The Phillips Curve: "Impossible! Recession and Rising Prices?"

"Impossible! Recession and Rising Prices?" stated a headline in the January 25, 1970 Sunday *New York Times*. This lead was typical of numerous complaints in the press that the laws of economics were no longer working. The phenomena that led to this outcry were the inflationary recessions of 1969–1970 and 1974–1975. During these years, both the rate of inflation and the unemployment rate increased simultaneously, seemingly in defiance of the predictions of economics. The traditional Keynesian model allows either a recession, characterized by unemployment, or inflation, but not both at the same time.

In particular, the purported stable trade-off between inflation and unemployment, known as the Phillips curve, seemed to be contradicted by the empirical evidence. The Phillips curve states that a trade-off exists between the rates of inflation and unemployment. If the government wishes to use economic policy to lower the rate of inflation, it can do so only at the cost of increased unemployment. During the 1960s the Phillips curve estimates for the United States indicated that a 4 percent full-employment rate of unemployment would be accompanied by a 4 percent rate of inflation. Inflation could be reduced to 2 percent at the cost of 5 percent unemployment and to zero at the cost of 7 percent unemployment. A reduction in the rate of inflation would always require an increase in the unemployment rate and vice versa.

Early in the 1970s it became painfully evident that these tradeoffs no longer applied. Contrary to the prediction of the Phillips curve, unemployment and inflation rates frequently moved together. For example, between 1968 and 1971 the unemployment rate, which increased from 3.6 to 5.9 percent, was accompanied not by a fall in inflation, as predicted by the Phillips curve, but by an increase in the inflation rate from 4.5 to 5.1 percent. Between 1973 and 1974 the unemployment rate increased from 4.9 to 5.6 percent and the rate of inflation also increased from 6.2 to 11.0 percent. The novel combination of inflation and unemployment increasing together was often referred to by the press as the inflation-unemployment dilemma and labeled an "inflationary recession" or, by some, "stagflation."

The inflation-unemployment dilemma was resolved by the development of the "natural rate of unemployment hypothesis." According to the natural rate hypothesis, market decisions are not influenced by the money price of goods, services, and resources, but by relative prices. People decide how much meat to buy after considering the price of meat relative to the prices of other foods that could be substituted for meat. Workers decide how much labor to offer by considering not the nominal (money) wage but the real wage, the actual purchasing power of the money wage.

Inflation, which leaves the relative prices of goods, services, and resources unchanged, would not alter anyone's market decisions to buy, sell or work. Consequently, changes in the rate of inflation would not lead to changes in output or unemployment. Therefore, the Phillips curve tradeoff between unemployment and inflation should not exist. Instead, the rate of unemployment in the economy should always tend toward the full-employment rate of unemployment (FEUR) and be independent of the rate of inflation. Any rate of inflation could coexist with the "natural" or full-employment rate of unemployment.

What, then, is the explanation for the evidence that at times the rate of inflation and the rate of unemployment have moved in opposite directions, the very evidence that established the Phillips Curve in the first place? According to the natural rate hypothesis, such movements are temporary and come about because people have imperfect information about the rate of inflation.

When the rate of inflation accelerates, for example, it proceeds from an increase in aggregate demand. Firms experience an increased demand for their output. They respond by raising the prices of the goods and services they produce and by attempting to increase output. In order to attract more workers, they offer higher money wages. Workers have very good knowledge of money wage rates, but only an imperfect knowledge about the prices of goods and services. Consequently, they believe initially that the higher money wages offered represent increases in the real wage; therefore more labor, in the aggregate, is supplied. The result is that the rate of unemployment falls below the FEUR and national output increases. Initially, therefore, as inflation accelerates, a Phillips curve relationship would be discovered. A higher rate of inflation will be associated with a decline in unemployment.

This positive result will, however, last only as long as workers believe that real wages have increased. Soon they begin to discover that the higher nominal wages they are earning, will, in fact, not buy any more goods and services than they previously could buy with lower money wages. The rate of unemployment will rise as workers reduce the amount of labor supplied, until the full-employment rate of unemployment once again prevails. The observed Phillips curve relationship, therefore, is a short-run phenomena and will not be observed in the long run.

The same relationship, only in reverse, between unemployment and inflation will be observed if the rate of inflation slows. Workers will not immediately recognize that the lower wages offered are, in fact, the same real wages as before. They will, therefore, invest more time searching for higher paying jobs that do not exist. Thus a fall in the rate of inflation is, for a short time, associated with a rise in unemployment. Once workers recognize the extent to which prices have ceased to rise at their former rate, they will begin to accept existing job offers and the rate of unemployment will once again tend toward the full-employment rate.

The imperfect knowledge workers have about the price level thus accounts for the existence of inflationary recessions and stagflation. Inflationary recessions are the periods of time required for workers to ascertain that the rate of inflation has, in fact, declined. The ultimate equilibrium position will find a lower rate of inflation and a rate of unemployment at the full-employment level.

Workers' expectations as to the rate of inflation are therefore very important in explaining the inflation-unemployment dilemma. The natural rate hypothesis suggests that the original Phillips curve analysis should be restated in terms of expected or anticipated changes in the rates of inflation. Thus, as the expected rate of inflation changes, the Phillips curve will shift. This reformulation is known as the expectations-augmented Phillips curve.

The expectations-augmented Phillips curve has important implications for economic policy. During the 1960s, monetary policy makers believed that it was possible to lower the unemployment rate if a somewhat higher inflation rate was tolerated. In fact, this belief is often made the culprit that caused the increasing inflation rate during the 1970s. The expectations-augmented Phillips curve reveals the fallacy of this belief. This analysis predicts that stimulating aggregate demand will only temporarily achieve lower rates of unemployment. A permanent decrease in the rate of unemployment below the full-employment rate would require the acceptance of a continually higher rate of inflation. An increase in the rate of inflation will, as noted above, stimulate a decline in the unemployment rate only until people correct their expectations. Once expectations adjust to the new higher rate of inflation, employment will decline to the full-employment rate. In order to keep this adjustment from taking place, it would be necessary for policy makers to fool workers by raising the rate of inflation still more. The price of attempting to reduce the rate of unemployment below the natural rate is to suffer ever increasing rates of inflation.

A second implication of the expectations-augmented Phillips curve analysis is that once, as a result of poor policy decisions, a high rate of inflation exists, it will be costly to quickly reduce the inflation rate. The rate of inflation can be reduced by reducing aggregate demand, but only at the cost of temporary unemployment until inflationary expectations adjust. The more determined the effort to reduce inflation (the greater the reduction in aggregate demand), the longer and more severe the inflationary recession that will result.

The inflationary recessions of 1969–1970 and 1974–1975 support this implication. The rate of inflation fell from 5.9 percent in 1970 to 4.3 percent in 1971, but only at the expense of an increase in the rate of unemployment from 4.9 to 5.9 percent. Similarly, the rate of inflation was reduced from 11.0 percent in 1974 to 5.3 percent in 1976, but the rate of unemployment increased from 5.6 in 1974 to 8.5 in 1975 and remained at 7.7 percent during 1976.

This historical experience serves to verify the implications of the expectations-augmented Phillips curve analysis. Any administration faced with the problem of inflation must weigh the benefits to be achieved from a lower rate of inflation against the short-term costs of higher unemployment. The inflation-unemployment trade-off explains why every administration, Republican or Democratic, during the 1970s chose to fight inflation by employing the strategy of "gradualism." Gradualism is the policy of gradually reducing aggregate demand through monetary and fiscal policies in order to slowly reduce the rate of inflation without severely increasing the rate of unemployment or bringing on another inflationary recession. The inflationary recessions of 1969–1970, 1974–1975, and 1980, and the trend toward higher rates of inflation testify to the difficulty of employing this strategy successfully.

The expectations-augmented Phillips curve adequately resolves the inflation-unemployment dilemma created by the inflationary recessions of the 1970s. Those observers and journalists who thought that the existence of stagflation demonstrated that the laws of economics no longer were obeyed were wrong. There is no law of economics that states that the inflation rate and the unemployment rate always move in opposite directions. Sometimes they do and sometimes they don't.

Additional Readings

Gittings, T. A. "The Inflation-Unemployment Tradeoff." *Economic Perspectives,* Federal Reserve Bank of Chicago, September–October 1979.

"Impossible! Recession and Rising Prices?" *New York Times,* January 25, 1970.

Preview

Is there a quick and inexpensive way to halt inflation? One school of economic thought thinks there is. This school of thought is called "rational expectations" after the distinguishing feature of this approach to economic thinking. Rational expectations assumes that individuals make use of all the available information when making economic decisions. In this chapter the implications of this approach for public policy are spelled out. If the assumptions of rational expectations are correct, then it is possible to design a macroeconomic policy that would quickly and relatively painlessly eliminate inflation.

Key Economic Points

How does the theory of rational expectations differ from conventional macroeconomic thinking?

What are the implications that rational expectations hold for the effectiveness of monetary policy?

The monetary policy of rational expectations is compared with the policy of Keynesian economists or monetarists.

Would the anti-inflation program described herein work or not, and at what cost?

28

Stabilization Policy: The Role Expectations Play

Is there a relatively inexpensive way to quickly eliminate inflation? Conventional economic thinking offers little hope that there is. In the opinion of most economists, any attempt to rapidly reduce the rate of inflation, to be successful, would entail suffering an unacceptably high rate of unemployment. But not all economists agree. Recently, a new school of thought called "rational expectations" has emerged that challenges the current orthodoxy. This view has attracted a great deal of attention, precisely because it offers the prospect of a quick, relatively painless solution to the inflation problem.

The theory of rational expectations challenges the conventional economic assumption as to how the public forms its expectations about the economic future. In particular, the expectations-augmented Phillips curve, which forms the basis for the existing explanation of stagflation and the intellectual underpinnings for gradualism comes under heavy attack from the new theory. The expectations-augmented Phillips curve assumes that the public's anticipations about the future have been formed by a process called "adaptive expectations." Individuals, according to this theory, have limited information about economic conditions outside the realm of their everyday experiences. They therefore base their expectations about future economic conditions solely on their current and past experience.

One way an individual could do this would be to predict that next year's rate of inflation would be some weighted average of current and past rates of inflation. Because past rates of inflation are used in formulating expectations, individuals adapt their expectations to actual conditions relatively slowly. Only if the rate of inflation had held steady for a period of time would the level of expected inflation equal the actual inflation.

The short-run inflation-unemployment trade-off implied by the expectations-augmented Phillips curve exists only if the expected rate of inflation differs from the actual rate. It is widely recognized that the spending and work decisions of individuals depend upon relative prices. Therefore, neither spending nor employment decisions are affected by a general rise in the price level provided the public correctly anticipates the rate of inflation.

It is highly unlikely that people will correctly anticipate the actual rate of inflation if they formulate their expectations as the adaptive expectations hypothesis suggests they do. Consequently, when the Federal Reserve increases the rate of growth of the money supply to combat a rising unemployment rate, the inevitable inflation will initially not be recognized as such, but will be misinterpreted as a favorable change in relative prices. Output and employment will temporarily increase until people recognize their mistake and revise their inflation expectations and the behavior based upon them.

The effectiveness of monetary policy as a countercyclical tool thus depends upon the ability of the monetary authorities to "fool" the people. If people correctly anticipated the rate of monetary expansion, they would immediately adjust their inflation expectations accordingly, and the price level would change but no employment or spending decisions would be affected.

Is it possible in a country with an open government and instant mass communications for a public agency to consistently fool the public? Is it conceivable that the private sector would not eventually catch on that a recession always brings forth an expansion of the money supply and then an increase in inflation, and immediately adjust their expectations accordingly? These are questions that proponents of rational expectations frequently ask.

President Lincoln more than a century ago stated that "you cannot fool all of the people all of the time." Rational expectations theory agrees. This theory states that people use all the available information, not just current and past inflation rates, when forming their anticipations about the future rate of inflation. The history of government stabilization policies is itself vital and valuable information used by the public in forecasting inflation.

According to rational expectations theory, the public will appreciate that whenever unemployment increases, monetary growth and inflation will accelerate. Individuals will incorporate this information in their inflation expectations. When the next recession occurs and the Federal Reserve takes the appropriate, but now anticipated, action, the results will not be what the authorities expect. The effect will be that the price level will quickly adjust to the increase in the money supply, but neither the real output of the economy nor the rate of unemployment will change as a consequence of the ease in monetary policy. If the public correctly antici- pates the behavior of the monetary authorities and no one is fooled, no trade-off between inflation and unemployment exists, and monetary poli- cy cannot affect anything but the rate of inflation.

The past policy failures of the Federal Reserve, according to rational expectations theorists, are in large part the result of failure to appreciate the role expectations play in the macroeconomy. The effectiveness of monetary policy, however, cannot be restored by the attempt by policy makers to carefully consider the public's expectations in their policy delib- erations.

First, it is difficult to measure expectations. If the estimated public expectations are incorrect, the outcome of a policy action might be the opposite of the desired results. If, for example, the authorities wish to stimulate employment and output, and estimate that the public expects monetary growth to be 6 percent, they will increase the money growth rate to 8 percent. But suppose the true public expectation was 10 percent, then an 8 percent growth rate provides less money than anticipated, and em- ployment and output will fall rather than rise.

Second, the theory of rational expectations suggests that even if policy makers knew the economy's expectations, the problem of using monetary policy to control the economy would not be solved. Suppose the Federal Reserve adopted a policy of always supplying more money than expected when a recession occurred. People would catch on to this strategy relative- ly quickly and adjust their expectations accordingly. While it may be possible to fool all of the people some of the time, it is impossible to fool all of the people all of the time.

The major implications of rational expectations is that monetary policy can only affect the general price level. Therefore, the Federal Reserve should be singularly devoted to the problem of controlling inflation. Furthermore, since inflation resulted from bad policy—the attempt by the Federal Reserve to control what it was impossible to control—inflation can be controlled only by good policy. It is theoretically possible to quickly and painlessly eliminate inflation by severely reducing the rate of growth of the money supply provided that the public correctly anticipates the reduction.

The Federal Reserve could announce that after some future date the money supply would grow at a rate of 3 to 4 percent a year, the rate of economic growth of the economy, and follow through on that promise. If the public believed this announcement, they would immediately alter inflation expectations. The increase in the quantity of money, in this case, would be precisely the amount required to finance the additional output produced by economic growth. There would be no additional money to fuel price and inflationary wage increases. The public would realize this and not attempt to raise wages above the increase in productivity or prices. Inflation would, in a short time, abate without any serious fall in the nation's output or rise in the unemployment rate.

However, it is unlikely that this announcement would be widely believed. More likely people would adopt a "wait-and-see" attitude. In this event, when the Federal Reserve carried through on its promise, both employment and output would be seriously affected. The Federal Reserve would not be believed because in the past it has always pursued a stop-and-go monetary policy. Restrictive monetary policies have in the past always been followed by a more stimulative policy. The public is not apt to ignore this information. There are, after all, no checks on the Federal Reserve that prohibit this possibility. The basic independence of the Federal Reserve allows the Board of Governors the freedom to change its mind.

One way to enhance the credibility of the Federal Reserve would be to eliminate this independence. Congress could pass a law setting rules for the conduct of monetary policy. This law could require that the money supply grow at a prescribed rate and hold the Board of Governors of the Federal Reserve responsible. It is probable that the impact of such a law would be to quickly alter the public's inflation expectations. When the Federal Reserve followed through on its legal obligation, inflation would disappear quickly and without the accompanying severe unemployment feared by many today. The theory of rational expectations, when coupled with appropriate institutional changes, thus offers the hope of a quick, painless cure for the inflation problem.

Most of the economics profession remains skeptical of such claims. Many critics question the realism of the rational expectations theory. Some critics contend that it requires the common person to have as much information as economic experts. Proponents of rational expectations reply that all that is required is that people have access to information, be well informed, and act rationally. Other critics question the extent to which in the real world wages and prices are free to adjust quickly. These critics assert that institutional factors, such as labor and financial contracts, seniority rules, minimum wage laws, regulated prices, and imperfect competition in product and factor markets prevent wages and prices from adjusting quickly to changes in monetary policy. Because of these institutional rigidities, monetary policy will continue to affect the levels of output and employment in the short run. In sum, the Phillips curve trade-off between inflation and unemployment exists for a variety of reasons, among which lagging expectations is only one.

It is fair to say that most economists have not accepted the theory of rational expectations. Most still believe that monetary policy can, in the short run, affect employment and output levels. Moreover, most economists do not believe that the public's expectations immediately respond to changes in economic conditions. Rational expectations theory has, however, had some influence on the economics profession. Many economists no longer feel comfortable with their previous assumptions about the role expectations play in macroeconomics. If the assumptions of rational expectations are too broad to be generally accepted, the assumptions of adaptive expectations are now generally considered too narrow. It is increasingly believed that the economic policies of government do affect expectations. In response to soaring inflation during 1980, an attempt was made to balance the 1981 federal budget. The effect of this action, according to proponents of a balanced budget, was designed to influence inflationary expectations. There was little support for a balanced budget solely because it was believed to be the correct fiscal policy for fighting inflation.

In the past, economic policies were analyzed without consideration of the effect the policies had on the public's expectations of future economic conditions. Both economists and policy makers assumed the public would continue to anticipate future conditions as if nothing had changed. Many economists, even those who do not hold with rational expectations as such, now feel uncomfortable with this assumption.

Additional Readings

McCallum, B. T. "The Significance of Rational Expectations Theory." *Challenge,* January–February 1980.

McElhattan, R., and C. Pigott. "Rational Expectations: The Tradeoff." *Weekly Letter,* Federal Reserve Bank of San Francisco, June 22, 1979.

Plosser, C., and C. Smith, Jr. "The People Can't Be Fooled." *Wall Street Journal,* June 25, 1979.

Preview

Wage and price controls have been used to combat inflation for centuries, always without success. Recently, a significant percentage of the public and even a number of economists have recommended that controls be tried once again. There are many things we can do today that our forefathers could not; perhaps wage and price controls are one of them. This chapter explores the United States' most recent experience with wage and price controls during the Nixon administration. Then the use of controls to reverse inflationary expectations is examined.

Key Economic Points

The efficiency costs of wage and price controls are specified.
Why do controls fail to eliminate inflation?
The proposal to impose controls to reverse inflationary expectations in combination with restrictive fiscal and monetary policy is evaluated.
What are the efficiency costs of controls in terms of the costs of a recession or continued high rates of inflation?

29

Incomes Policy: Wage and Price Controls

The overall rate of inflation during 1979 was 13.3 percent, which was bad enough, but for most consumers the news was even worse. The prices of energy, food, housing and health care, items on which two-thirds of American families spend 80 percent of their income, rose an astounding 17.6 percent. The skyrocketing prices of these basic items accounted for virtually all of the rise of the inflation rate to double-digit levels. The prices of all other goods included in the consumer price index rose only 6.8 percent, just slightly more than in 1978 and actually less than in 1976.

Early in 1980, public opinion pollsters reported that 65 percent of all Americans favored the imposition of wage and price controls and believed that controls were the best, perhaps the only, way to curb inflation. Opposed to controls were the Carter administration and a majority of all economists who believed that controls had never worked in the past, wouldn't work now, and would prove, if enacted, to be costly and burdensome to the economy. A growing number of economists, however, including the former head of President Carter's Council on Wage and Price Stability, were defecting from the ranks and openly advocating the use of controls to battle the worse peacetime inflation in the nation's history.

The increasing political support for controls, reinforced by the recommendations of a growing number of professional economists, raises the question: can wage and price controls work today? This question is explored in this chapter. In addition, the history of price controls is briefly traced, and our country's most recent experience with price controls is examined to determine if controls worked and at what cost. The answers to these questions will help to answer the more basic question of whether controls can work today or not.

Wage and price controls have a long, if not exactly honorable, tradition. They existed in ancient Babylon, were periodically tried by the Greeks and Romans, were improved by the Mongol Jublai Khan, and were a prominent feature of the European medieval economy.

The Puritans brought the concept with them to the New World. Here wage and price controls have been used from time to time, especially during wartime when inflation became a problem. The Continental Congress tried to set prices before and during the American Revolution as did the Confederacy during the Civil War. The U.S. government employed wage and price controls during the two world wars and again during the Korean War. Here in America, as elsewhere, wage and price controls have never been considered to have been successful.

But there are many things our ancestors could not do that we can do successfully. Perhaps wage and price controls are one of those things. The most recent U.S. experience with controls may cast some light on whether our current ability to control prices has improved over that of our forefathers.

Wage and price controls were suddenly imposed by President Nixon on the 15th of August, 1971, when he announced his "New Economic Policy." This action took the country by surprise, because the Nixon administration had previously rejected a controls program as unfeasible. Prior to the middle of August, the administration had relied upon a policy of gradualism to reduce inflation without precipitating a recession. By the summer of 1971, gradualism was widely considered to have been a failure.

The New Economic Policy began with a 90-day freeze on all wages, prices, and rents, with the exception of taxes, agricultural prices, and mortgage interest rates. During the 3-months freeze, known as phase I, the necessary administrative machinery was established to control wages and prices during phase II. Two chief administrative units, the Pay Board and the Price Commission, were set up as part of the Cost of Living Council. Given the complexities of the U.S. economy and the absolute necessity for public support of the controls program, the program was designed to be basically self-administered by the public. In order to ensure political support, representatives of labor, business, and the public were included on the stabilization boards.

Phase II followed the end of the freeze and lasted for 14 months. The price control administrators attempted to apply broad standards for wage and price increases consistent with a reduced rate of inflation. Wage increases were limited to 5.5 percent, with some exceptions for gross inequities. Prices could be raised only as a consequence of rising costs. Cost increases could be passed through to higher prices provided that the margin of profit did not increase.

Phase II, begun in January 1973, was intended to be a transition period to decontrol. Larger than standard price increases were accepted if evidence was provided that such increases were necessary for the efficient allocation of resources or to maintain adequate levels of supply. Inflation accelerated early in 1973, and phase III was reconsidered by the administration. The result was a second freeze on prices, imposed in June 1973. This freeze was gradually lifted and ended entirely 2 months later.

Phase IV followed the end of the second freeze, bringing regulations more stringent than those of phase II. A policy of gradual decontrol on a sector-by-sector basis was implemented. Controls expired on April 20, 1974; at that time only 12 percent of the goods whose prices are measured by the consumer price index were still being regulated.

Were the Nixon controls successful in containing or at least restraining inflation and at what cost? A number of studies attempting to evaluate the effectiveness of the Nixon controls program have been done. In order to measure the impact that controls had on the inflation rate, it is necessary to predict what the rate would have been in the absence of the controls program. The predicted rate of inflation in the absence of controls, known as the counterfactual alternative, is then compared with the actual rate of inflation to determine the impact of controls. A number of different methods have been used in these studies to obtain the counterfactual alternative. As a consequence, the results reported differ somewhat between studies.

Most studies did find that the phase I freeze reduced the measured rate of inflation from what it would have been. During the freeze, the consumer price index increased at the annual rate of 1.7 percent, the wholesale price index actually fell, and wages increased at the rate of 2.2 percent. Wages and prices could rise during the freeze because not all prices were subject to control. In the quarter prior to the unexpected freeze, the annual rate of inflation, as measured by the consumer price index, was almost 5 percent and rising. Depending on the methods used to obtain the counterfactual alternative, most studies found that the freeze lowered the measured rate of inflation by 2 to 3 percent.

The measured rate of inflation, as reflected in price indicators such as the consumer price index, probably does not accurately reflect the actual rate of inflation when price controls are in effect. Price controls, if effective, create shortages; that is, insufficient amounts of a good are available at the controlled price. What is the actual price of a good that can be purchased not at all or only after spending hours waiting in line? Producers also have an incentive to introduce at higher prices new products not yet subject to price guidelines that are in fact only thinly disguised versions of existing price-controlled goods. Furthermore, producers will tend to reduce the quality of products that are price-controlled, in effect selling a cheaper good at the price-controlled price, which amounts to the same thing as raising prices. The measured rate of inflation will fail to reflect these actual price increases. Price controls thus repress inflation, shifting the effects of inflation into areas that are not measured by price indexes. Repressing inflation in these ways does not eliminate the social costs of inflation, but makes them worse.

There is less agreement about the effectiveness of the controls program during subsequent phases. During phase II and generally thereafter, the price control program allowed business firms to pass along cost increases to consumers. There is a modicum of agreement that controls succeeded in depressing the price level through the end of phase III. The amount of this reduction varies from study to study, with the amount ranging from 1.5 to 3 percent off the inflation rate. Thereafter, as controls were progressively relaxed during phase IV, the rate of inflation accelerated as prices raced to catch up with what they would have been had controls never been imposed.

Some of the studies even found that during this period of "catch-up," prices rose to a level higher than they would have been had controls not been employed. One study estimated that the effect of controls was to cause the consumer price index to be 1 percent higher than it would have been.

These findings answer, at least in part, the question of the effectiveness of wage and price controls. But why would controls, if they were effective in temporarily restraining inflation, cause the price level to be permanently higher over the long term? The answer is to be found in the perverse incentives that effective controls create. In theory, just about everything is wrong with wage and price controls. Controls interfere with the vital signals usually conveyed by the free market system, resulting in the misallocation of resources. Controls, if effective, create shortages and reduce the incentive to undertake capital investment. Business and labor waste resources and ingenuity devising ways to circumvent the regulations, which in response become increasingly complex. The overall result is to reduce the overall productivity of the economy, which, if nothing else changes, results in a higher price level.

The end of the Nixon price control program saw the beginning of double-digit inflation as the catch-up arrived. Surveying these results, former Secretary of the Treasury George Schulz described the 3 years of controls as "the biggest failure in the history of economics." Even the avowed proponents of wage and price controls thought the Nixon controls a failure, but they attributed the lack of success to half-hearted efforts on the part of the administrators themselves. John Kenneth Galbraith expressed the view that "any controls program run by Republicans is bound to be fouled up."

Whatever the reasons for the failure of the Nixon controls program, the lack of success did demonstrate that wage and price controls by themselves cannot halt inflation. The Nixon administration apparently believed that they could. The 1972 Economic Report of the President stated: "The establishment of the direct wage-price controls created room for some expansionary measures." Monetary policy was certainly expansionary during the period of controls. The rate of growth of the money supply was 40 percent higher during the years of controlled prices than it was during the 5 years prior to the imposition of controls. There was little designed use of fiscal policy during the period. The high-employment budget was mildly expansionary during 1971 and 1972 and mildly contractionary during 1975. The overall effect of monetary and fiscal policy was expansionary, so expansionary that the control program was undermined. Wage and price controls, all by themselves, obviously cannot control inflation without creating serious shortages and reducing the productivity of the economy. There is nothing in the record of the Nixon New Economic Policy to support the contention that we can use wage and price controls any more effectively than could our forefathers.

There is, however, another possible role that wage and price controls could play in macroeconomic policy making. Controls could potentially be used to ease the impact of the restrictive monetary and fiscal policy required to halt inflation. Current economic opinion believes that before fiscal and monetary policy can affect the rate of inflation, existing inflationary expectations must be reversed. In order to reverse the existing level of expectations, it is thought that both business and labor will require strong evidence that the rate of inflation is actually going to decline before they will moderate their price and wage increases. Moreover, it is feared that only a recession, with the high social costs involved, will provide the hard evidence required. The prospect of society bearing these costs has generally persuaded policy makers to pursue a policy of gradualism; meanwhile, society bears the costs of prolonged inflation.

Imposing controls on wages and prices at the same time that restrictive monetary and fiscal policies are implemented may allow inflation expectations to adjust downward without the necessity of a recession. Ordinarily when wage and price controls have been employed in the past, excess demands for goods, expressed as shortages, have occurred because the underlying causes of inflation have not been treated. If, however, restrictive economic policies keep severe shortages from developing, business firms will feel no pressure to raise prices when the controls are lifted. Labor, not having suffered a decline in real wages, will have no incentive to demand inflationary wage increases. Wage and price controls will be substituted for a recession to reverse inflationary expectations. Supporters of this view suggest that the cost imposed on society by the inefficiency of temporary controls would be less than the costs of a recession.

There is some evidence that inflationary expectations did temporarily moderate when the phase I freeze was imposed. Long-term interest rates, which include an inflation premium, fell when price controls were first implemented. This suggests that lenders expected lower rates of inflation in the future. This impression was supported by surveys that reported a decline in the inflationary expectations of the persons polled. Both long-term interest rates and survey results, however, suggested a rise in inflationary expectations when the second freeze was imposed during phase III. This suggests that few persons, after experiencing the Nixon controls, believed that controls by themselves would contain inflation.

What, then, can be said about the effectiveness of wage and price controls in restraining inflation? It is perhaps safe to conclude that controls by themselves will only work temporarily and at some cost in terms of economic efficiency. Even then it is possible that this short-term relief will be purchased at the cost of a price level permanently higher than would exist if price controls had not been imposed. Furthermore, controls cannot be effective against inflation unless they are accompanied by restrictive monetary and fiscal policies. Whether controls would work in this case to reverse inflationary expectations remains a matter for speculation because it has never been tried.

Additional Readings

Blinder, A. S., and W. J. Newton. *The 1971–74 Controls Program and the Price Level: An Econometric Post-Mortem.* Working Paper No. 279, National Bureau of Economic Research, September 1978.

Collins, J. M. "Price Controls: Forty Centuries of Failure." *Business Week,* December 18, 1978.

Feige, E. L. and D. K. Pearce. "The Wage-Price Control Experiment—Did It Work?" *Challenge,* July–August 1973.

Grayson, C. J., Jr. "Controls Are Not the Answer." *Challenge,* November–December 1974.

Guzzardi, W., Jr. "What We Should Have Learned About Controls." *Fortune,* March 1975.

Lekachman, R. "The Inevitability of Controls." *Challenge,* November–December 1974.

Preview

A tax-based incomes policy has been described as the only new idea for combating inflation that has been proposed in the last two decades. President Carter attempted, without success, to get Congress to employ this type of program in 1978. A tax-based incomes policy employs taxes to create an incentive for business firms to resist granting inflationary wage increases to workers. Wages and salaries are the largest single cost of production, so if wage increases are moderated, so will be the rise in the cost of production, and therefore product price increases will slow. This chapter explores the pros and cons of this novel proposal.

Key Economic Points

How can we evaluate the claim that excessive wage increases lie at the heart of inflation?

How would a tax-based incomes policy (TIP) work?

A TIP program is compared with a wage and price control program.

Would TIP by itself reduce or increase the rate of inflation?

Is'TIP an effective program to revise inflationary expectations?

30

Incomes Policy:
A Tip for Fighting Inflation

Beset by a soaring price level, President Carter, late in 1978, announced an innovative program designed to check inflation. The President's new inflation program consisted of voluntary wage and price guidelines, which, of course, were not new, and a proposed real-wage insurance program, which was novel in its conception. The real-wage insurance program would guarantee workers who voluntarily adhered to the wage guidelines against a fall in their real wage should the rate of inflation exceed the price guidelines. In that event, these workers would receive a tax rebate equal to the amount of real income lost to inflation. The real-wage insurance program would, in the President's words, "remove the only legitimate reason not to cooperate with the wage guidelines."

The President chose to install a tax-based incomes policy (TIP) as the heart of his anti-inflation program because the policies employed in the past had either not worked or were considered socially too expensive. Voluntary wage and price guidelines in the recent past had been widely ignored, actual wage and price controls had not worked, and a deliberate recession to halt inflation was rejected as socially too costly.

The Congress of the United States did not approve the President's TIP program and the fight against inflation limped on with only voluntary guidelines as the main battle weapon. The result was that the present decade began with the economy once again suffering from double-digit inflation.

A tax-based incomes policy has been described as the only new idea for combating inflation that has been proposed in the last 20 years. TIP is designed to get to the heart of the inflation problem by creating incentives for business to limit wage increases. Wages, according to this view, are the single most important price in the economy because wages and salaries make up about three-quarters of the costs of production. When wages increase, business firms pass on their increased costs by raising prices. Thus, if wage increases are moderated, so will be the rate of inflation. If any anti-inflation strategy is to be successful, according to the proponents of TIP, it must avoid this upward pressure on the prices from excessive wage increases. TIP would accomplish this by employing taxes to create the incentive to follow the wage guidelines.

A tax-based incomes policy was first proposed a decade ago by Henry Wallich, now a governor of the Federal Reserve system, and Sidney Weintraub, an economics professor at the University of Pennsylvania. Since then many variations of the same basic idea have been put forward. In many ways the Wallich-Weintraub proposal remains the most attractive, and we concentrate upon it in this chapter.

Their proposal would impose a surcharge on the corporate income tax of any large corporation that agreed to grant wage increases to its workers above the national wage guidelines. Thus the business firm that agrees to a labor contract in violation of the guidelines would be penalized by tax increases. The firm would thus have an added incentive to resist granting inflationary wage increases. TIP would work as follows. Suppose the wage guideline is 7 percent. If a corporation grants a 7 percent wage increase, its income rate will remain at the current level. However, if the firm grants a wage increase of 8 percent, the corporation will have a surcharge added to its income tax rate—say 6 percent for every 1 percent wage increase greater than the wage guidelines. A 9 percent wage increase, 2 percent above the guideline, would entail a penalty surcharge of 12 percent. And so on.

The prospect of a TIP tax penalty would provide an additional incentive for management to resist inflationary wage increases above the guidelines. Increased management resistance in labor negotiations should result, on average, in lower wage settlements. These lower wage settlements would quickly be passed on to consumers in the form of lower prices. The lower money wage settlements, therefore, do not result in lower real wages because prices are also lower than they would be in the absence of TIP. TIP would thus reduce inflation without imposing costs on either business or labor. In order to ensure that voluntary compliance with the wage guidelines would not result in a decline in real wages for workers, a wage insurance program, similar to the one proposed by President Carter, could be enacted as part of TIP.

As the inflation rate slows, the wage and price guidelines would be adjusted downward until a zero inflation rate was achieved. Wage increases with a zero rate of inflation would be limited to the rate of labor productivity growth. If wage increases are not to be inflationary, they must be limited to the increase in labor productivity. In recent years a growing gap has appeared between the money wage and the increase in labor productivity. The rate of inflation has, on average, been equal to the difference between money wage increases and the increase in labor productivity. Proponents of TIP cite this historical fact as evidence that inflation will quickly moderate if only a reduction in the rate of wage increases can be accomplished.

Critics of TIP doubt that wage increases per se cause inflation. It can be argued, as labor leaders have argued, that rising prices cause higher wages. More likely both rising prices and excessive wage increases have a common cause: a too high growth rate of the money supply. Recently, TIP proponents appear to have accepted the view that excessive money expansion is the basic cause of inflation, but still see a starring role for a tax-based incomes policy in combating inflation. TIP by itself, it is now admitted, would not control inflation, unless it were accompanied by a tight money policy. What TIP would do, if accompanied by a tight money policy, would be to reduce the social cost of adjusting to a lower rate of inflation.

TIP supporters do not deny that a reduction in the rate of monetary growth would eventually reduce the rate of inflation. They believe, however, that a tight money policy by itself is a lengthy and costly way to fight inflation. The initial effect of a reduced rate of monetary growth is likely to be concentrated in a higher unemployment rate and a lower standard of living before any effect on inflation will be noticed. Thus the economy will be forced to suffer an expensive recession before the inflationary expectations of business and labor abate.

Combining a tight monetary policy with a tax-based incomes policy, supporters suggest, will cause inflationary expectations to adjust more quickly, perhaps sparing the economy a costly recession. They insist that prices are slow to adjust to slower monetary growth because wages, for a time, keep rising independent of what is happening in the economy. The price expectations of labor are based on past experience, so that workers and unions insist upon inflationary wage increases until a rising rate of unemployment proves these expectations unfounded. TIP proponents propose to use taxes to break the inflation expectations of labor. As inflationary wage increases abate, the rate of price increases will also slow.

TIP supporters suggest that a tax-based incomes policy is superior to outright wage and price controls as a program to contain inflationary expectations. Controls inhibit the freedom of business and labor to make their own wage and price decisions, and they stop the reallocation of resources in response to market forces. The economic consequences of wage and price controls can be fairly severe. The essence of TIP is that it differs fundamentally from the usual kind of wage and price controls. Business and labor are free to bargain for any wage income they choose. Only the weight of market forces is changed, with the tax surcharge doing the weighting. The TIP penalty for exceeding the wage guidelines is significant but not prohibitive. Where market forces call for a relative wage increase to attract labor to an expanding industry, TIP allows this to be done as long as the tax penalty is paid. Wage controls would not allow this change to even take place. If those who favor TIP are correct, their program would cut the costs of employing a tight monetary policy, avoid the serious inefficiency of wage and price controls, and achieve its aim—a lower rate of inflation.

But not all economists believe that TIP will work as its supporters suggest. Some economists suggest that the TIP surcharges would simply be passed on to consumers in the form of higher prices. Others think that TIP would impose an unfair burden on labor. Still others feel that TIP is in reality a form of wage controls that would require a large bureaucracy to administer and still be unenforceable.

The supporters of TIP deny that a business firm paying a tax surcharge for granting an excessive wage increase would be able to pass on its costs as higher prices. The surcharge is levied on net income or profits, and a profits tax is notoriously hard to pass on in the form of higher prices. But critics suggest that in reality the surcharge is a tax on labor because it is only paid when excessive wage increases are granted. A firm attempting to expand will have to offer higher wages to attract workers. Besides the higher wages, the firm will have to pay the tax penalty. As a result, expanding firms will hire less labor than they would in the absence of TIP. They will offer fewer goods for sale and command a higher price for what they do sell. Therefore, according to the critics, the effect of TIP will be to reduce wages (unfair to labor) but increase prices (not reduce inflation), thus destroying the normally stable wage–price relationship relied on by TIP proponents.

Still other critics feel that a TIP program is unenforceable because business and labor have ample room to maneuver to avoid the tax. A firm might disguise a wage increase as another business cost. An employee, for example, could be provided a company automobile in lieu of a wage increase. Or a business firm could reduce the work day to 7 hours and pay overtime for the eighth hour of work each day. Whatever the methods employed, business firms would have a strong incentive to reduce their TIP tax payments. TIP supporters counter with the expert opinion of tax administrators who think that they can do the job.

Both the proponents and opponents of TIP have the same goal: to lower the rate of inflation. Although they obviously disagree about the prospective effectiveness of a tax-based incomes policy in achieving the goal, both sides would agree that TIP is the only new idea for dealing with inflation to be proposed in some time. There is some doubt as to whether it is a good idea or not.

Additional Readings

Gillum, G. P. "TIP Is Not the Answer to Inflation." *Business Review,* Federal Reserve Bank of Philadelphia, January–February 1980.

Jianakoplos, N. A. "A Tax-Based Incomes Policy (TIP): What's It All About?" *Review,* Federal Reserve Bank of St. Louis, February 1978.

Miller, P. "TIP: The Wrong Way to Fight Inflation." *Quarterly Review,* Federal Reserve Bank of Minneapolis, Spring 1978.

Seidman, L. "Fighting Inflation With a Tax-Based Incomes Policy." *Business Review,* Federal Reserve Bank of Philadelphia, January–February 1980.

Preview

The 1978 Humphrey-Hawkins Bill set for our country ambitious goals for simultaneous reduction in both the unemployment rate and the rate of inflation. This bill left it to the President and Congress to design and implement a means for achieving these goals. This task, although not easy, is by no means impossible. This chapter employs the modern theory of unemployment to identify and analyze the steps that might be taken to allow the economy to meet the goals of Humphrey-Hawkins.

Key Economic Points

The unemployment rate does not measure the unavailability of jobs but rather the extent to which the labor force is between jobs.

The full-employment unemployment rate limits the effectiveness of fiscal or monetary policy in reducing the rate of unemployment.

What specific factors have caused the full-employment unemployment rate to rise in the last two decades?

The unemployment rate goal set by the Humphrey-Hawkins Bill requires that the full-employment rate of unemployment be reduced.

31

Unemployment and Inflation: Meeting the Goals Set by Humphrey-Hawkins

The Humphrey-Hawkins Full-Employment Act was overwhelmingly passed by both houses of Congress and signed into law by the President in October 1978. The most widely known feature of this legislation is to set as a national goal the reduction of the rate of unemployment to below 4 percent by 1983. In addition, this bill sets as a national goal the reduction of the rate of inflation to 3 percent by 1985 and to zero by 1988. In order to meet these goals, the existing trend in both the unemployment rate and the rate of inflation will have to be reversed. The average rate of unemployment during the 1950s was 4.5 percent, during the 1960s it was 4.8 percent, but during the 1970s the average rate of unemployment soared to 6.2 percent. The rate of inflation during the decade of the 1950s averaged 2.2 percent, during the 1960s 2.5 percent, but during the 1970s over 7.3 percent. The Humphrey-Hawkins Bill thus legislated ambitious goals but initiated no new programs, leaving it up to the President and Congress to determine the best means of accomplishing these goals.

The determination of the best means of accomplishing these goals is no small task. Recent developments in the theory of unemployment suggest that designing a program to reduce the unemployment rate to less than 4 percent without simultaneously causing the rate of inflation to accelerate, while not impossible, will require the restructuring of past government policies and programs. In this chapter, the modern theory of unemployment is used to identify and analyze the steps that might be taken if the goals of Humphrey-Hawkins are to become a reality.

In order to do this, it is necessary to first clear up a common misconception as to what the rate of unemployment actually measures. Next, the different types of unemployment are identified and the concept of full-employment rate of unemployment is discussed. The question of why the unemployment rate is currently so high at full employment is then addressed. Finally it becomes possible to discuss the steps that must be taken to reduce the unemployment rate to below 4 percent without simultaneously increasing the rate of inflation.

It is a common misconception that the unemployment rate measures the percentage of the labor force for whom there are no jobs available. In fact, the unemployment rate is a more accurate indicator of the extent to which the labor force is in transition between jobs than it is a measure of job unavailability. An individual is considered unemployed by the Bureau of Labor Statistics if he or she does not have a job and is actively looking for one or has been laid off and is waiting to be recalled. There are always some people who are temporarily between jobs, having voluntarily left old jobs and are about to take new jobs, and some people who are on temporary lay-offs and are soon to be recalled. It is not unusual, for these reasons, that more than half of the unemployed during prosperous times are out of work for less than 5 weeks. Unemployment for most people is a temporary affair—a period of time spent waiting or searching for an acceptable job opportunity. Persons who voluntarily pass up lower paying jobs to wait or search for a better job are called the frictionally unemployed.

Besides frictional unemployment, there is another kind of unemployment called structural unemployment. In the American economy there are always some industries that are expanding and some that are contracting. If, for example, consumers decide to purchase more television sets and fewer books, workers will be laid off in the printing trades at the same time that more workers are being hired by television manufacturers. It takes time for the newly unemployed printers to find other acceptable jobs. Persons who are temporarily unemployed for this reason are known as the structurally unemployed.

Some frictional and structural unemployment is desirable in a free, unregimented society that values highly the freedom to choose when and where a person is going to work, and the freedom to spend income as an individual chooses. Given this freedom of choice, some people will always be between jobs and others temporarily unemployed as the economy fluctuates, reallocating resources to better correspond to the demands of consumers. Furthermore, both types of unemployment will occur even when there are sufficient jobs available to reemploy everyone because it takes time to match people with jobs.

This is not to suggest that unemployment cannot impose severe financial hardships on some people. Even during prosperous times, one unemployed worker in twelve is out of work for 6 months or more. The unemployment rate, however, is not a good measure of the extent of this suffering. The unemployment rate does not, for example, include the workers who have grown weary of looking for a suitable job and are no longer actively searching for employment. During the 1970s there were on average over 1 million of these discouraged workers. Discouraged workers, instead of being counted among the unemployed, are classified along with children, housewives, and the retired as non-labor-market participants. The unemployment rate is simply not a good measure of the extent to which jobs are unavailable; rather, it is a better measure of the extent to which the labor force is in transition between jobs.

When the number of frictionally and structurally unemployed persons equals the number of job vacancies, the rate of unemployment is said to be at the full-employment unemployment rate (FEUR) or, as it is sometimes called, the natural rate of unemployment. There are enough jobs for all the unemployed, but they haven't found them yet. Another way to view the full-employment unemployment rate is as the unemployment rate that determines the capacity of the economy to produce goods and services. Any attempt to reduce the unemployment rate below this natural rate of unemployment will result in increasing the rate of inflation rather than expanding real gross national product.

Crucial to the problem of developing a program to achieve the goals set by Humphrey-Hawkins is the determination of the current full-employment rate of unemployment. If the current FEUR is greater than the 4 percent Humphrey-Hawkins goal, then attempts to reduce the unemployment rate by conventional fiscal and monetary policies will result in increasing the rate of inflation, which would make the inflation rate goal unattainable.

During the 1950s and 1960s the full-employment unemployment rate was estimated to be about 4.0 percent. Recent studies now find that the original figure was probably too low and that 4.8 percent more accurately measures the natural rate of unemployment at that time.

But whatever the FEUR may have been two decades ago, the full-employment unemployment rate today is substantially higher. The Council of Economic Advisors has calculated that the 1978 FEUR, comparable to the 4.0 percent of the 1950s, was 4.9 percent. Further indications suggest that factors in the current market could push the natural rate of unemployment to 5.5 percent or even higher. A somewhat higher figure would be consistent with the findings of other economists who place the current natural rate of unemployment somewhere between 5.5 and 6.0 percent.

The rise in the FEUR since the 1950s is the result, according to these studies, of changes in the composition of the labor force and institutional factors that influence how people conduct job searches. The composition of the labor force is important because there are large differences in the unemployment rates experienced by different groups identified by age, sex, race, and marital status. As the proportion of the labor force that experience high unemployment rates increases, so will the FEUR. Institutional factors, such as the minimum wage, unemployment insurance, and subsidies, will also affect the duration of unemployment and therefore the FEUR.

How have these factors that influence the full-employment rate of unemployment changed since the 1950s? Married men, for example, have more stable employment patterns than other groups in the labor force. However, their proportion of the labor force has declined. This decline is the result of increased numbers of teenagers and young adults entering the work force and the increased participation of adult women in the labor force. Both groups have historically experienced relatively high rates of unemployment. Teenagers and young adults as a group are quite mobile and are relatively frequently in transition between jobs and nonmarket activities, such as attending school. Many have financial support from their families and seek part-time or short-term jobs rather than career opportunities. Consequently, the group as a whole exhibits a higher rate of unemployment. In the past two decades teenagers and young adults have increased as a proportion of the labor force from 15 to 24 percent; as a consequence the FEUR has increased.

Women as a group have also increased as a proportion of the labor force, from 28 percent two decades ago to 35 percent during the 1970s. This increase is largely the result of the rise in the participation rate for women in the labor force, from a third to almost half of all adult women. Adult women as a group, partially because they are often the second wage earner in a family and because they often have strong family obligations, experience unemployment rates much higher than those of adult males, voluntarily entering and leaving the labor force more frequently than their male counterparts.

As teenagers, young adults, and adult women increased as a proportion of the labor force, the FEUR increased. One estimate suggests that the FEUR has increased by 0.46 percent as a consequence of these shifts in the composition of the labor force.

Institutional factors have also been at work that tend to increase the natural or full-employment rate of unemployment either by encouraging longer periods of job search for the unemployed or by making it more difficult for certain groups to find jobs.

The Fair Labor Standards Act, usually known as the minimum wage law, makes it more difficult for teenagers and young adults to find jobs, increasing the time spent before finding a job. The minimum wage reduces the number of jobs available to low-skilled workers, predominantly teenagers and young adults with little work experience whose work efforts are not worth the mandated minimum wage. The effect of the minimum wage may be to raise the FEUR by 0.5 percent.

Welfare recipients, in order to qualify for continued assistance, are now required to register as available for work, whether in fact they are or not. Thus many welfare-receiving mothers are counted among the unemployed when they are not actively looking for work. Possibly another 0.2 percent of the increase in the FEUR is attributable to the work registration requirement.

Another major factor that has increased FEUR has been the extension and liberalization of unemployment insurance benefits. Unemployment insurance benefits during 1975, for example, were extended to seasonal workers. An even more important factor has been the liberalization of benefits. If a person qualifies for unemployment compensation, the price of leisure is much lower than if the unemployed worker does not qualify. Therefore, workers covered by unemployment compensation are more likely to take the time to paint the house, or go hunting or fishing when laid off than immediately search for work. Furthermore, as the difference between a worker's take-home pay and unemployment benefits narrows, the incentive to obtain a new job declines while unemployment benefits last. Expanded benefits that reduce the cost of leisure may have increased the FEUR by as much as 0.55 percentage point.

Because of these changes in demographic and institutional factors, the full-employment rate of unemployment today may be as high as 5.6 to 6.3 percent. When the unemployment rate rises above this figure, as it did during the recessions of 1975 and 1980, then another type of unemployment, called cyclical unemployment, exists alongside the frictional and structural unemployment. Cyclical unemployment is created when the total demand for the economy's goods and services falls below the amount the nation's businesses desire to produce. Cyclical unemployment is the source of any excess unemployment above the full-employment unemployment rate. The government by employing fiscal or monetary policy to stimulate the total demand for the economy's output may be able to reduce cyclical unemployment and push the unemployment rate down to the natural level.

Once the natural rate of unemployment is reached, a completely different set of policies must be employed if the rate of unemployment is to be permanently reduced further. Once the economy is at the full-employment unemployment rate the only way to lower long-term unemployment is to reduce the natural rate itself. Since the current FEUR is approximately 2 percentage points greater than the goal set by the Humphrey-Hawkins Bill, appropriate government policies designed to meet this goal must be directed at reducing the full-employment unemployment rate.

While the government cannot affect the demographic characteristics of its people that cause the FEUR to be higher, the passage of time can affect demographics. The American population is aging, and therefore the number of youths (16–24) will decline during the 1980s in absolute numbers and as a percentage of the labor force. If labor force participation rates remain constant through 1985, the FEUR could decline by a full percentage point because of aging. If, however, participation rates increase, as they have in the recent past, the FEUR decline will be closer to a half percentage point. The aging of the U.S. population will by itself cause the reduction of the FEUR during the 1980s.

The full-employment unemployment rate could also be lowered by elimination or reduction of the minimum wage. Potentially another 0.5 percentage point could be shaved off the FEUR by eliminating this restriction on the ability of young persons to find jobs. Similarly, the elimination of the recent increases and extensions of unemployment compensation benefits could reduce the FEUR by a full percentage point. Such institutional changes are, however, likely to be highly controversial.

Also controversial, but less effective, would be the elimination of the mandatory work registration requirement for welfare mothers who otherwise would not be looking for work, reducing the FEUR by 0.2 percentage point. The government could also introduce effective manpower programs to reduce the amount of structural unemployment, as a means of helping the unemployed in locating and qualifying for available jobs. Such programs might be able to reduce the FEUR by another 0.3 percentage point.

Thus it is feasible for the President and Congress to design a comprehensive program that, in combination with demographic changes, will lower the full-employment unemployment rate below 4 percent. Such a program would require the repeal or modification of the minimum wage law, the reduction of unemployment compensation benefits, the elimination of the mandatory work registration requirement for welfare mothers, and the implementation of an effective manpower training program. This combination of policy changes and programs along with demographic developments could reduce the FEUR by 2.5 to 3.0 percentage points, or well below the goal of 4 percent unemployment. These changes would then allow fiscal and monetary policy to be used, if needed, to reduce the unemployment rate to the FEUR without causing the rate of inflation to accelerate.

Additional Readings

Cagan, Phillip. "The Reduction of Inflation and the Magnitude of Unemployment." *Contemporary Economic Problems, 1977*, W. Fellner, ed. American Enterprise Institute, 1977.

McElhatten, Rose. "Fully Employed?" *Weekly Letter*, Federal Reserve Bank of San Francisco, March 17, 1978.

Pearce, James E. "The Rise In Unemployment Since the 1950s." *Voice*, Federal Reserve Bank of Dallas, January 1979.

Seater, John J. "Coping With Unemployment." *Business Review*, Federal Reserve Bank of Philadelphia, January–February 1977.

VI

ECONOMIC GROWTH AND INTERNATIONAL TRADE

Preview

The rate of economic growth in the United States has slowed significantly during the last decade. If this trend continues it means that the standard of living for modern Americans will not rise as rapidly as it did for our forefathers. The reason that the economy is not growing as rapidly today as in the past is because the rate of productivity increase has fallen. But why this occurred remains a mystery. In this chapter the sources of economic growth are explored. In particular, the reasons that have been suggested for the decline in production are examined.

Key Economic Points

Two ways that our economy can grow are identified.

The main determinants of productivity change remain unknown.

There are two possible explanations for the decline in productivity growth: (1) it is the result of a combination of small effects or (2) it is the result of a factor that also affected the world economy.

How could a specific factor in the world economy result in reduced productivity growth in the United States?

32

Economic Growth: The Mystery of the Recent Decline in U.S. Productivity

Economic growth in the United States has slowed dramatically during the past decade. This is a cause for concern because it was the rapid economic growth of the past that had raised the standard of living of Americans to the present high level. National income per person employed in the private sector had increased, during the quarter century that spanned the years 1948–1973, by an average of 2.4 percent a year. This average rate of growth may on first sight appear unimpressive, but it translates into a doubling of income every generation. Had this rate of growth continued, productivity and income would in 1979 have been about 16 percent greater than it was in 1973. Instead, in 1979, the national level of productivity was actually below the 1973 level.

The decline in productivity has potentially serious consequences for all Americans. Should the decline in productivity, which has averaged about 0.5 percent between 1973 and 1976, continue, our standard of living will actually begin to fall. Solving the mystery of the causes of the decline in productivity would allow the opportunity for appropriate steps to be taken to remedy the situation. Failure to solve the mystery, should the decline continue, will have policy makers fumbling in the dark for a solution.

Economic growth can come about in many ways. The growth of the nation's output can be obtained by employing more factors of production, which is called extensive growth, or by increasing the output obtained from a given quantity of factors, which is termed intensive growth. Extensive growth would be affected by changes in the level of employment, working hours, and in the average level of skills of the labor force. Also, changes in the quantity of capital or the amount of resources available will affect extensive growth. Intensive growth represents a change in the efficiency with which the factors of production can be transformed into outputs. Technological change (improvements in the state of knowledge), changes in the efficiency of resource allocation, and economies of scale, among other things, determine the amount of output obtainable from a given quantity of inputs.

It is fairly easy to measure the growth of national income per person employed in the private sector by simply dividing the change in national income by the change in employment. Edward Denison has done this calculation. He found that the annual rate of productivity increase for the period 1948–1973 was 2.43 percent. He found that it was much more difficult to appropriate to each of the determining forces its proper share of the total. Denison was able to account for only a bit more than two-fifths of the total 2.43 percent. He found that increased educational levels of workers, increases in the amount of capital per worker, improved resource allocation, and economies of scale contributed to rapid growth during this period. The rate of growth would have been even larger except for reductions in the average hours of work and shifts in the composition of the labor force toward younger and less experienced workers. Nevertheless, 1.41 percent, or almost three-fifths, of the 2.43 percent growth rate remained unassigned among the possible sources of economic growth. Denison believes that this unexplained residual is mainly accounted for by "advances in knowledge," the gains in measured output that results from technological change or from improvements in managerial efficiency.

This unexplained residual category accounted for most of the growth between 1948 and 1973. This same category accounted for most of the decline in growth during the 1970s. The residual showed an almost constant growth rate during the quarter century ending in 1973 because the determinants that can be measured directly account for most of the irregularities in productivity growth over the period. But after 1973, the residual departs abruptly from past experience. The change in productivity assigned to the residual category, instead of showing a more or less constant growth of 1.4 percent, declined by a −0.75 percent between 1973 and 1976, years for which data are available. Preliminary data for the years 1977–1979 suggest that this decline has continued.

The mystery is why the forces, as yet unidentified, that are lumped into the residual category stopped contributing to productivity growth after 1973 and actually became a negative factor. Solving the mystery is not made easier by the fact that the identities of these factors remain unknown.

The mystery of the declining productivity of the U.S. economy has not suffered from a lack of detectives. Denison reports no less than 17 possible solutions or hypotheses that have been suggested by his fellow economists, the most popular of these was the "people don't want to work hard anymore" explanation. The problem with this explanation is that it has been heard for generations and is heard today in such unlikely places as Japan and West Germany. Furthermore, it was probably true each time it was heard. After all, who has ever wanted to work hard? The difficulty with this explanation lies in the timing; the observation is ages old, but the decline in productivity begins in the 1970s.

The same problem with timing argues against the following suggested explanations: the decline in productivity is due to (1) a decline in Yankee ingenuity or (2) a decline in the opportunities for major new advances in the state of knowledge. The first possibility is that Americans are not as inventive as they used to be, which may or may not be true, but it is unlikely that this deficiency would suddenly develop in 1973. The second possible explanation suggests that diminishing returns to the existing stock of basic scientific knowledge is occurring. According to this hypothesis, most of the possibilities for increasing productivity that were available from existing knowledge have already been exploited. Subsequent advances will be less productive until major new scientific discoveries are made. Again, this possible development may be true or false, but if it is true, then the effect upon productivity is apt to be gradual and would not suddenly appear in 1973.

A much larger number of proposed solutions to the mystery fail individually because their individual effect is too small. The following proposed explanations are suspect for this reason: the decline in investment expenditures devoted to research and development; the delay in the application of new knowledge because the rate of capital accumulation has slowed; the diversion of resources away from productivity-increasing activities to comply with government regulations and, in particular, the diversion of managerial resources in this fashion; the delay in undertaking new investments because of government regulations; the increase in government-required paperwork; the disincentive effects of high tax rates and, in particular, the capital gains tax; the rise of monopoly with the consequent decline in competitive pressures to be efficient; and the shift of resources into the service sector where possible productivity gains are limited.

This is not to suggest that the above developments did not retard the rate of economic growth. It is possible that everything went wrong at once and that each of the possible explanations subtracted a bit from the growth rate, the result of which was a substantial decline in productivity.

There is, however, a further clue that should be considered. The decline in productivity in the United States, while of particular interest to Americans, is not unique to this country. Every major industrialized country has to varying degrees experienced the same decline. This development suggests that if a major cause of the decline in productivity is to be found, it will be a factor that affected the world economy, not just the United States. There are two possibilities: the energy crisis with the consequent rapid rise in fuel prices, and the onset of a worldwide inflation. In both instances the timing is correct and the effect worldwide. The Organization of Petroleum Exporting Countries (OPEC) began to increase oil prices significantly during 1973 and inflation was recognized as a worldwide problem at about the same time.

The rapid increase in energy prices after 1973 would be expected to have the following effects upon the developed economies of the world. The prices of goods that use a relatively large amount of the now more expensive energy to produce will rise more rapidly than the prices of goods that use less energy to produce. Consumers and businesses will tend to substitute the relatively less expensive goods for the now more expensive energy-intensive goods. The costs of adjusting to such a change in consumer and business demand may show up in the form of reduced productivity. Furthermore, within the business sector, firms will try to substitute other resources for the relatively expensive energy. In the short run, there are more possibilities to substitute labor for energy than to substitute capital for energy, since energy and capital are closely allied in the production process. Thus the initial effect of rising prices is to encourage the more intensive use of labor until more energy-efficient capital goods are developed and installed. The decline in the availability of capital and energy per unit of labor would be reflected in a decline in labor productivity. Higher energy prices represent a once and for all decline in productivity, hence in the potential income of the economy.

Does the sharp rise in energy prices account for the decline in productivity? Some empirical studies suggest that it does. In fact, according to these studies, higher energy prices would account for all of the observed decline in productivity. It would be doubly satisfying to accept this explanation because it would not only solve the mystery of declining productivity, it would also be reassuring about the future. The decline in productivity would be limited to the period required to adjust the capital stock to the fact of relatively higher energy prices. Once that was accomplished, the economy probably would return to the previous trend of productivity growth, barring, of course, future petroleum price increases.

Unfortunately, not all economists agree with this explanation. And their contrary opinion is also based upon empirical research. These studies suggest that the effect of higher energy prices accounts for about 0.1 percent of the decline in productivity, or about one-twentieth of the total decline. The fact that there have been several investigations of the effects of higher energy prices upon productivity should not create the false impression that the subject has been exhaustively studied. It hasn't. While all economists agree that the effect of higher energy prices has been to reduce the productivity of the economy, they do not agree about how much of the decline is attributable to higher energy prices. The range of opinion runs from all of it to no more than any of the numerous negative factors dismissed above as not significant enough to account for much of the decline.

The second worldwide phenomenon that might account for the mysterious decline in productivity is inflation. Although inflation in the United States dates from 1966, it became recognized as a persistent problem early in the 1970s. The public recognition of the problem, here as well as abroad, in the form of anticipation of future inflation can be reasonably dated as beginning in 1973.

The fundamental function of the price system is to provide, at low social cost, the information decision makers require in order to make fundamental economic decisions: which goods and services to produce, and how much of each; how to produce each good and service; and how to employ the factors of production. The information required is knowledge of relative prices: the price of one product compared with the prices of others, the cost of one factor of production relative to others, and the present prices of goods relative to their prices in the future.

This information is transmitted in absolute prices, for example, so many dollars a pound. If the overall price level is not changing or is changing at a steady, expected rate, it is relatively easy for individuals to compute the relative prices from observed absolute prices. However, when the rate of inflation is high and fluctuating, it becomes much more difficult to extract the relative price signals from the distortions created by inflation. Inflation thus interferes with the market's ability to provide the information required to make correct economic decisions and renders the economy less efficient.

This source of inefficiency is reinforced by legal restrictions on price changes. The government is itself a producer of goods and services, from postal services to electricity. Other prices are regulated by government and cannot be changed without prior approval. These range from public utilities, to airline and taxicab fares. Labor unions as well as business enterprises are locked into long-term contracts. These restrictions, during periods of rapid and fluctuating inflation, limit the ability of the price system to accurately reflect and transmit reliable information about relative scarcities in the economy. That a volatile inflation rate impairs productivity seems certain, but no one seems to know by how much it may have done so after 1973.

The mystery of the decline in productivity remains unsolved so far. The number of potential suspects is large, but inflation and the rise in energy prices appear more likely to be guilty than the others. The possibility remains, however, that most, or perhaps all, of the listed suspects are to some extent guilty of causing the decline in productivity. Each reduced the rate of productivity change a small amount, but when totaled they could account for the whole crime.

CHAPTER 32

Additional Readings

Bennett, Paul. "American Productivity Growth: Perspectives on the Slowdown." *Quarterly Review,* Federal Reserve Bank of New York, Autumn 1979, pp. 25–31.

Burke, William. "The Mystery." *Weekly Letter,* Federal Reserve Bank of San Francisco, November 2, 1979.

Denison, Edward F. "Explanations of Declining Productivity Growth." *The Survey of Current Business,* Department of Commerce, August 1979, Part II, pp. 1–23.

Hannan, T. "The Productivity Perplex: A Concern For the Supply Side." *Business Review,* Federal Reserve Bank of Philadelphia, March–April 1980.

Perry, George L. *Potential Output: Recent Issues and Present Trends.* Reprint 336 of the Brookings Institution.

Rascle, Robert H., and John A. Tatum. "The Effects of the New Energy Regime on Economic Capacity, Production, and Prices." *Review,* Federal Reserve Bank of St. Louis, May 1977.

Tatum, J. A. "The Productivity Problem." *Review,* Federal Reserve Bank of St. Louis, September 1979.

Preview

The United States, until recently, has been firmly committed to reducing the barriers to international trade. The belief has been that there were significant gains to be earned from following the principle of comparative advantage. Recently, however, organized labor has joined with management in certain key industries to lobby for increased protection from foreign corporations. They cite the loss of thousands of jobs as the reason protection is needed. The loss of jobs due to importing is but one side of the coin; the other is the gain in employment in the expanding export sector. This chapter investigates the effect of increases in foreign trade on domestic employment and identifies the winners and losers from trade. The gains from trade are benefits that all enjoy, but the costs of the necessary reallocation of resources fall on a few. The gains from trade are net gains, but the costs should not be ignored. It is the costs that stir opposition to free trade. Existing and proposed programs to share and reduce these costs are considered.

Key Economic Points

There are gains from trade inherent in following comparative advantage.

Why does organized labor now oppose foreign trade?

The loss of jobs due to foreign trade is weighed against the resulting gain in employment opportunities.

The costs of reallocating workers falls on a particular group.

The benefits of a program for sharing the costs of resource reallocation resulting from foreign trade are weighed.

33

Gains from Trade: The Coming Political Assault on Free Trade

Until relatively recently, the trend in the world has been toward freer trade. This was especially true in the United States, whose leaders have been instrumental in pushing the world's governments toward fewer trade restrictions. Our leaders were reflecting the views of business and labor that free trade was beneficial to all.

This consensus began to break down in the late 1960s when some labor leaders began to actively oppose further tariff reductions and the removal of other restrictive trade measures. In 1967, union leaders joined with the steel industry in supporting the imposition of import quotas on foreign steel. Organized labor itself had completely reversed its position by 1973, when AFL-CIO President George Meany publicly opposed free-trade policies. Labor's new opposition to free trade was based on the alleged loss of jobs that free trade had caused. The AFL-CIO estimated that the reduction of tariff barriers had cost U.S. workers 1 million jobs. Labor was joined by the management of several industries that still faced foreign competition. Executives of the steel, textile, shoe, and consumer electronics industries lobbied actively for increased protection from foreign competition.

The latest union to change its mind about the benefits of free trade is the United Auto Workers (UAW). Early in 1980, slumping sales of domestically produced automobiles had indefinitely idled 25 percent of the

UAW's 750,000 members. Union leaders feared that many of these layoffs could become permanent if imported cars continued to expand their sales in the United States at the expense of Detroit-built automobiles. Imported cars, mostly from Japan, had captured 27 percent of all new car sales in the United States and their share was increasing.

In an attempt to avoid an enormous loss of jobs, the union has reversed its traditional free-trade philosophy and is seeking restrictive legislation to stem the tide of imports. There are signs that the manufacturers themselves, previously favoring free trade, are about to join the union's efforts and urge that import cars be assigned quotas. The UAW's position is that either imports should be restrained or foreign producers should be required to manufacture in the United States at least 75 percent of each car they sell here.

The benefits of free trade between nations have been known since the days of the classical economists. Adam Smith, David Ricardo and John Stuart Mill each stressed the advantages that would accrue to nations which allowed their foreign commerce to remain unfettered by tariffs, taxes, or restrictive legislation. The gains from free trade were revealed by applying the principle of comparative advantage: nations of the world would benefit most if countries everywhere were allowed to specialize in those goods which they produced with the greatest relative efficiency. All nations, whether rich or poor, would gain from free mutual trade because no nation, no matter how efficient, would possess a comparative advantage in producing every good it desires to consume.

While the principle of comparative advantage is the cornerstone of modern economic thought, it has not become a basic principle of political action. Benjamin Disraeli, the English statesman, once said, "Free trade is not a principle. It is an expedient. . . . Protection is not a principle but an expedient." History has proven Disraeli correct, for the world has on several occasions turned toward free trade when it became expedient, and turned away when it was no longer so.

An important factor in the arguments of labor and industry for the rejection of continued free trade was the resulting loss of jobs for American workers as imported goods replaced domestically produced ones. There is no doubt that there have been job losses, especially in the iron and steel industry, clothing and shoe industry, automobile industry, and television manufacturing industry. Entire factories employing thousands of workers in these industries have been closed, in some cases threatening the continued existence of the towns or cities in which the closed factories were located.

The loss of jobs to foreign competition is, of course, only one side of the free-trade coin, but it is a highly visible side. The other side of the coin is the jobs created by expanding export industries and the added wealth created by free trade. A country exports for only one reason—so that it can in turn purchase goods produced by a foreign country. A foreign country

GAINS FROM TRADE

sells to the United States so that it can buy goods in the United States and other countries with the proceeds. Because nations export in order to import, jobs must be created in the United States by foreign trade at the same time as jobs are lost due to imports. Whether on balance more jobs are lost than created is both a theoretical and empirical question that is considered below.

There is no question that every nation in the world is better off as a consequence of participating in foreign trade. This conclusion is implied by the principle of comparative advantage which governs trade. As foreign trade expands, and nations gain and lose comparative advantage, resources must be reallocated. This requires that labor and capital move from occupations that are less productive to activities that are more productive.

International trade has become a more important part of the economic activity of the United States. Imports as a percentage of gross national product (GNP) increased by 46 percent between 1960 and 1975, rising from 4.6 percent of GNP to 6.7 percent. The rising importance of international trade has required some resources to be reallocated in the U.S. economy. Jobs have been lost in the sectors that face increasing competition from imports while other jobs have been created in the export sector.

Federal Reserve economist C. B. Luttrell has studied the effects of increasing foreign trade on the total level of employment in the United States. Luttrell's estimates of jobs lost is presented in Table 1. Column 1

Table 1

Number of Employees in Domestic Industries with Rising Competition from Imports and Jobs Lost in These Industries from Imports (thousands)

Industry group	(1) Actual number 1964–1965 (annual average)	(2) Number required for 1975–1976 purchases assuming no change in percentage imported	(3) Actual number 1975–1976 (annual average)	(4) Estimated loss from increased imports
Radio and TV receiving equipment	124	139.3	125	14.3
Automobiles	743	809.0	742	67.0
Blast furnaces and basic steel products	641	561.0	544	17.0
Iron and steel foundries	220	227.9	221	6.9
Clothing	1,332	1,306.7	1,267	39.7
Footwear, except rubber	236	185.7	166	19.7
Mining	634	849.5	764	85.5
Total	3,930	4,079.1	3,829	250.1

Source: C. B. Luttrell, "Imports and Jobs — The Observed and the Unobserved." *Review,* Federal Reserve Bank of St. Louis, June 1978, p. 4.

presents the average annual employment by industry for 1964–1965. Column 2 shows the estimated number of workers required to produce the amount of goods domestically that were consumed in 1975–1976. Column 3 gives the average number of workers actually employed in 1975–1976 in these industries. The difference between what it would have taken to produce the goods consumed in that year and the actual number of U.S. workers employed is the jobs lost to foreign imports. This is shown in column 4.

Mining and the automobile industry suffered the biggest losses in potential jobs. In percentage terms, radio and television reception equipment lost 10 percent of the potential jobs available, footwear 11 percent, mining 10 percent, automobiles 8 percent, and the other industries about 3 percent. In all, 250,000 jobs were lost to import competition during the decade.

Countering this loss of jobs was the expansion of employment opportunities in an expanding export sector. Table 2 provides estimates of the jobs created in this sector. The industry that has gained most from expanding exports has been farming. Almost as many jobs were created in agriculture as were lost in the manufacturing sector because of competition from imported goods. In total, more jobs were created in export industries than were lost to imports for a net gain of almost 120,000 jobs.

These estimates are in line with what would be theoretically expected.

Table 2

Number of Employees in Industries with Sizable Gains in Net Exports

Industry Group	(1) Actual number of employees, 1964–1965 (annual average)	(2) Number of employees in 1975–1976 assuming 1964–1965 levels of exports	(3) Actual number of employees, 1975–1976 (annual average)	(4) Estimated gain in direct employment from increased exports
Transport equipment other than new automobiles	939	905.0	949	44.0
Nonelectrical machinery	1,674	2,013.9	2,072	58.1
Chemicals	893	1,016.2	1,023	6.8
Food, live animals, soybeans, and textile fibers	4,442	3,103.1	3,339	235.9
Professional, scientific, photo, and controlling instruments	379	494.7	499	4.3
Textiles other than clothing	912	913.6	934	20.4
Total	9,239	8,446.5	8,816	369.5

Source: C. B. Luttrell, "Imports and Jobs — The Observed and the Unobserved." *Review,* Federal Reserve Bank of St. Louis, June 1978, p. 8.

Free international trade would be expected not to permanently reduce the overall employment in the United States or elsewhere. The dollar earned by foreign countries by selling goods in the U.S. market must eventually be spent in the United States, creating jobs as a result. Any tendency for industries facing increased foreign competition to reduce employment will likely be offset by the expansion of jobs in the export sector.

The reallocation of resources in the United States in response to increased trade has also doubtless created gains in economic well-being for Americans. These gains come from the greater specialization of resources that result from following the principle of comparative advantage.

The leaders in the movement to overthrow free trade as U.S. policy have fallen into a logical fallacy of composition, reasoning that what is true for the part must therefore be true for the whole. Since radio and television manufacturing, iron and steel production, and clothing and shoe manufacturing have lost jobs to foreign competition, the whole economy must also have lost employment opportunities. This reasoning ignores the expansion of job opportunities in the export sector.

Fallacious reasoning, of course, is not responsible for the increasing opposition to free trade. Exposing a fallacy of composition will not cause the opposition to change its opinions. The gains from trade are net gains. The costs of reallocating resources have so far been ignored in the above analysis. These costs are real and fall upon a few, while the benefits of free trade are general and shared by almost everyone. It is reasonable to expect those who are obliged to shift occupations to resist the required changes.

It is not easy for a Youngstown, Ohio steelworker who has lost his job to become a Boeing assembly line worker in Seattle. Nor can a garment worker become a computer programmer overnight. Individuals, while following their occupations, acquire skills that are in many cases specific to that job. When their industry loses its comparative advantage, these specific skills become worthless. Such persons are not rendered better off by the increased specialization that accompanies a growing foreign trade. In the words of Sol C. Chalkin, President of the International Ladies Garment Workers Union, one of the unions threatened by foreign competition: "The real world is composed of men and women who can't become electronic or hydraulic specialists, who aren't slim and trim and don't have a great command of the language. These people (I represent them) have to work and they are entitled to decent worthwhile jobs."

Comparative advantage is established primarily because of differences in relative factor proportions between trading partners. The United States, in comparison with most of the world, is heavily endowed with capital, highly skilled labor, and land suitable for agriculture. It is little wonder that the U.S. export industries that are expanding are those that use the resources we have in relative abundance. Nor should it come as a surprise that the industries threatened by imports are those that do not rely heavily on these resources.

A recent study of the industries affected by foreign trade found that those favorably affected employed, in large proportion, highly skilled, educated workers whose wage was above the national average. Industries that were adversely affected by foreign trade on average employed fewer skilled workers and paid less than the national average. These industries employed proportionally more females, more minorities, and fewer educated workers than the national average. This study found that increased international trade produced gains for the nation as a whole, but that these gains are reduced by the costs of resource reallocation. These adjustment costs fall heaviest on the workers who can least afford them and who, as a group, have the fewest alternative sources of employment.

This fact suggests that programs such as the Trade Adjustment Assistance Program serve a useful function. The purpose of this program is to aid firms and workers adversely affected by international trade. An ideal program, however, would retrain these workers, increasing their skill levels so that they could qualify for jobs in sectors in which the United States has a comparative advantage. To date, the United States has not adopted such a program, and until it does the adjustment costs of foreign trade will continue to fall on the workers who, in one sense, are least able to bear these costs.

International trade, of course, is not the only cause of resource reallocation and the resultant losses to businesses and workers. It goes on all the time as a necessary—but not costless—reaction to changes in consumer demands and in the costs of production. But in this ongoing process, seldom do entire industries lose their comparative advantage almost overnight as occurs when trade barriers are suddenly reduced. When this happens, the cost of reallocating resources is apt to be geographically concentrated, breeding organized political opposition.

When this happens, both the labor unions and the industries directly affected demand immediate relief from the government. If it happens on a broad enough scale, the political opposition to continued free trade is apt to become very strong. A glance at Tables 1 and 2 is sufficient to explain why organized labor turned against continued free trade in the 1970s. The industries that were losing jobs to foreign competition were highly organized and the industries that were gaining jobs were not. In the process of reallocating resources in response to increasing trade, labor unions were losing members.

As Disraeli stated, "free trade is not a principle. It is an expedient. . . ." If the costs of reallocating resources are sufficient to generate effective political opposition, it may become politically expedient to turn away from free trade toward the protection of domestic industries. If that happens, all the countries of the world will be poorer for it. A comprehensive trade adjustment program would be a small price to pay to avoid the return of protective tariffs, quotas, or nontariff barriers to trade.

Additional Readings

Aho, C. M. and J. Orr. "The Burdens of Free Trade." *Collegiate Forum,* Dow Jones, Summer 1979.

Krauss, M. B. "Stagnation and the New Protectionism." *Challenge,* January–February 1978.

Luttrell, C. B. "Imports and Jobs — The Observed and the Unobserved." *Review,* Federal Reserve Bank of St. Louis, June 1978.

Preview

In the past tariffs were the main instrument used to erect barriers to international trade. Today, however, because of international agreements, tariffs are less frequently used. In their place nontariff barriers are often employed. The United States has taken the lead in attempting to negotiate international agreements to reduce both tariffs and nontariff barriers to trade. But even while these negotiations were proceeding, the United States erected substantial nontariff barriers to certain foreign imports. Thus it would appear that U.S. trade policy is at best inconsistent and perhaps even contradictory. This chapter reviews the recent spread of the use of nontariff barriers to trade, explores the reasons for this development, and explains the U.S. reaction to this situation. You can then decide whether U.S. trade policy is as inconsistent as it appears on the surface.

Key Economic Points

What are the functions of nontariff barriers to trade?

What are the economic circumstances that create political pressure for a government to grant protection?

Should the United States follow a policy of free trade even if subsidized foreign imports threaten a domestic industry?

Has U.S. international trade policy been inconsistent?

34

Nontariff Barriers to Trade: The New Protectionism

The international trade policy of the United States appears to have been both inconsistent and contradictory. On the one hand, the United States is publicly committed to free trade. It took the lead in attempting to obtain the signatures of the eighty-seven member countries to ratify both the General Agreement on Tariffs and Trade (GATT) and the complex Multilateral Trade Negotiation (MTN), the purpose of which was to further reduce the trade barriers between nations. However, concurrent with these negotiations, the United States imposed quotas on the imports of television sets, textiles, and shoes, imposed a "trigger price system" on steel imports and granted increased price supports to protect U.S. sugar producers. Thus, while attempting to reduce tariff barriers, the administration has itself simultaneously erected substantial nontariff barriers to world trade.

The substitution of nontariff barriers (NTBs) for explicit tariffs has been called the most significant development in international trade policy during the 1970s. A tariff is an explicit tax levied upon specified foreign goods when imported. Nontariff barriers to trade take various forms, such as preferential government procurement regulations, discriminating product standards, state subsidies, tax rebates, orderly marketing agreements, and unreasonable customs regulations and procedures. The purpose of NTBs is the same as a tariff, that is, to protect domestic industry from foreign competition. So prevalent has the use of NTBs become that the practice has been labeled the "new protectionism."

Nontariff barriers to trade are much more insidious than tariffs because they are often disguised as programs or rules and regulations that are ostensively designed to serve other purposes. Tariffs are highly visible and therefore can be easily recognized by exporters, importers, and the general public; nontariff barriers are more difficult to identify. It is, for instance, against existing foreign trade agreements and U.S. law to "dump" foreign-produced goods in the United States. Dumping is the practice of price discrimination, of selling abroad for less than the product sells for at home. U.S. textile and steel manufacturers firmly believe, and have convinced the U.S. government, that certain foreign governments subsidize by tax policies and rebates their exports of steel and cloth. This provides foreign producers with an artificial competitive advantage in the U.S. market. The Japanese government, as well as others, burdens American imports with numerous restrictions (NTBs) that foreign imports do not encounter in the United States.

The existence of the new protectionism confuses the determination of which country actually has the comparative advantage in the manufacture of a good. Nontariff barriers to trade thus present a difficult policy problem for the U.S. government: should the government continue to pursue a policy of free trade while its industries are placed in an artificially created, competitive disadvantage? This chapter considers the problem. An attempt is also made to reconcile the apparent contradictions of current U.S. international trade policy, which ostensively favors free trade at the same time it grants protection to domestic industries.

The increasingly frequent use of NTBs to encourage exports and discourage imports clearly threatens the continued expansion of world trade. During the past quarter of a century, international trade has grown faster than world output. This expansion of trade was facilitated by a major reduction in tariffs under the auspices of the GATT. The Kennedy round of these negotiations, completed in 1967, resulted in a one-third reduction in the level of tariffs around the world. During the last decade, the movement toward freer international trade has lagged somewhat. Between 1974 and 1980, trade barriers actually increased. The GATT Secretariat has estimated that new trade barriers have been imposed on 3 to 5 percent of world trade. These new barriers are not tariffs, but nontariff restrictions.

The advantages of free world trade are widely acknowledged. Under free trade a country will export goods in which it has a comparative advantage and import goods in which it does not. The nations of the world benefit from sharing in the gains from trade that arise when production is carried on by the lowest cost producers. These benefits allow higher levels of world consumption and investment than would be possible if trade were restricted.

Despite the overall loss in economic welfare that trade barriers bring about, there are two circumstances that can lead a domestic industry to request protection and have it granted by the government. First, as economic growth occurs and international trade expands, inevitably some countries will lose their comparative advantage in some products while they acquire an advantage in others. Recently, as developing countries have entered world markets, they have done so by acquiring a comparative advantage in products that rely upon well-established technology. As a result, the more developed countries are finding that their comparative advantages have shifted away from these industries to products that require relatively more skilled labor and more advanced technology.

This shift generally requires that resources be reallocated away from older, established industries to newer, rapidly expanding industries. This adjustment is not without cost. The existing firms in the established industries have capital invested, and their workers possess specialized skills. Foreign competition decreases the value of both of these resources. The political demands of these businesses and their workers for protection from foreign competition are often more effectively voiced politically than the demands by consumers to be allowed to benefit from the lower prices imports allow. Protection may be granted even though the social gains from free trade are greater than the costs imposed on domestic businesses and their workers.

Second, pleas for protection are more likely to be heard when the economy is suffering through a recession, experiencing excess capacity and high rates of unemployment. In this event, the labor and capital displaced by foreign imports are not likely to be quickly reabsorbed into the economy. Imports that might have been considered a welcome supplement to domestic output in times of high employment are blamed for increasing domestic unemployment during periods of recession. This provides an additional incentive for governments to limit imports.

A worldwide recession such as that of 1974–1975 also creates the incentive for governments to develop programs that will stimulate their export industries in order to reduce domestic unemployment. Increasingly, this has been accomplished by direct state subsidies to producers or to entire industries by the granting of tax preferences. The aim is to export abroad the country's unemployment along with its products. When these goods are imported by other countries, they replace domestically produced goods, increasing unemployment there. The resulting foreign unemployment, however, generates a reciprocal demand for protecton in these countres.

The increased demand for protection, both here and abroad, thus stems from two sources: the loss of comparative advantage for valid economic reasons and the apparent loss of comparative advantage, which, in reality, is due to political subsidy. It is often difficult to distinguish between the two. Few economists feel that the loss of comparative advantage for purely economic reasons is grounds for protection. The loss of apparent advantage due to political subsidy is another matter, and the economics profession is divided on this issue.

One school of thought is that we should do nothing about this situation. If Great Britain chooses to subsidize its steel industry to the extent of $1 billion a year and France to guarantee over $5 billion in loans to its steel industry (which they have), then let U.S. consumers take advantage of the lower cost imported steel, paid for in part by European taxpayers. Foreign subsidization of exports, according to this view, does not constitute a problem for the United States but a blessing: to the usual gains from trade are added the benefits of the subsidy.

An alternative view, one held by the U.S. government, is that foreign subsidies of export industries do present a real problem. U.S. industry in this situation is faced with unfair competition, its profitability not determined by the law of comparative advantage and dependent upon the efficiency of resource allocation, but instead dependent upon the political whim of foreign governments. This view is supported by GATT rules, which allow countervailing action by a country whose domestic industry is damaged by foreign dumping practices.

The U.S. International Trade Commission (ITC) in 1977 investigated 26 petitions for import relief, covering nearly $5 billion in imports. The commission recommended increased protection in the form of tariffs or, more frequently, quota restrictions for $3 billion, or 66 percent of this trade. The most important of these items were shoes, color television sets, mushrooms, and above-the-ground swimming pools. In 1978 the number of complaints increased to 30, covering imports of $2 billion. The ITC recommended relief on more than $1.3 billion of these imports.

The U.S. government, while committed to free trade based upon comparative advantage, is also committed to defend domestic industry against foreign goods that owe their apparent comparative advantage to state subsidies. Distinguishing between the two in practice is often difficult. This problem is dramatized by the pleas for protection from the U.S. television, steel, and textile industries.

During the 1970s, U.S. imports of Japanese-manufactured television sets increased rapidly. By 1978, imports had captured more than a third of the domestic market. Five U.S. producers closed their doors, laying off 60,000 U.S. workers. Domestic manufacturers accused the Japanese of dumping and the U.S. Treasury agreed. In this case, dumping was not easy to establish because the imported price into the United States was the same as that charged in Japan, but the retail price was lower in the United States than in Japan. The explanation for this price differential proved to be a series of illegal "kickbacks," or rebates, which Japanese exporters paid to U.S. importers. These payments amounted to as much as $100 per set. The total penalties assessed against Japanese producers amounted to $500 million. In addition, U.S. retailers may still be fined a total of $1 billion.

The intermediate solution developed by the U.S. government was to negotiate a voluntary quota for Japanese television sets. These types of arrangements limit the imports of Japanese televisions to a specified number per year. This type of arrangement is called an orderly marketing agreement. Quantitative restrictions of this type are more damaging than an equivalent tariff to the U.S. consumer. During a recession, quotas provide less protection from imports (when business is depressed). During an expansion, quotas do not permit imports to limit domestic price increases when the industry is running at capacity.

During 1977, developments in the steel industry presented the U.S. government with a difficult problem. Steel industries throughout the world had been hard-hit by the 1974–1975 recession and the subsequent slow worldwide recovery. At the same time, significant new production capacity became operative, creating excess capacity worldwide that was likely to persist through the 1980s. Steel imports flooded into the United States, capturing 20 percent of the market. Entire domestic steel mills were closed in Ohio, Pennsylvania, and New York, unemploying thousands of workers. The steel industry, combined with the unions, claimed that foreign steel was being dumped in the U.S. market. The government agreed after an investigation.

The U.S. government responded by creating a trigger price system. The trigger price is determined by the costs of production of the most efficient foreign producer, currently Japan, plus the costs of shipping steel from Japan to the United States. If foreign steel is sold in the United States below this trigger price, antidumping fines and penalties will be assessed. The trigger price has significant advantages in practice over a quota. A quota would have undermined the incentive for U.S. producers to hold down prices and costs. The trigger price will decline if Japanese efficiency increases, so that domestic producers will continue to feel the discipline of foreign competition.

Once the U.S. government begins to grant relief from imports whose comparative advantage stems from the subsidies of foreign governments or from the practice of price discrimination (dumping) by foreign exporters, it is difficult to deny protection to other industries that have, for valid economic reasons, lost their comparative advantage. In the United States, the textile and clothing industries are in this position. Nevertheless, the U.S. government granted these industries protection under the U.S. Multifiber Agreement of 1974, which limits the growth of imports to 6 percent a year. In 1979, independent action was taken to limit textile imports from India, which had increased rapidly from $7 million in 1972 to more than $100 million in 1978. Red China was singled out for similar action in 1974.

The protection afforded textiles was designed or at least promoted as temporary relief, granted to ease the required reallocation of resources. The U.S. government has also implemented a program to facilitate the adjustment of workers, firms, and communities harmed by import competition. The federal Trade Adjustment Assistance Program provides readjustment allowances, training, and relocation payments for workers who have lost their jobs as the result of foreign imports. Technical and financial assistance is also provided to affected firms, and public works money is allocated to communities whose economies have been harmed by foreign imports.

The purpose of trade adjustment assistance programs is to ease the private costs of reallocating resources when an industry has lost its comparative advantage. In practice, such programs, especially if they rely on quotas and tariffs, are likely instead to delay the required adjustments. In the case of textiles, this is almost certainly the case. The textile industry is widely dispersed geographically in the United States, which ensures broad political support in the Congress.

The best hope of dealing with NTBs is the Multilateral Trade Negotiation. This agreement includes agreements on subsidies and foreign trade licensing. It also includes tariff reductions, which in the United States are projected to an average of 30 percent. The agreement on subsidies and countervailing duties will limit trade-distorting subsidies and provide for the right of a country to take action against such practices. The government procurement code is intended to reduce the scope for discrimination against foreign suppliers when governments purchase goods for their own use. This agreement represents the first time since the 1960s that the international community has reduced the barriers to trade across such a broad spectrum of tariff and nontariff measures. The long-term solution to the problems created by NTBs surely lies in such agreements and not in unilateral action that only creates greater barriers to trade.

Additional Readings

Cheng, H. S. "The Tokyo Round." *Weekly Letter,* Federal Reserve Bank of San Francisco, July 13, 1979.

Gaines, T. "Mistaken Ideas." *Economic Report,* Manufacturers Hanover Trust, March 1979.

Krauss, M. B. "Stagnation and the New Protectionism." *Challenge,* January–February 1978.

Preview

During the second half of the 1970s, the United States' foreign trade sector experienced severe difficulties, running record deficits on the balance of payments current account while at the same time the dollar fell drastically in value relative to other foreign currencies. The coincidence of record balance-of-payments deficits with a falling dollar called into question whether flexible exchange rates were working as they were supposed to do. It was commonly expected that the value of the dollar would adjust so that there would be a balance of trade and the value of exports would be approximately equal to the value of imports. In theory, there was never any reason to expect that this would always be so, as this chapter reveals. These expectations also ignore the J-curve effect, which describes the path the balance-of-payments current account will follow in response to a decline in the foreign exchange value of a nation's currency.

Key Economic Points

In theory, there is no reason for the balance-of-payments current account to always balance exactly.

The total balance of payments is always in balance.

The current account of the balance of payments responds to a decline in the foreign exchange value of a nation's currency.

Time plays a role in this adjustment process.

When the J-curve effect is considered, flexible exchange rates are working exactly as theory would predict, contrary to popular opinion.

35

The J Curve Effect: Record Trade Deficits and the Depreciation of the Dollar

Everything appeared to go wrong at once for the U.S. international trade sector during the second half of the 1970s. The balance of payments recorded succeeded record deficits, while at the same time the bottom seemed to fall out from under the value of the dollar. The merchandise trade balance went from a $9 billion surplus in 1975 to a $9 billion deficit in 1976. Then the deficit increased to a record-breaking $31 billion in 1977, which was broken the very next year when the deficit rose to $34 billion. Accompanying the record trade deficits was the now famous fall in value of the U.S. dollar, relative to other so-called hard currencies. Beginning in 1977 and continuing through 1978, the German mark, the Swiss franc, and the Japanese yen appreciated relative to the dollar. By the end of 1978 it took 20 percent more dollars to buy a German mark, 50 percent more dollars to buy a Swiss franc, and 53 percent more dollars to buy a Japanese yen.

The record trade deficits and the decline in the dollar were considered a national disaster by international traders and brokers. They called into question the sytem of flexible exchange rates that had been established in the early 1970s. The major advantage of flexible exchange rates was supposed to be the freedom this system gave to countries to tailor their domestic economic policies to their own requirements. The exchange rate was relied upon to fluctuate to maintain a balance of payments equilibrium, thus freeing a country from concern over this sector.

Two years of record U.S. deficits, coupled with a year and a half of rapid depreciation in the dollar's international value, called the system of flexible exchange rates into question. Business publications ran numerous articles entitled "Why Floating Exchange Rates Aren't Doing Their Job" (*Forbes,* October 2, 1978), or something similar. These articles attempted to explain why the decline in the value of the dollar had not resulted in expanded U.S. exports and reduced imports to restore equality in the balance of payments. These articles explained that the cause of the problem was that the Germans liked to save, the Japanese did not like to consume foreign-manufactured goods, or currency speculators were the source of the trouble.

The critics of flexible exchange rates assumed that the flexible exchange rates were not working because of the time that had elapsed without the balance of payments on current account deficit being eliminated or even substantially reduced. International trade economists, however, were not surprised by these events because they were consistent with a theoretical concept called the J curve. The J curve describes the process of balance-of-payments adjustment in response to a falling exchange rate. The purpose of this chapter is to describe and apply the concept of the J curve to the U.S. balance-of-payments problem of the late 1970s.

The balance-of-payments accounts of a country summarize its transactions with the rest of the world. It is often useful to subdivide these transactions into three categories: the current account, which reports the balance of merchandise trade, the exchange of services, and the exchange of gifts; the capital account, which records international capital movements into and out of the country; and the intervention account, which registers the movement of funds between governments for the purpose of influencing exchange rates.

The merchandise trade portion of the current account usually receives the most attention because it is the largest single component of the U.S. balance of payments. When the merchandise account registered record deficits of $31 billion in 1977 and $34 billion in 1978, it was widely noted by the nation's press. The deficit on current account was much less, $15.4 billion in 1977 and $18 billion in 1978, because the United States ran a substantial surplus on the exchange of services. Nevertheless, the U.S. balance of payments was substantially in the red, indicating that the United States was spending more dollars abroad for goods than foreigners wanted for purposes of buying U.S. goods.

The United States or any nation must pay for an excess purchase of foreign goods in exactly the same manner that an individual would make good expenditures that exceeded personal income. The U.S. must either sell assets (stocks, bonds, or real estate) to foreigners, borrow from them sufficient funds, or both to pay for excess purchases. The balance of payments must always balance; therefore, a deficit on current account must be made good by a surplus in the capital account or the intervention account.

Thus there is no necessary connection between a deficit in current accounts and the fall in the value of the nation's currency. A deficit on current account can be covered by offsetting capital movements, or by the intervention of foreign governments to support the exchange rate, or a combination of both. However, despite the large short-term capital movements into the United States and substantial intervention by foreign central banks in support of the dollar, there was, during 1977 and 1978, an excess supply of dollars on the foreign exchange market. This excess supply caused the dollar to fall in value, especially against the German mark, the Swiss franc, and the Japanese yen.

The dollar declined in value because the U.S. importers tried to supply more dollars to purchase foreign goods than foreign nations required to finance their purchases of U.S. goods, stocks, bonds, and real estate. The excess supply of dollars was also greater than foreign bankers wished to acquire as reserves, and as a result the value of the dollar fell.

The depreciation of the dollar would, of course, eventually eliminate the excess supply of dollars in the foreign exchange market by stimulating U.S. exports and discouraging imports. The price of U.S. produced goods exported to foreign countries would decline, increasing the quantity demanded. U.S. exports of food, machinery, chemicals, and computers would therefore increase. Simultaneously, U.S. imports of televisions, stereo equipment, steel, automobiles, and clothing would decline as they became more expensive in U.S. markets. As exports expanded and imports contracted, the deficit on current account would be reduced and the excess supply of dollars would disappear. The exchange rate would have moved from one equilibrium to another, reducing, in the process, the balance of payments on current account deficit.

But this movement from one equilibrium position to another would not occur overnight. Trades do not take place instantaneously, but over a period of time. International trade, because of the distance involved, takes even longer. Goods traded internationally are often contracted for months, even years, in advance of delivery. A falling exchange rate does not affect the quantity of goods already contracted for, but it does affect their cost. Thus imports cost more and the value of imports in the merchandise account temporarily increases. Meanwhile the exports that were already contracted for decline in value for the same reason. The short-run effect of a depreciating currency is to make the current account deficit worse, not better.

The old saying that "things will get worse before they get better" aptly describes the behavior of the current account in response to a depreciating currency. It also describes the J curve. The shape of the letter J droops

247

down before it slopes upward, which is how the current account deficit behaves in response to a depreciating exchange rate. First it gets worse, then it gets better.

Eventually the resulting cheaper exports, and more expensive imports, will have their effect upon the deficit on current account. The deficit will decline as exports increase and imports decline. The trade balance will begin to follow the upward swing of the letter J. The deficit will decline to the point where an excess supply of dollars no longer exists on the foreign exchange market. The deficit on current account may or may not disappear. This depends upon whether the United States wishes to invest more or less in foreign countries than foreign countries wish to invest in the United States. The United States may run a deficit on current account for long periods of time, as it did in the nineteenth century, if foreigners wish to invest more in the United States than the United States wishes to invest abroad.

The balance-of-payments deficit on current account corresponded to the J curve between 1977 and 1979. The record trade deficit of $15.4 billion in 1977 caused the depreciation of the dollar, which made the 1978 trade deficit even worse ($18 billion). The depreciation of the dollar then led to a reduced deficit for 1979 of $0.3 billion and to a surplus during the last quarter of that year. If you were to plot these deficits on a graph, the pattern that would be traced out would be recognizable as the letter J.

The actual appearance of the J curve in the foreign trade statistics depends, however, on certain assumptions. The most important of these is that events do not change during the time period required for the depreciation of a currency to work its effects on the foreign trade sector. In a world of increasing foreign trade influenced by business fluctuations, international cartels, and so on, this is not apt to happen. Nevertheless, the J-curve effect is present, representing, as it does, the reaction of markets to changes in relative prices.

Innocence of the J-curve effect can account for the belief that flexible exchange rates were not working as expected in correcting the excess supply of dollars on the foreign exchange rate that developed in 1977. The fact that the deficit on current account worsened in 1978 was mistakenly read as evidence that flexible exchange rates were not working, when in fact it was to be expected according to the J-curve effect. The nature of foreign trade means that the balance-of-payments reaction to a falling exchange rate will occur over a considerable period of time. Adjustments in the balance of payments should not be expected to occur quickly.

Additional Readings

"The Case For a Stronger Dollar." *Business Week,* October 2, 1978.

"Economic Diary." *Business Week,* May 21, 1979.

"Why Floating Exchange Rates Aren't Doing Their Job." *Forbes,* October 2, 1978.

"Why 1979's Trade Balance Should Look Better." *Business Week,* December 18, 1978.

Index

HB
172.5
T47

Thomas, Robert Paul.

Macroeconomic
applications

47030

DATE			
DE1 8 '90			
MY 1 '98			
MY 05 '0			